I0890301

Hard Times in an American Workhouse, 1853–1920

HARD TIMES IN AN AMERICAN WORKHOUSE 1853–1920

Gregg Andrews

Louisiana State University Press | Baton Rouge

Published by Louisiana State University Press
lsupress.org

Copyright © 2024 by Louisiana State University Press
All rights reserved. Except in the case of brief quotations used in articles or reviews, no part of this publication may be reproduced or transmitted in any format or by any means without written permission of Louisiana State University Press.

Manufactured in the United States of America
First printing

Designer: Michelle A. Neustrom
Typefaces: Sentinel, text; DIN 2014 Narrow, display
Printer and binder: Sheridan Books, Inc.

Jacket photograph: The shackled legs of a workhouse prisoner. Courtesy *St. Louis Post-Dispatch,* April 16, 1905.

Cataloging-in-Publication Data are available at the Library of Congress.

ISBN 978-0-8071-8278-9 (cloth) | ISBN 978-0-8071-8278-9 (pdf) | ISBN 978-0-8071-8327-4 (epub)

CONTENTS

Hard Times in an American Workhouse, 1853–1920

INTRODUCTION

The chilling, heartbreaking stories of brutal abuse, hard luck, and hard times you're about to read come from the dark, dank dungeons of the old St. Louis Workhouse. Perched high on the lonesome limestone bluffs of Point Breeze, the workhouse overlooked the Mississippi River on the city's south levee. Amazingly, although its quarry played out in 1953, the institution on Point Breeze operated from 1853 until 1966, when it was replaced by a penitentiary, the Medium Security Institution. But locals still called it the Workhouse.

We know only a mere fraction of the names of those who were locked up in the old workhouse, but what we do know about them says much about the city's carceral regime. Those who were penned up in workhouse garb mostly represented the down-and-out, the downtrodden, and the damned during the rise of industrial St. Louis. As casualties in the war against poor people, many inmates fell victim to the rottenness that corrupted the city's very own soul. By that, I mean the wormy core of a corrupt penal system that criminalized poverty, Blackness, vagrancy, homelessness, and dissent. Breaking up rock in the city quarry for fifty cents a day minus room and board was the police court remedy for what ailed the city's poor. If you did not have the money to pay a fine, off to the workhouse you went.

Forced labor on the rock pile and in the sewing rooms and brush factory furnished important resources to the city. Judges tossed the "feeble-minded," the insane, and those who eked out a living on the levee and in the slums into overcrowded cells with hardened felons to work off their fines in the quarry. From the beginning, the workhouse was ill-equipped to handle felons, but on plea deals the criminal courts often sent violent criminals there instead of the penitentiary in Jefferson City. Felons joined "levee rats," petty thieves, peace disturbers, confidence men, adulterers, "Sunday drunks," "morphine eaters," and a long line of police court misdemeanants who broke city ordinances. Squeezed into cells with them were sex workers, political dissenters of various types, and women arrested for defying social convention by wearing men's clothing.

In violation of the ordinance that authorized the workhouse in 1843, overseers and guards committed unspeakable cruelty in the punishment of prisoners. In a moldy, diseased institution where sadism, side hustles, and corruption went unchecked, racism and contempt for the poor made canings, lashings, and the use of torture seem acceptable somehow. The workhouse offered ready employment to many ex-police officers fired for drunkenness, corruption, and cavorting with prostitutes while on duty. In some cases, officers on patrol abused citizens they were sworn to protect. Drunken guards beat inmates with rawhide whips and canes filled with lead. In case the sting of lashes on prisoners' backs did not bite deeply enough into the flesh, guards sometimes strung inmates up by their thumbs in sheds and outbuildings. They used ropes and pulleys from the ceiling to ratchet up the torture. Cries for mercy mostly went unheard, and in some cases guards beat prisoners to death. Such savagery by those who committed it, and by those who condoned it, calls to mind Mark Twain's observation by way of Pudd'nhead Wilson's Calendar: "There is a Moral Sense and there is an Immoral Sense. History shows us that the Moral Sense enables us to perceive morality and how to avoid it, and that the Immoral Sense enables us to perceive immorality and how to enjoy it."[1]

Such horrors in a badly fragmented city touted as the "Babylon of the New World" were far worse than even Charles Dickens's fictionalized portraits of cruelty in the prisons and workhouses of Victorian England. Low-browed guards and low-salaried superintendents on Point Breeze hid behind red tape while barefooted prisoners begged for socks and shoes in temperatures as low as twenty degrees below zero. In the early years of the St. Louis Workhouse, superintendents were elected annually, but after a revised city ordinance in 1861, the mayor appointed them to a one-year term, later increased to two-year terms. Ward political patronage determined the appointments—and just about everything else in city government. Despair and hopelessness drove many prisoners to commit suicide or to run for their life amid a fusillade of bullets and buckshot in desperate escape attempts. If luck was on their side, a slow-moving Iron Mountain freight train or an unattended skiff at the river's edge might carry them to freedom. For some, a stretch in Missouri's infamous state penitentiary was more appealing than doing hard time in the St. Louis Workhouse.[2]

Unlike illegal beatings and other torture in the hot, hellish chambers of the workhouse, solitary confinement on a diet of bread and water was an authorized form of punishment. The practice originated as an alternative to physical punishment, but it drew increasing fire from critics. In *American Notes for General Circulation,* Dickens blasted solitary confinement as a well-intentioned, Quaker-inspired reform initiative gone awry. After touring Philadelphia's Eastern State Prison in 1842, he described the inhuman effects of the practice, which was conceived as an alternative to laying the whip to prisoners in the City of Brotherly Love. "I believe that very few men are capable of estimating the immense amount of torture and agony which this dreadful punishment, prolonged for years, inflicts upon the sufferers," he wrote. He pointed to "a depth of terrible endurance in which none but the sufferers themselves can fathom, and which no man has a right to inflict upon his fellow creature." Continuing, Dickens made it clear he regarded the practice unacceptable as a form of punishment: "I hold this slow and daily tampering with the mysteries of the brain to be immeasurably worse than any torture of the body; and because its ghastly signs and tokens are not so palpable to the eye and sense of touch as scars upon the flesh; because its wounds are not upon the surface, and it extorts few cries that human ears can hear; therefore the more I denounce it, as a secret punishment which slumbering humanity is not roused up to stay."[3]

A half century later, the U.S. Supreme Court agreed with Dickens, ruling in 1890 that solitary confinement was inhumane and amounted to torture in American prisons. In reference to the first experimental use of the practice in the United States, at Walnut-Street Penitentiary, Justice Samuel Freeman Miller wrote in the high court's majority opinion: "A considerable number of the prisoners fell, after even a short confinement, into a semi-fatuous condition, from which it was next to impossible to arouse them, and others became violently insane; others still, committed suicide; while those who stood the ordeal better were not generally reformed, and in most cases did not recover sufficient mental activity to be of any subsequent service to the community."[4] Punishment by forced labor, not reform, was the goal of workhouse officers and those who hired them. Although solitary confinement was intended as an acceptable alternative to the whipping post, officers on Point Breeze used both with great relish to punish inmates.

In a city rife with boodling and rapacious grafters at the top, there was nothing too grand for its Gilded Age rulers and political bosses, and no punishment too brutal for its unruly masses, especially after the interracial radicalism of the St. Louis Commune and general strike of 1877. Many of the strikers, especially steamboat roustabouts, stevedores, and others on the levee who joined them, ended up in the workhouse for their efforts. In August 1877, the *St. Louis Post-Dispatch* complained that "the alleged leaders of the late riots are turned loose upon the community, while the poor dupes who did their bidding, are sent to the Work-house." The newspaper editorialized that the workhouse was an ideal cure for "idleness."[5]

From top to bottom, corruption was the name of the game in St. Louis, where open bribery in city contracts and railway franchises was rampant. Crookedness was widespread in the issuance of city permits and peddler licenses, and corrupt officeholders and city suppliers looted public funds and supplies. Likewise, corruption tainted the remitting of fines and nearly every other transaction in the workhouse. If prisoners had money on file in the workhouse office, guards might see to it that they enjoyed all kinds of special perks. In "Tweed Days in St. Louis" (1902), journalists Claude H. Wetmore and Lincoln Steffens contextualized the city's embarrassing scandals, some of which were exposed and prosecuted by circuit attorney Joseph W. Folk at the time: "In all cities, the better classes—the businessmen—are the sources of corruption; but they are so rarely pursued and caught that we do not fully realize whence the trouble comes. Thus most cities blame the politicians and the ignorant and vicious poor."[6]

Much of the corruption was rooted in the ward-based patronage structure of the city's political life. The 1876 home rule charter in St. Louis and the "divorce" between the city and county left the city decentralized politically, with weak mayors and a state-mandated bicameral municipal assembly that often kept city affairs in gridlock. Members of the house of delegates, representing each of the city's twenty-eight wards, were elected every two years, and a thirteen-member city council and its president were elected at large to serve four-year terms. The system contained so many checks and balances that often the only way to get anything done was through ward politics. Class and ethnic/neighborhood divisions were based on immigration patterns in the city's history. Representatives of German and Irish immigrants, who typically dominated ward political structures, doled out jobs based on political loyalties and how many votes one could deliver. Power brokers and the two major political parties feasted on the "boodle," or bribes, that came from control of ward politics. The result was a notoriously corrupt, badly fragmented political culture in which loyalties were determined more by neighborhood/ethnic considerations at the ward level and less by allegiances to the municipal unit. A neighborhood saloon was often the center of political gravity.[7]

Naked corruption in St. Louis was a powerful aphrodisiac and a way of life. It emanated from the city's elites, or the "Big Cinch," as they were dubbed. Thanks to weakened mayors and machine politics, the Big Cinch exercised its financial and political prerogatives with a sense of entitlement. The corruption filtered down through powerful political brokers like the Irish immigrant boss Edward Butler to ward heelers, city administrators, and the Four Courts Building itself, the criminal justice complex that housed judicial chambers, the county jail, city detention wards, the district attorney's office, the chief of police, the chief of detectives, and a "reporters' room." American novelist Theodore Dreiser, who dutifully went to the Four Courts once or twice a month as a cub reporter in the 1890s, said he always felt "a sicky and sinking sensation." He described the building as a "horrible place, a pest-hole of suffering and error and trickery, and yet necessary enough, I know."[8]

While corruption and arbitrariness flourished, the city's penal institutions suffered from overcrowding, neglect, and underfunding. Inmates paid the price. Dreiser called attention to the corrupting influence of the Four Courts on all who were caught in the web of administering justice, including the agents of justice themselves: "The petty tyrannies that are practiced by underlings and minor officials! The 'grafting' of low, swinish brains! The tawdry pomp of ignorant officials! The cruelty and cunning of agents of justice," he wrote. "Clothe these officials as you will, in whatsoever uniforms of whatsoever splendor or sobriety; give them desks of rosewood and walls of flowered damask; entitle them as you choose, High and Mightiness This and That—still they remain the degraded things they have always been, equals of the criminals and the crimes they are supposed to do away with."[9]

In Dreiser's autobiography, he remembered that behind a line of waterfront mills lay "wretched tenements, as poor and grimy and dingy as I have ever seen."[10] While the slums of Kerry Patch, Clabber Alley, Wild Cat Chute,

Deep Morgan, and others cried out for mercy and relief in the swelling, fast-industrializing city, St. Louis's political kingpins and merchant and bond-holding boodlers fattened their accounts and retreated to their homes on the West End. They lived it up in palatial style with Irish and Black household servants, butlers, and carriage drivers while the waterfront masses endured squalor and degraded living conditions. The message to the masses was pointed and clear: "If you can't pay the fine, don't do the crime."

Criminals at the top grew rich in St. Louis, but to steal a bite to eat or a lump of coal, to fall asleep in a freight car or someone's barn, or to appear staggering drunk on the street risked arrest and confinement in the workhouse. The police court system was toxic for poor people. When it came to paying court costs and fines, money and political connections bought freedom, but if you were poor, friendless, and did not know the right folks in your ward, it meant hard time and hard labor on the workhouse rock pile in what amounted to debtors' prison.

Broadly defined, widely abused vagrancy laws were a favorite police tool to control criminal behavior, impose morality, and sweep the city's poor off the streets. Shooting craps, "idling," "lounging," or nodding off in a poolroom chair might be all it took for a sleep-deprived steamboat roustabout to get "vagged," or arrested for vagrancy, and thrown into the workhouse. A political dissenter who gave a street corner soapbox speech to protest the inequities of capitalism might be clubbed, fined, and dragged off to the workhouse rock pile and clubbed some more. The workhouse might well be the landing place for a homeless teenage girl arrested at night as a suspected prostitute. Likewise, a Black washerwoman delivering a basket of clothes at night might find herself hauled in by the police, fined, and consigned to a workhouse cell as a suspected prostitute. Police court justice meant the rock pile for "river riffraff," alcoholics, trespassers, peace disturbers, drifters, and those whose only crime was old age, homelessness, or unemployment, if they could not pay the fine for minor infractions of city ordinances. "A miserable wretch who climbs into an empty freight car on a rainy night and is fined $25," wrote a *St. Louis Post-Dispatch* reporter in 1886, "will have to do seventy-two days of hard labor to make up for his indiscretion. This is very near a mockery of justice, but is the simon-pure article of Police Court justice nevertheless."[11]

Yet there were voices of resilience, resistance, protest, and perseverance inside the cells and stockade walls of the workhouse. On the outside, humanitarian voices objected to the torture of prisoners and other deplorable practices of the institution. Even guards occasionally broke the code of silence about what went on behind its walls, sometimes behind the backs of superintendents. Calls to reform the workhouse persisted as officials ignored public revelations of abuse and graft—unless they caused too much embarrassment for the political party in charge of municipal governance. Petty grafters at the ward level regarded the workhouse as easy pickings. The *St. Louis Post-Dispatch,* after Joseph Pulitzer bought it in 1878, became a leading critic and voice for reform of the workhouse. A persistent thorn in the side of successive workhouse superintendents and their guards and officers, no matter the party in power, the Democratic newspaper published endless exposés of conditions in the institution to prick the conscience of the public. Later, so did the *St. Louis Star.*

Abuses of women in city penal institutions triggered activism among club women. The Woman's Christian Temperance Union (WCTU), the Humanity Club, the Tuesday Literary Club, the Women's Trade Union League, and other organizations pressured mayors to promote the rehabilitation of women inmates and to improve conditions in the workhouse. In the late 1890s, their intervention in the disturbing case of a woman who was an anarchist sympathizer, former teacher, writer, and self-described "mental science healer" led to a lawsuit against the workhouse superintendent and the City of St. Louis. The woman, known as a "police character," was kept far past her sentenced time in solitary confinement. Without the WCTU's intervention, she might well have died in the workhouse's dreaded "bullring," or "bull pen," as the solitary confinement dungeon was often called.

Not until the first two decades of the 1900s did St. Louis take tentative steps toward modernizing the workhouse along lines suggested by penal reformers and criminologists. Most popular among Progressive calls for criminal justice reform was a municipal farm to replace the urban industrial model for petty criminals and alcoholics. The municipal farm concept captured the imagination of civic groups, policymakers, and even some politicians. They puzzled over how to rehabilitate addicts and alcoholics. Penal reformers focused on how to separate hardened criminals from those who broke minor ordinances and those whose main crime was poverty. A hard-fought new city charter in 1914 brought only marginal improvements in the administration, organization, and conduct of the workhouse. St. Louis's limited Progressivism proved no match for nearly three-quarters of a century of ward political corruption, public weariness, and fragmentation. When a 1920 bond issue to fund a municipal farm to replace the workhouse failed, the defeat spelled doom for those who hoped for cleansing reform of the antiquated institution.

1

DAILY LIFE AND LABOR IN THE WORKHOUSE

On September 5, 1843, the St. Louis City Council approved a municipal ordinance to set aside blocks 46 and 47 in Carondelet's city commons for the creation of a workhouse. The city's first workhouse, a one-story brick building with a log calaboose (jail) and belfry, was at South Eighteenth Street and Park Avenue, east of the city hospital, west of Second Carondelet Avenue, and near Lafayette Park between Park and Lafayette Avenues. Male convicts planted trees, graded Lafayette Park, and hauled rock to macadamize streets. Women prisoners washed, scrubbed, and made workhouse clothing. With only limited work possibilities for inmates at the location and an increasing population, the workhouse moved to a new site in 1853.

The new location was on the city commons at the intersection of Carondelet Road (South Broadway) and Meramec Street. The original cell house reportedly was a former French monastery with a bell tower that was used until about 1960. From high atop the craggy limestone bluff of Point Breeze, in a rather remote location, the workhouse looked down on the Iron Mountain Railway tracks, steamboat traffic on the Mississippi, and the shantyboats of Chickentown at Workhouse Landing. Upriver about a half mile was the U.S. Marine Hospital, and across the Mississippi lay Cahokia, Illinois, once the center of Indigenous Mississippian culture, centuries earlier. In 1895, a reporter described the workhouse's bucolic setting and commanding view of the river: "Both from the river approach on the east and Broadway on the west, picturesqueness is its chief characteristic. As one glances up from the river a cluster of white buildings, surrounded by whitewashed fences, lies high on a bluff, which is level with the street on the western approach. Beyond the Illinois banks of the Mississippi the eye sweeps without interruption over a beautiful line of hills which fringe the horizon, and on all sides the view upon the city, Carondelet, and down to the lazily dragging waters of the broad river is charming."[1]

The main attraction of the site was a quarry of St. Louis limestone, where inmates trudged to the rock pile, many of them in shackles. There also were clay deposits in the rugged terrain. Inmates graded roads, blasted, and busted up rock in the quarry. Trusties were assigned less strenuous work. Women, too, worked on road crews and the rock pile in the early years of the workhouse. With spalling hammers and sledgehammers, both sexes worked twelve-hour days from April through September and ten-hour days from October through March to pay their costs and fine at a rate of fifty cents daily (approximately $12.50 in today's money) minus about thirty cents a day for food and boarding costs. By 1871, a revised ordinance set the workday at ten hours. Prisoners whose fines were higher than ten dollars (about $250 today) wore a heavy ball and chain.

High, whitewashed plank walls with guard towers that looked like castle turrets surrounded all the buildings on the site. In the outer yard of the villa were stables for horses and mules used in quarrying and road grading. The workhouse building was about fifty feet wide and one hundred feet long with a corridor in the center. Two tiers of cells lined each side. Each cell customarily held eighteen prisoners and six double beds. At times, as many as twenty-four inmates squeezed into a cell, sleeping four to a double bed. A dining room and a laundry room were on the enclosed grounds, as well as a house where the superintendent and his family lived. Above the door to the inner yard of the workhouse, a sign reading "Ring the Bell" greeted visitors and new inmate arrivals. It was a mournful bell that did not stop reverberating any too soon. For many prisoners, it sounded a death knell.[2]

As early as the 1850s, there were repeated but unheeded calls for a new branch workhouse in north St. Louis. From the workhouse's inception, its abuses and corrupt practices raised public concerns. When a reporter for the *Daily Missouri Democrat* visited in June 1855, there were 190 prisoners packed into the workhouse's eleven cells, three of which held women. The reporter condemned the practice of firing at prisoners who attempted to escape, cautioning superintendents not to make up for security deficiencies by resorting to illegal remedies. There was a built-in temptation for superintendents to appropriate workhouse horses, corn, hay, and other city supplies for their own uses. The decision whether to act on the temptation depended entirely on the honesty of superintendents and officers. The reporter, critical of the degrading practice of forcing women to break rocks in the quarry, urged more suitable kinds of labor for them. Expressing moral concerns about corrupting influences, he warned, too, of the temptations to sexually abuse women prisoners and called for the hiring of a female matron: "We do not conceive it possible for a young woman to be sent to the workhouse for her first offense, without returning tenfold more the child of Satan than before. Her hardened companions corrupt her, and she cannot shun their company if she would—for there are sometimes twenty-four unfortunates in one cell."[3]

In 1856, abuses and corrupt practices at the workhouse were exposed when Mayor Washington King, of the nativist Know-Nothing Party that captured control of municipal politics, removed fellow Know-Nothing William Lingo from his elected position as superintendent of the workhouse. Lingo refused to vacate his office when King's newly appointed replacement showed up for duty, but King prepared nineteen articles of impeachment against him in January, accusing him first and foremost of "brutal and inhuman treatment" of prisoners. At a trial in the chambers of the city council, numerous witnesses, including a workhouse guard, corroborated Mayor King's charges.

The mayor testified that on a visit to the workhouse on December 18, 1855, he found two men being tortured in the bullring with no nearby fire to keep them warm. When they moaned and cried out to him for mercy, he ordered their immediate release. Superintendent Lingo was away at the time, but he had left his son, Edward Lingo, in charge. Witnesses confirmed that Edward was drunk on duty every day, and they called attention to the filthy conditions in the vermin-infested institution. King further testified that he had ordered Superintendent Lingo to remove Edward from the workhouse payroll on account of his repeated displays of drunkenness downtown. Other charges against the superintendent included appropriating the labor of inmates for his personal household and benefit, as well as intermingling his own hogs, cows, and horses with city-owned livestock on the grounds and feeding them city-purchased corn. King observed that it was easier to find Lingo downtown than at the workhouse, pointing out that the superintendent was often away from the grounds in neglect of his duties. Finally,

King emphasized Lingo's failure to consult him on a single appointment of workhouse guards or clerks, or to report escaped prisoners as required by city ordinance.[4]

Amid growing nationwide concern over vagrancy after the Civil War, the power to arrest suspects on charges of vagrancy expanded as a popular policing tool to control who was on the streets. Before 1865, the subjects of vagrancy arrests in St. Louis typically were prostitutes, petty thieves, and those who displayed public drunkenness. In the context of the abolition of slavery, the tool provided a way to control and command labor as freedmen searched for work and as Black families separated during enslavement tried to find each other and assert rights of citizenship. Combined with prevailing racist beliefs that Blacks were inherently lazy and shiftless, state vagrancy statutes and local ordinances handed police wide discretionary powers when it came to making arrests. No warrant was necessary. If police lacked solid evidence and merely suspected someone of being up to no good, they were empowered to make the arrest, even in the absence of a crime. Suspects who failed to convince officers that they held a steady job or had a legitimate home address likely faced arrest, a hasty police court trial, a fine, and a stretch in the workhouse.

St. Louis, because of its river location and important role in the steamboat trade, attracted freedmen looking for work on the levee as stevedores and steamboat firemen, stewards, cabin crews, and roustabouts. The latter often lodged in Black and Italian saloons in the waterfront district, a hopping place with musical entertainment and countless raucous saloons, pool halls, pushcart peddlers, secondhand shops, and bawdy houses. Police made surprise visits to waterfront pool halls to arrest steamboat roustabouts who fell asleep in chairs. Thanks to hasty police court justice and poverty, the workhouse rock pile awaited roustabouts and other day laborers and drifters on the levee.[5]

Vagrancy arrests skyrocketed in the 1870s and 1880s. Even charity reformers and philanthropists urged compulsory labor as an antidote for begging on the streets. Veterans of the Civil War who were missing an arm or leg and who were reduced to begging might well find themselves swept off the streets and shipped off to the workhouse to work for wages at a rate of fifty cents per day. Traditions of unfree pauper labor melded with ideas of free labor and the marketplace in the late nineteenth century. The growing use of vagrancy as a tool for sentencing a person to the workhouse rested on shaky legal ground. Typically, in such cases, police arrested someone they suspected was likely to commit a crime, although no crime had been committed. Police often arrested suspects on charges of vagrancy if they were without visible means of support and kept company with prostitutes, gamblers, "immoral persons," thieves, or other criminals.

In the eyes of the police, unemployment meant you were either a criminal or a criminal in waiting. The underlying assumption was that if you were jobless with too much leisure time and too little money, you would steal to get your hands on some money. In St. Louis, police court (or earlier, recorder's court) judges often hit arrested suspects with a large fine but offered to remit the fine and grant reprieve with stipulations. If the suspects agreed to clear out of the city within a specified number of hours or days, they were set free. If they agreed but failed to leave, they were subject to rearrest and a much longer stint in the workhouse—called the "vag. pen" by a *St. Louis Globe-Democrat* reporter in 1878. On the court docket, the cases simply were notated as "vagrancy" or "V.C.O. No. __, Art. __, Sec. __, in relation to vags."[6]

The long-standing practice gave police and police court judges arbitrary latitude to control who was on the streets, but by the late 1860s, it faced legal and political challenges. In December 1868, Judge Wilson A. Primm of the criminal court freed Owen Hines, who was in the workhouse on a charge of vagrancy. Judge Primm accused the police court of carelessly keeping improper records by using notations such as "vag," "ditto," and the like. He emphasized that every prisoner had a right to know the specific charge against him. The police court did not change its policies, but in 1869 an attorney representing workhouse prisoner William Dempsey questioned the legality of the practice. In July 1869, Judge Primm ordered Dempsey's release, ruling that the fine of $500 and rearrest of Dempsey were illegal, even though Dempsey agreed to accept the arrangement. The charge of "vagrancy" or "v.c.o. in relation to vags" had no legal foundation. "If this be an abbreviated statement of an offense against the city ordinances," ruled Judge Primm, "it is one which may be understood by the officers of the Police court, but which is certainly not recognized by law."[7]

At a time of broader conflicts over Radical Reconstruction, a power struggle was under way between the mayor's office and the police justice apparatus. Radical Republican mayor James Thomas was engaged in a bitter conflict with the police commissioners. Much to the resentment of Union political forces, secessionists hostile to St. Louis in the Missouri legislature in 1861 had vested in the governor the power to appoint members of the St. Louis Board of Police Commissioners. Judge Primm's rulings, if enforced, tilted the power to remit workhouse fines more decidedly toward the mayor's office and away from the police court system. Acting Mayor Elon G. Smith complied, remitting the fines of Samuel Banyard (v.c.o.), Edward McKnight (v.c.o.), and Mary Ann Thorp, a prostitute charged with vagrancy. Smith ordered city marshal Frances Romer, who was an officer of the police court, to release the three inmates from the workhouse. The acting mayor, who emphasized that those charged with vagrancy had violated no law or city ordinance, notified Romer that all future remits of fines and stays of execution would be invalid if they did not originate in the mayor's office.[8]

Judge Primm's ruling did not stop the practice. In fact, the ruling was ignored immediately. To cite but one of many examples, a police officer soon arrested a fifty-year-old Black woman for being out late at night. She had committed no crime. At her arraignment on a charge of vagrancy in police court, the arresting officer testified that within the past six months he had seen her in dramshops and on the streets late at night in the company of a Black man. Three "respectable looking" witnesses testified that she was a washerwoman who simply was out delivering clothes with an elderly Black man to escort her. She feared that if she walked the streets alone, police would arrest her. The *Missouri Democrat* was sympathetic to the woman but shrugged off her conviction as a matter of bad luck: "Upon this evidence the court saw fit to fine the poor creature ten dollars . . . A hard decision . . . but all cannot be lucky and some must be unfortunate."[9]

Legal challenges to vagrancy arrests of "unfortunates" appeared again in St. Louis near the turn of the twentieth century. In May 1896, an attorney implemented habeas corpus proceedings in the St. Louis criminal court on behalf of Walter Smith, a Black workhouse inmate who, although he had committed no crime, was slapped with a draconian fine of $500 plus three dollars in costs. First District police judge Thomas H. Peabody sentenced Smith to the rock pile on a charge of vagrancy, for associating with known criminals. Smith was also serving a workhouse sentence to work off a fine of ten dollars plus three dollars in costs on a minor infraction of a city ordinance.

He appealed to the Missouri Supreme Court, which declared that the eighth clause of section 1533, article 6, chapter 25 of St. Louis's revised ordinances of 1887 was unconstitutional. The state court was remarkably clear and forceful in its ruling, determining that the eighth clause violated an individual's right of free association and jeopardized personal liberties. The high court ordered Smith's release as soon as he worked off the smaller judgment, on or about July 3, 1896. As the supreme court justices pointed out, he would have fared better if he had committed a felony and served time in the penitentiary. To work off the $500 fine would have required that Smith remain in the workhouse for six years, ten months, and twenty-five days.

In a separate case soon afterward, St. Louis circuit judge William Zachritz freed another workhouse prisoner, ruling that the "idling" section of the statute, too, was unconstitutional. He emphasized that it was a mockery of justice to criminalize unemployment. In an Audrain County case in which a justice of the peace ordered the sheriff to auction off a Black man arrested for vagrancy, the Missouri Supreme Court ruled that the practice violated the federal and state constitutions. In 1897, the legislature repealed a section of the state's vagrancy statute that allowed the sale of vagrants on courthouse steps for six months to the highest bidder, but the vagrancy statute itself remained intact.[10]

In the 1871 annual report of the workhouse superintendent, Frank G. Fitzgerald emphasized that overcrowding was at a critical stage, with as many as twelve inmates in a cell. Noting, too, that the quarries were nearly played out, he recommended the sale of the workhouse property and buildings and the construction of a new workhouse on a new site. At the end of July 1872, Mayor Joseph Brown, the workhouse committee, and the city comptroller visited the institution to discuss plans for expansion. Concerned that the supply of St. Louis limestone rock in the quarry was nearly exhausted, the officials considered a possible new location, but the lack of accessible quarries elsewhere discouraged them from pursuing a new site. During the visit, the mayor, comptroller, and committee ate lunch with Superintendent Fitzgerald and toured the facility. There were 152 men and 103 women imprisoned in the workhouse at the time. On duty in sentry boxes were nine guards, including two night sentries armed with loaded muskets. While Mayor Brown was on the grounds, he exercised executive clemency to pardon and release about seventy inmates.[11]

Instead of moving the workhouse to a new location, city officers opted to renovate and expand the existing site and facilities. In 1873, a new brick building with three tiers of cells was added. With four prisoners in a cell, it was calculated to hold 168 inmates. The eastern end of the structure consisted of only two stories with added baths, a boiler room, and sleeping quarters for the guards. The improvements included a new two-story, Gothic-style brick house for the superintendent and his family. The seven-room house, surrounded by trees and beautiful flower beds tended by workhouse trusties, was built by workhouse labor just outside the gate and walls of the grounds, partly so the walls would further shield superintendents' children from the prisoners and the daily workhouse routines and practices.[12]

Yet there was nothing bucolic about what lay behind the stone walls at Point Breeze. Most workhouse inmates had broken city ordinances. They were petty criminals from police courts—"Sunday drunks," "police characters," peace disturbers, vagrants, unlicensed peddlers, and "fallen women" who refused to pay shakedown money for police protection. Many were repeat offenders who suffered from alcohol and drug abuse, and many were casualties of homelessness and poverty. When police court judges did not know what else to do with them, they sent them to the workhouse to break rock in the quarry. If a person who was "deaf and dumb" did not respond quickly enough to a police officer's questions or commands on the streets, the workhouse rock pile might be the punishment. Among the inmates, some suffered from epilepsy or the frailties of old age. Despite the opening of the St. Louis County Lunatic Asylum in 1869, the workhouse continued to house prisoners who suffered from insanity.

Mayor John How, who oversaw the relocation of the workhouse to Point Breeze in 1853, complained that it was disgraceful to pen up the insane with vicious criminals and others. On April 21, 1868, the *Daily Missouri Republican* noted that among approximately 350 inmates were fourteen male and sixteen female "lunatics." On a traditional Independence Day "turn-out," or remitting-of-fines tour of the institution, with Republican mayor James S. Thomas and several city officers in July 1868, a reporter for the *Missouri Democrat* noted thirty-five prisoners who were deemed insane. Twenty of them were women under the supervision of Elizabeth King, a nurse. As the reporter and other visitors walked through the area that housed insane women, one of the so-called insane gave a speech on women's rights.[13]

In October 1869, Republican mayor Nathan Cole pointed out that there were eighteen insane people and "idiots" in the workhouse. He, too, considered such treatment of the mentally ill a disgrace. A judge emphasized that some of them had been locked up in the workhouse for at least four years. He charged that outsiders dumped some of them in the city, where they were left on the streets, arrested for some trifling violation, and then sent to the workhouse. He urged the stationing of police at depots and steamboat landings to curb the practice. Despite modest efforts to find better care and more humane treatment of the mentally ill by placing them in other institutions, the workhouse continued to house prisoners who were there because of their insanity.[14]

A few inmates were incorrigibles whose families had tired of them and thus refused to pay their fines in the courts. Some of the women had infants with them. When Mary Barrett's relatives charged her with peace disturbance, she showed up in the Second District police court with her infant on September 7, 1888, unable to pay the five-dollar fine. The judge showed no mercy and sent her and the baby to the workhouse.

Some inmates were guilty of assault and battery and other felonious activities, but for more than a few, life in the dreary workhouse was easier than life on St. Louis's Gilded Age streets. In this sense, the workhouse at times functioned as a safety net. In 1867, seventy-year-old Timothy Hurley, homeless, hungry, and unemployed, asked Mayor Thomas to send him to the workhouse. The mayor gave Hurley a letter to take to James Luddington, superintendent of the workhouse. The letter instructed Luddington to put Hurley to work on the rock pile and to release him whenever Hurley asked to leave. A destitute old person like Hurley, on the ragged edge of starvation with no food or place to sleep, might beg the mayor to send him to the workhouse, but to do so exacted a price. The homeless, hungry, and feeble old men were thrown into crowded cells with convicted felons and young street toughs who often bullied them. Many prisoners wore a ball and chain.[15]

Women prisoners worked off their fines in several ways. In 1868, the "better class" of women sewed prisoners' clothing while the "more abandoned" broke rocks in the quarry. A few did some tailoring. Later, until contracts dried up around 1890, some of the women toiled in a brush factory on the third floor of the women's quarters. Of approximately one hundred women prisoners at the time of a report by an undercover reporter in 1886, about twenty worked in the factory. By 1890, after ongoing public criticism of forcing women to work on the rock pile, women mostly washed, scrubbed, sewed, and mended the gowns worn by women prisoners and the pants and shirts worn by the imprisoned men.[16]

The workhouse received prisoners from the Court of Criminal Correction and from three divisions of the circuit court, but nine out of ten inmates came from the notorious police courts. Of the 1,528 prisoners (815 men and 713 women) confined during a six-month period in 1872, 1,418 had been sent by police courts. Irish immigrants and Black residents of the city bore the brunt of such confinements. Among the total number in 1872 were 747 Irish immigrants, 284 Blacks, 235 nonimmigrant whites, and 143 immigrants from Germany. Spectators gathered about the Four Courts when prisoners were loaded into the police patrol wagon, or the Black Maria, as it was commonly called, for transport to the workhouse.[17]

A city ordinance required that no sentence from a police court be longer than six months, or a year in the case of prisoners sent by the criminal courts, whether felons or those convicted of a misdemeanor. Police court judges had no authority to send a person directly to the workhouse, but the fines they imposed, if unpaid, meant confinement. As a *St. Louis Post-Dispatch* reporter observed in 1886, "It is only the poor man who cannot pay his fine, or the unfortunate who cannot get word to his friends, or is deserted by them, who goes down to break rocks." As a subcommittee of the Social Service Committee of the St. Louis Civic League pointed out in 1911, "The commitments from police courts come from the quasi-criminal nature of police court procedure, by which offenders against city ordinances *are virtually imprisoned for debt*—that is, for inability to pay the city the amount owed as a fine." The committee further explained, "This system of commitment from the various courts under really different theories, results in a fundamental practical reality in dealing with the problem of the workhouse as a social institution, *because the system oftentimes frees the habitual offender who has money, or friends with money to pay fines, while those too poor to pay are compelled to serve time. Many are committed from whom society does not need protection, and who are in no sense criminal, and many escape commitment who need the corrective influence of imprisonment*" (emphasis in original).[18]

After the mournful signal bell announced that the Black Maria was about to dump its daily batch of fresh arrivals at the workhouse, a clerk recorded their names and noted their crimes and sentences as they stood in line. Then guards and trusties marched them to the bathrooms, where they were stripped of their clothing. In many cases, the prisoners' tattered, vermin-infested clothing had to be cut off and thrown away. Each male prisoner donned a prison garb of brown canvas pants and a blue shirt, along with brogans and a cap. Women wore a bluish-gray checked gown. Two large bathing tanks filled with muddy Mississippi River water awaited them. Each tank, one for men and the other for women, had a capacity of fifteen bathers. After their bath, new inmates were assigned to a cell based on racial and gender segregation as stipulated by city ordinance.

On the following day, guards took men whose sentences exceeded four months to the "shackle shop," where a blacksmith riveted ten-pound shackles and chains on them. A prisoner with a fine of at least fifty dollars wore a shackle and chain on both legs, but men whose fine ranged between twenty-five and fifty dollars wore a shackle on one leg only. A fine under twenty-five dollars meant no shackling of the prisoner was required. Those who served long sentences in shackles and chains often developed a shuffle and foot-dragging style of walking that marked them for life.[19]

At six o'clock in the morning, guards marched prisoners in a line to the dining room for a breakfast of black coffee, a cold corn dodger that was "somewhat heavier than zinc," with "the tenacity of wrought-iron," and a pie plate half filled with heavily watered-down molasses to wet the cornbread. An undercover reporter wrote that the cornbread "would make good macadam if it could be broken." The sweetened water was made at a ratio of eight buckets of water to a bucket of molasses. "Whoever discovered this nauseating and transparent fluid to be an article of food deserves a medal," he noted with sarcasm. Not much could be said for the coffee, either, but it was hot. So little coffee was used in brewing that it hardly turned the color of the water. Added essence of coffee chemicals and acids darkened it during preparation, but the taste was nearly as awful as early efforts to provide soldiers with instant coffee in the Civil War. Workhouse coffee, served in the same tin bowls that had held soup the previous night, always contained a "greasy scum" on account of the kitchen's speedy, easy dishwashing system, which consisted of putting all the tinware into a large tub and pouring hot water over it.[20]

At seven a.m., guards marched inmates to the quarry, where the prisoners broke rock and loaded riprap for use in grading and improving city streets. Men broke the big rocks while women used hammers to break the rock into still smaller pieces, to add to nine-foot-high piles of riprap in the quarry. To quench their thirst in the quarry, prisoners drank hydrant water hauled from the mule trough at the stables, where about forty mules, a few cows, and a horse or two also drank. Under the supervision of guards, selected prisoners in street crews known as "clay-banks" regularly crossed congested streets in a procession of mule-drawn carts filled with riprap to grade and improve streets.

At noon, prisoners on the workhouse grounds marched to the dining hall, where a paid steward, aided by a handful of prisoners, served a fare consisting of three-quarters of a pound of tough but welcomed soup meat and a hunk of white bread from the poorhouse bakery. The best cut of beef went to the officers and guards' kitchen for preparation. Seated on crowded benches jammed against long tables, male prisoners in the cell buildings washed down their food with hydrant water cooled in a deep cistern. The clay-banks, whose noon meal was delivered in wagons to the work site in the city, usually received higher-quality food than what was served in the dining hall. Street crews knocked off work at about four p.m. to get back to the workhouse in time for a supper of "skilly" at six o'clock.

In 1872, a reporter for the *Missouri Republican* was at the workhouse to witness the return of a chain gang from the quarry. "The gang marched in twos, each one having his legs loosely chained together," he observed, "the clanking of which was heard some distance as they marched along." The evening skilly consisted of whatever was left from the dinner's soup "boiled up with the bones and diluted plentifully with water." "Sometimes it is so thin at supper," wrote an undercover reporter in 1886, "that the bottom of the bowl can be seen through it, but generally it looks and tastes like hot hydrant water thickened with a little salt and with a few drops of grease sprinkled on top."[21]

The time nominally allotted for prisoners to eat was ten minutes, but hungry guards pushed them away from the tables in about four or five minutes. Inmates often had to gulp down the liquids and grab the solids on their way to the quarry or back to their cell. A paid gardener with prison labor at his disposal produced a large summer garden, but typically the vegetables went to the officers' kitchen. Not until late in the growing season, if then, did vegetables appear on the table of inmates. Strawberries never did find their way there. "Unless a man is a rather large eater," concluded the reporter, "the quantity of food supplied is sufficient. The general complaint is to the sloppiness of the food, soup twice and coffee and sweetened water once a day, giving too constant a run of spoon victuals. The meat is also rather scarce and often quite fatty or gristly."[22]

On a day-to-day basis, prisoners washed up in tin basins at a few pumps on the grounds. Four towels, to be shared by all the men, were distributed each morning and night. Inmates had no opportunity to wash up at noon. On Saturday evenings at five o'clock, they took their weekly bath in a tank, or "sinkhole," that was about six feet high and five feet wide. For men, there were two racially segregated tanks. Guards hustled the men in and out of the tanks in squads. The tanks were filled with four feet of water that was often extremely cold. In each of the two segregated tanks, the inmates, many of whom were afflicted with open sores, bacterial infections, and other ailments, bathed in the same water because the guards did not want to be bothered to change it. "It is not the dirtiest men but the cleanest who shudder most at the thought of the weekly cold bath," a reporter observed, "and it is cold, unmercifully cold in May before the hydrant water turns warm."[23]

Skilled male prisoners were assigned to carpenter and blacksmith shops and construction and repair projects on the grounds. Trusties, who were doled out special favors and privileges, worked in the vegetable garden under the supervision of a paid gardener, or they landscaped the grounds and around the outside of the walls. Some of the trusties worked in the superintendent's home on the grounds, or they performed other less onerous tasks. Men who were emaciated, scrawny, and frail, or who had serious ailments, usually worked in the kitchen or dining room, or they did lighter work on the grounds and in the stable. Male prisoners on short-term sentences were assigned lighter work in the vegetable garden and yard on the assumption that short-term inmates were less likely to try to escape.[24]

On November 23, 1880, the Board of Public Improvements (BPI), upon the recommendation of the workhouse superintendent, requested appropriations to create a brush factory on the grounds to find more suitable employment for women inmates. The board authorized the superintendent to begin discussions with brush manufacturers and dealers who might be interested in setting up the operations in exchange for the brushes and compensation for labor. The authorization came in response to a public outcry and grand jury report that recommended a more humane way than breaking rocks in the quarry to put women inmates to work.[25]

The brush factory began operations on January 1, 1881. In the first six months, women inmates and a few from the men's quarters manufactured 23,000 brushes valued at $387, but by 1890, the number of contracts began to dry up. In February 1890, the BPI refused to accede to a request from the Corner Manufacturing Company of Columbus, Ohio, to cancel a brush contract. The company complained that at the time the contract was signed, there were more than one hundred women prisoners available for labor at the workhouse. In the meantime, the number of women inmates dropped to around fifty. As a result of its unprofitability, the company had eliminated the position of its foreman at the workhouse.

After the workhouse factory closed, the main employment of white women consisted of mending and making prison clothes in a sixteen-by-twelve-foot sewing room on the third floor of the women's "extremely primitive" prison. Some of them also cooked and worked in the officers' and guards' kitchen and dining room under the direction of a kitchen supervisor. Other women prisoners cleaned the men's cells, made the beds, and worked in the laundry. Black women, given the racial pecking order, were compelled to clean the cells of white women inmates as well as their own and to scrub the floors and wash the walls, bedding, and clothing. "When I first came to this place they made us break rock just the same as the men," recalled Ellen Maher in 1907. "We got our clothes most tore off of us doin' it, too. It was the awfullest work I ever done. An' then they made us make brushes, women an' men. I got to be a pretty good brushmaker before they stopped that and put us at somethin' else . . . I guess I've done about all the kinds of work women ever did here, and some that men did, too."[26]

On Saturday afternoons, work ended early to allow prisoners to line up, two by two, for their weekly bath and fresh change of clothes. After a tin bowl of soup for supper, the guards marched them back to their cells to be locked up for the night. All lights were extinguished in the cell buildings at nine p.m. between April and October, and at eight p.m. during the other months. Workhouse officers claimed the food was more than adequate, but an investigation in 1910 concluded that the food was of inferior quality, completely inadequate for the work required. In 1898, when a reporter asked about the food, a young prisoner complained, "For breakfast we get bread and molasses that tastes like sweetened water. For supper we have what they call pea soup. It is hot water with a few dried peas thrown in. To eat this soup means to lie awake all night with cramps."[27]

An undercover reporter in 1886 estimated that 75 percent of inmates suffered from diarrhea. He noted that "a medical student or some new-fledged pill-maker is supposed to visit the place daily, but he is as difficult to see as a king."[28] About three times a week, a doctor hired by the superintendent made rounds at the workhouse or was summoned to examine prisoners in the "sick cell," which was anything but a place for the sick. In some cases, the doctor prescribed medicine or suggested that prisoners be sent to the city hospital, but workhouse officers did not always follow his instructions and recommendations. To make sure inmates were not feigning illness to avoid the rock pile, officers made the sick cell appear more like a place of punishment. At times, it went unheated. And in fact, those who complained of sickness were assumed to be faking. "That sick-cell ought to appeal to the humane," an inmate recalled in 1897. "I was in it for a day. The floor is of concrete and the furnishings consist of two wooden benches and a bucket of water. There was no bed or bedding in it . . . They don't care anything about a sick man down there."[29] Insane inmates, too, were chucked into the room. Epileptics were suspected of staging seizures to get out of work. "Just as policemen sometimes arrest a man in a fit [seizure] as drunk," wrote the undercover reporter, "so do the brilliant police judges sometimes fine a stark mad man for assault and battery or some other offense."[30]

Although the costs of room and board went up over the years, the wage of fifty cents per day prevailed until a new charter in 1914 hiked it to three dollars. No credits were given for Sundays. In fact, half of Saturday's credits were subtracted to pay for Sunday's two meals. On days when sickness or bad weather prevented work in the quarry, inmates were still entitled to compensation, but they had to subtract room and board charges. Unruly prisoners who refused to work or who were punished in solitary confinement did not get credit for those days, but costs of rooming were added to the amount of their fine to be worked off. Escapees, when recaptured, forfeited credit for what they had worked off prior to their escape. Once again, they had to work off the original amount of their fine. The city ordinance required the superintendent of the workhouse to notify the mayor and the city marshal within twenty-four hours when a prisoner escaped, and to provide a description of the escapee and the manner of escape. Failure to do so meant that the superintendent was personally liable for the prisoner's fine and costs.[31]

Oversight of the workhouse was at first vested in a board of managers, then in the Board of Public Improvements. After the new city charter in 1914, the director of the Public Welfare department assumed oversight. The mayor appointed superintendents, who required confirmation by the city council, but after 1914, an efficiency board examination was required, and the director of Public Welfare appointed them. The city ordinance prohibited work on Sundays and stipulated that no prisoner was to be assigned to work for private parties unless the board approved a full written contract specifying the details of the arrangement.

The use of solitary confinement, irons, and a diet of bread and water in the calaboose as a form of punishment was spelled out in the ordinance. In 1879, a reporter described what lay in store for a prisoner locked in the bull-ring on a diet of bread and water, with only a tiny hole in the top of the door for light: "It is next to impossible for him to obtain any rest while confined, as there is no furniture in the room, and on every four inches of the floor there is a small board about an inch in height, which makes the surface so uneven that it would more torture to attempt to lie down than refresh him. Should this not subdue the prisoner, his arms are tied up to a post at his back. This never fails to bring him under control."[32]

On Sundays in the workhouse, cells remained closed, except at mealtimes. Only two meals were served, breakfast at nine o'clock and supper at three thirty. The workhouse had no chapel until the second decade of the 1900s. Nor was there a regularly appointed chaplain, but several ministers and priests donated their time. Thomas Harvey Hagerty, a Methodist minister, devoted more than thirty years of service to the spiritual needs of inmates in the workhouse and other city institutions. For Catholic prisoners, Father Martin of St. Anthony's Church and the Franciscan Monastery on Meramec Street held services at eight a.m., one week for men and the next week for women. The Queen's Daughters and women from the Christian Willing Workers sometimes distributed religious literature in the afternoons, and other Protestant preachers showed up to sermonize and to lead prisoners in the singing of hymns.

Prisoners passed the time as best they could. There was no opportunity for exercise. Those with family and friends were allowed visitors. Some of the prisoners read a newspaper, religious tract, or other piece of available literature. A few played cards in their cells, but to do so required special permission. As a reporter noted in 1886, "The principal feature of the day is the fearful noise and ribaldry which is kept up between the cells by the toughs and hoodlums. The greater portion of the day is a perfect pandemonium."[33]

Daily life in the workhouse changed little from year to year, despite an occasional modest attempt by superintendents to improve conditions. Typically, reform-minded initiatives came only in response to bad publicity after incidents of outrageous brutality or revelations of horrid conditions hit newspapers. Even for superintendents whose attempts at reform were genuine, the life of prisoners in the workhouse was more often determined by the methods of discipline and cruelty of guards and clerks employed at the institution. Superintendents came and went regularly, but guards, especially those known for brutality and corruption, often remained on the workhouse payroll from one superintendency to the next, sometimes for a decade or two.

2

GUARDIANS OF BRUTALITY

The St. Louis Workhouse was plagued by racism, scandal, nepotism, cronyism, patronage, and trigger-happy guards with their own side hustles. The guards seemed to relish whipping and torturing the institution's "moral lepers." A wrong look or wrong word, a split second of hesitation in responding to a command, or a weakened stumble by a sick prisoner might set off a guard and provoke a clubbing or worse. Savage beatings were the flip side of lax discipline that led to frequent escapes and suicide attempts. Far too many guards in the age of social Darwinism shared views of the down-and-out and afflicted as animals, the unfit of the species who deserved every beating they got. It was a coal smoke–darkened world that often brought out the worst in humanity. A dog-eat-dog philosophy prevailed. Many observers believed that prostitutes, drug users, or a poor woman who picked up a few lumps of coal in a rail yard to heat her river shanty deserved whatever punishment was meted out. Poor record keeping, carefully stacked coroner's juries, and political cover by friends in the mayor's office and city hall shielded the workhouse's petty tyrants from scrutiny and dismissal.

Superintendents guarded workhouse secrets carefully. They put up walls to shield the institution from newspaper reporters who came poking around. Until the late 1880s, reportage on the workhouse was rarely critical of its inner workings. The public knew little about its practices or the conditions of its prisoners. Reporters who requested to visit the workhouse typically were given sugarcoated tours by its officers on Sundays, when the institution looked its best. Rarely did reporters get a chance to interview inmates without the intimidating presence of the superintendent or one of his clerks or scowling guards. Such was the case when a *St. Louis Globe-Democrat* reporter wrote a favorable piece on the workhouse on July 19, 1875.

Henry Stussel, the newly appointed superintendent who was the Democratic Party's recent nominee for alderman of the Third Ward, was not available for an interview. A Prussian immigrant, he was the joint owner of Stussel & Meyer, undertakers who operated a livery stable business. In his absence, Michael Carey, a longtime workhouse guard, and John Merz, the foreman, showed the reporter around the grounds and the quarry, answering questions along the way. The result was an overall favorable Sunday picture of the institution, a mainly descriptive article with images of prisoners lounging in their cells, preachers in the corridors, and a few women prisoners bantering with Merz or joyously singing "Shall We Gather at the River?"[1]

After controversial killings in the workhouse and deaths of prisoners under questionable circumstances, reporters began to adopt a more critical perspective. On August 2, 1878, several guards fired on and killed George Stevens, a twenty-nine-year-old epileptic who resisted their authority. Stevens, intelligent but of doubtful sanity, was in the workhouse on peace disturbance charges brought by his brother-in-law and a couple of others. It was not his first time inside the walls. Previously, Stevens's brother-in-law had also filed assault charges against him, but Stevens at the time was in such a pitiful, weakened state that the prosecuting attorney and judge of the Court of Criminal Correction set him free. Several officers at the Four Courts who were familiar with Stevens thought he should be sent to the insane asylum. After he was freed, police found him asleep in a gutter and rearrested him on a vagrancy charge. Off to the workhouse he went, where he was killed.[2]

The *Globe-Democrat* immediately blamed the victim, "a veritable vagrant, one of those lousy, idle characters who roam around the streets at daytime and at night sleep on the Court House steps or in alleys." The newspaper justified the killing on grounds that the guards shot Stevens in self-defense. To dehumanize Stevens further, the newspaper's coverage of the killing emphasized that he faked epileptic seizures, or "fits," as they were commonly known at the time, to get out of work. The newspaper also claimed that he often violently attacked guards. After two days in the "black hole" with his arms tied to a post, Stevens was sent to break rock in the quarry under the supervision of guard John H. Coy. After a confrontation with a guard, Stevens started throwing large rocks and injuring several guards who tried to subdue him. Finally, guards pulled their revolvers and blazed away. Coy fired at Stevens, who finally dropped after quite a battle, according to the *Globe-Democrat.* Two workhouse prisoners were wounded by stray bullets.[3]

On the scene at the time was workhouse superintendent Charles H. L. Groffman, a Republican grocer and saloon keeper who was confirmed in 1878 after the city council rejected eight of Mayor Henry Overstolz's nominees for the superintendency. Upon the summoning of doctors, Groffman reportedly dashed off to the mayor's office, unavailable to answer questions from reporters. After a coroner's inquest, guard Coy was charged with assault with intent to kill. A jury in the Court of Criminal Correction found him guilty, but he was fined only $100, which his friends posted immediately. A few weeks later, it was business as usual at the Four Courts when Coy's light punishment became even lighter. His sentence was quietly commuted to two hours in the city jail.[4]

In addition to the customary financial, statistical, and informational materials provided by workhouse officials, a *Post-Dispatch* reporter on a guided Sunday tour of the institution in 1879 did capture a few brief profiles of prisoners who were frequently confined there. Among them were Blanche Shoemaker, often arrested for peace disturbance when she drank too much, and Eliza Wells. Wells was known for a well-established practice of "going to butchers' stands and after depositing five cents for a soup-bone quietly walking off with a ham valued at a few dollars dangling under her apron." Sixty-five-year-old James Daily, who had averaged about three confinements per year over eighteen years on charges of drunk and disorderly conduct, suggested that when things on the outside got too rough, it was easy to get confined "just by taking some little thing so that the owner will catch you." The reporter, in his reflections on the visit to the workhouse, may have said more about the desperate living conditions of the city's toilers than about the inmates of Point Breeze: "To an outsider it would appear that the prisoners confined in the Work-house enjoy life better than many of the laboring classes who inhabit the hovels and tenements throughout the city, but the simple fact that they have not their liberty is sufficient punishment for their offenses."[5]

For a few inmates, the workhouse provided a sense of community. In the case of German-born William Henry Nolte, a thirty-day sentence in the workhouse turned into a lifetime as a trusty when he repeatedly pleaded with officers not to force him to leave. When he immigrated to the United States from Württemberg in 1865 at age seventeen, he left behind Freda

Meyerchord, the young daughter of a shopkeeper to whom he had pledged his troth. A master brewer, Nolte found a job in St. Louis at the Lemp Brewery. He and Freda exchanged letters, and soon her family arrived in St. Louis, where her father opened a bakery. Nolte boarded with them, and he and Freda became engaged.

When the depression of 1873 hit, Nolte lost all his savings in an investment, and he lost his job, too. Unable to find steady employment in the mid-1870s, he continued to drift from one temporary job to the next while Freda waited. In the meantime, the Meyerchord family fell on hard times, and Freda turned to another suitor. In summer 1878, when Nolte discovered that she had jilted him, he angrily created a drunken disturbance in the neighborhood. Freda served as a prosecution witness against him in police court. In July, the judge sent him to the workhouse for thirty days under Superintendent Groffman's tenure. At the end of Nolte's sentence, he insisted he would not leave until Freda came to seek his pardon. Years passed, and in the meantime he settled in as a trusty who gained the nickname "Sweet Water" for his work mixing molasses and water and serving food in the dining room.[6]

Nearly thirty-nine years after Nolte entered the workhouse on a thirty-day sentence, he was forced out into the world at age seventy-five, in 1907. By then, even his name was lost to those around him. Friendless and without family, he was known only as Sweet Water. Addled and confused upon dismissal, he sought the help of former workhouse superintendent Andrew Scully, who persuaded the superintendent of the industrial school to give Nolte a job doing chores and to let him sleep in a shed at the institution. Soon fired, Nolte was distraught. "If they would only let me fix the meat and potatoes and lay out the salt for the boys," he pleaded, "I think I could please them. I am the best man in the world for that job." He opposed going to the poorhouse, but Scully convinced him it was necessary. Reflecting on Nolte's being kicked out of the workhouse as an old man, Scully told a *Post-Dispatch* reporter: "His dismissal after all these years has almost driven him insane. He has told me he was 'bug house' from drink when he was sent there, but I know plenty of men walking around loose who are not as sane. I regret that such a faithful, inoffensive servant of the city has been turned out into the world where he is helpless after having given 38 years of free service to the city which really owes him money enough today to keep him out of the Poorhouse."[7]

Nolte's case, though unique in its characteristics, underscored a much larger problem for the poorest of workhouse inmates without resources and a supportive network of family and friends. What would be the fate of the penniless upon release? In 1912, the Reverend Thomas Hagerty, Methodist chaplain of city institutions, called attention to the contradictions of a policy that left prisoners with nothing when they left the workhouse. "Having served the term," he pointed out in a letter to the editor of the *Globe-Democrat,* "they are turned out, not having a cent, many of them, or a place to sleep. What can they do? To beg will endanger an arrest as vagrants, or to sleep in some box or empty car, they are in danger of an arrest. To seek employment and tell that they are just out of the Workhouse, who will employ them?" Hagerty suggested that the city provide inmates with a voucher for lodging and food and help them look for work at the end of their confinement. Or, alternatively, he urged the city to allow them to live at the workhouse for a few days and to pay them decent wages in order that they might have at least a modicum of support when they went out to look for work.[8]

Superintendent Groffman turned the workhouse into a self-sustaining, even profitable institution, but the brutality of his regime created such an uproar that he was removed from the superintendency. In 1880, Samuel Marchbank threatened to sue Groffman and the city for abuse he suffered while locked up in the workhouse for six months on a charge of adultery. What sparked the abuse was a visit by Sarah "March," with whom Marchbank was cohabiting in St. Louis. Both were fined $500, but Sarah, after twenty days in jail, was released on account of health problems and insolvency. She obtained a permit from the mayor's office to visit Marchbank in the workhouse. When Marchbank was brought in her presence, she spontaneously threw her arms around him and kissed him, promising to get money somehow to pay his fine. Afterward, a guard told Groffman about the kiss.

That night, after the prisoners were asleep, Groffman called Marchbank from his cell bed into the corridor. Cussing and ranting that the prisoner was not going to turn his workhouse into a "whorehouse," Groffman belted Marchbank in the mouth with his fist and struck him twice in the stomach with a club. The blows staggered Marchbank against the cell door and left a lump on his head and a cut inside his lip. The abuse did not end there. Marchbank was strung up in the bullring with his hands drawn behind him for about eighteen hours. Lice-infested and denied a bath, he made it clear to a reporter he would kill himself if he thought he had to endure another three months in the workhouse.[9]

Upon hearing about the abuse from an anonymous source, a determined *Post-Dispatch* reporter paid a visit to the workhouse with a special permit to interview Marchbank privately, without a guard standing nearby. The reporter was shocked when the clerk brought before him a dirty, disheveled, heavily bearded, and heavily shackled inmate. He could scarcely believe it was the same well-dressed man he had seen in the Court of Criminal Correction a few months earlier. Through the reporter, the public learned the frank account of Marchbank's abuse at the hands of Groffman. "You mark my words," the prisoner told the reporter. "As soon as you leave I will get a worse dose than the first one; but damn him, when I get out of this he will pay for it."[10]

From the time of Marchbank's arrest and sentencing in the Court of Criminal Correction in January 1880, the case drew enormous publicity. Formerly of New Jersey, he was a well-dressed supervisor of cutters at the shirtwaist factory of F. A. Steers on a monthly salary of $100. Elizabeth Marchbank, his legal wife whom he left behind in New Jersey, showed up in court with their three children to press charges against him, but she was remorseful immediately after he was sentenced. She even went to the capital, Jeff City, to plead for a pardon on his behalf. On May 6, Missouri governor John Smith Phelps denied the request for a pardon but noted that Marchbank could use city courts in St. Louis to punish workhouse officers if they abused him.[11]

To calm the public storm, Mayor Henry Overstolz appointed Wilhelm "Billy" Kunz to replace Groffman. Kunz was a police sergeant with a cork leg as the result of a wound sustained in the line of duty on the force. Drawing a monthly salary of $100, he implemented an incentive-based system that relied less on brutal exploitation to increase work output and to make the workhouse profitable. He set a daily rock-breaking quota of one hundred feet of riprap in the quarry, adding financial rewards to shorten a sentence if a prisoner's output exceeded the quota. Kunz argued that the new system would increase the workhouse's profitability as well as alleviate overcrowding via shorter confinements. From time to time in the past, mayors had ordered the release of a mass number of prisoners to relieve overcrowding. Under Kunz, the mayor exercised the power of executive clemency in a different way. Nearly every week, during visits by the mayor to the workhouse, the chief guard lined up the convicts and singled out for praise those whose good behavior and work output warranted clemency. The mayor pardoned them on the spot. Such a system rewarded good behavior and moved deserving prisoners out of the institution earlier, avoiding mass releases without regard to a prisoner's behavior.[12]

Unless an occasional ex-inmate of the workhouse stopped by a newspaper office to tell of the dark side of life in the institution, the public knew only what officials fed reporters. Even when a shocking incident of brutality hit the public from time to time, workhouse officers typically dug in their heels and waited for the storm of controversy to blow over. Required reports by grand juries and the Board of Health were mostly perfunctory. Rarely did they spark meaningful reforms. In fact, they often were a farce. On prearranged tours of the workhouse, reporters generally received a royal reception, and maybe a box of cigars as a gift. The *Post-Dispatch* made several futile efforts to plant an undercover reporter inside the workhouse as a prisoner. Someone at the Four Courts usually spotted him as a fake when he appeared before a judge on a misdemeanor charge. In 1886, six years after the Marchbank affair and Kunz's implementation of a rewards system, an undercover *Post-Dispatch* writer slipped past judges and officers of the Four Courts and was sent to the workhouse to work off his fine on a trivial charge.

At the time the reporter entered the workhouse, Kunz was still the superintendent, reappointed by Mayor William L. Ewing. Ida Kunz, the superintendent's wife, also was on the city's bloated payroll, drawing a monthly salary as the officers' cook and matron, and Johnny Kunz, the superintendent's brother, was a guard. The reporter praised Superintendent Kunz's "many admirable reforms," including greater attention to the cleanliness and comfort of the cells. The mattresses and bedding were nearly new. Women prisoners washed the floors daily and whitewashed the walls regularly. Although the building was old, pests were not a serious problem at the time. The reporter also lauded the quarry foreman as a reasonable taskmaster who rarely cussed the men at work breaking rock.

In "Work-House Woes," a front-page story in the *Post-Dispatch,* the reporter emphasized that although Kunz was well-intentioned and deserved praise for improving conditions, he spent most of his time in the office, shielded from abuses inflicted by guards. The man who truly managed the prisoners was Joe Galen, the "burly, big-voiced" inside foreman and chief assistant who was a Democratic operative from the Eleventh Ward and kin to Kunz. "He [Galen] aspires to be a terror, and having plenty of power and the men being helpless he succeeds fairly well," observed the reporter. "He has good executive ability and is well acquainted with the kind of men he has to deal with. His drawback is his natural and acquired brutality. In this respect he is totally unfit for the position."[13]

In the presence of the undercover reporter, an English prisoner, George Saplin (or Charles Penrose), was suffering mightily from dysentery and flux when he asked Galen for some medicine. Galen knocked Saplin down, and ordered him to keep working, even though the prisoner could barely stand. Then he threw Saplin into the sick cell, where the prisoner lingered without medical attention. On June 3, workhouse officials sent Saplin to the city hospital, where he died the next morning.

George Wilson, a machinist sentenced in late March 1886 to work off a fine of $100, suffered a serious injury in the quarry when pieces of frozen clay fell on his leg and ankle. In serious pain as his shackled ankle swelled, he repeatedly requested medical attention, but Galen kept him on the job and refused to remove the shackle from the injured foot and leg. Afterward, Wilson went to Superintendent Kunz, who called for a doctor. Wilson ended up in the city hospital, where he was treated and sent back to the workhouse. The mayor pardoned him on May 26, but when Wilson was released from the workhouse, he left with a permanently crippled leg.[14]

As the case of Adolphus F. "Frank" Ulrich illustrates, there was no legal compensation for injuries sustained in the workhouse. A Union veteran who had served on the western frontier after the war, he suffered a series of misfortunes on St. Louis's dangerous streets. In 1886, he ended up in the city hospital after being waylaid, beaten, and robbed of forty dollars on the corner of Seventeenth and Pine Streets. While walking near the Union Market on a bright, moonlit night in 1887, he accidentally dropped a few small coins into a gutter and bent over to search for them. "While doing this," Ulrich wrote in his diary, "a big brute of a police officer came up and demanded to know what I was doing. Before I had time to reply he struck me on my left arm with his club and then struck me on the left leg, laming me so I could scarcely walk. Either by accident or otherwise, he ran the end of the billy into my eye, nearly gouging the eye from its socket." When Ulrich cried out in pain, the officer clubbed him again and locked him up in the Biddle Street police station, but the police judge freed him the next morning. On another occasion, three men who claimed to be police officers stripped him of three silver dollars and personal items such as his honorable military discharge. The men warned that if he reported the incident, they would see that he spent six months in confinement.[15]

On May 7, 1889, Ulrich was arrested for test firing a new revolver he had bought for protection. In the backyard of his boarding house, enclosed by a sturdy high brick wall, he propped an old door against the wall and fired three shots into it. He was quickly arrested and hustled off to Judge Cady's police court, where the amused judge allowed him to read from a verbose statement outlining his previous misfortunes in the city. Judge Cady fined Ulrich twenty-five dollars and sent him to the workhouse without an opportunity to contact family or friends to help him pay the fine.

Ulrich was assigned six mules to feed, water, groom, and hitch and harness to carts for use in the quarry. Two of the mules were known to be particularly ill-tempered. On May 14, one of them kicked Ulrich on the left breast and right arm. Staggered and knocked about twenty feet, Ulrich briefly lost consciousness. When he regained consciousness, the stable guard was standing over him, cursing and kicking him. Barely able to move, Ulrich requested medical aid but was ordered to keep working in the stable. Over the next two weeks, Ulrich was repeatedly beaten by John N. Baumgartner, the main mule driver, when he was assigned heavy physical tasks that he was unable to perform. The beatings reopened the wound on Ulrich's left breast.[16]

With three broken ribs from the mule kicks, Ulrich begged foreman Joseph Geller [Galen] and clerk John Stansbury to take him out of the stable and give him some other kind of job to do, but they ordered him back to the stable. On a rainy June 17, when all prisoners were ordered to sit down in a narrow hallway, Ulrich was unable to lower himself to the floor on account of the pain in his ribs. In response, Galen belted him twice with a club. "I could not raise my arm for ten days and carried the marks of the blows for a month," Ulrich recalled.

After completing his forty-five-day sentence, Ulrich told his story to Charles P. Johnson, former lieutenant governor of Missouri and one of St. Louis's finest attorneys. Johnson later recounted:

> Poor Ulrich was injured for life by the mule and by the brutal treatment he afterward received at the hands of the Work-house guards. His lungs became diseased and his spine was injured. Through sickness and from the

suffering he endured in the Work-house he became temporarily deranged and for three weeks was confined in the City Insane Asylum. One day he came to me and told me of his troubles. I investigated and found that he had told the truth and though he was without money I undertook, through sympathy for his unfortunate condition, to recover damages for him through the courts.[17]

On November 16, 1889, Johnson filed a suit in the St. Louis Circuit Court against the City of St. Louis, John Baumgartner, and Joseph Geller [Galen] for $20,000. Three years later, the Missouri Supreme Court affirmed the lower court's decision against Ulrich, ruling that a municipal corporation was not liable for the actions of its officers. Justice Francis Marion Black dissented, arguing that Ulrich deserved compensation. In 1894, less than two years after the state supreme court's ruling, Ulrich died in a poorhouse in Edwardsville, Illinois. "His case is one of the greatest outrages that has ever come to my attention," attorney Johnson told a reporter.[18]

No matter the superintendent in charge, the workhouse was incapable of reforming itself. Galen's brutality continued under the controversial superintendency of James J. "Choctaw Jim" Carroll, a Democratic operative from the Fourteenth Ward. Carroll, indicted for election fraud in 1886, was narrowly confirmed in September 1888 as successor to Superintendent Kunz upon Kunz's death on August 2. In November 1889, Michael Walsh, an ex-guard fired recently by Superintendent Carroll, blew the whistle on Galen's corruption and brutality. Walsh, hired as a workhouse guard in January 1887, pointed out that Galen drew a salary of sixty dollars monthly but made more from the sale of tobacco to prisoners at twice the going price. Walsh recalled an incident in which Jim Ray, a Black prisoner, gave a silk handkerchief and a pair of gold earrings to a guard to give to Sadie Truehart, who was imprisoned in the women's quarters. Truehart received the handkerchief but not the earrings. Ray complained to a sympathetic guard, who made the charges known to the superintendent, but nothing was done about the stolen earrings. On another occasion, when Ray complained to Galen about the food, the latter beat him on the head with a heavy cane, inflicting a large gash. Galen reportedly remarked, "I have been laying for you since that earring matter."[19]

"Work-House Woes" exposed arbitrariness and contradictions in the institution's practices and routines, as well as corruption on the part of guards. Shooting craps on the levee might mean a stint in the workhouse for a steamboat roustabout, but guards gambled frequently in the halls. An occasional prisoner was arrested, fined, and sentenced for riding a lame horse, but guards often worked a lame mule in the quarry. Heavy use of alcohol on the outside might mean confinement to work off a sentence, but guards indulged in drunkenness on the job with few if any restraints. They were often guilty of criminal assaults on prisoners, some of whom had been convicted of assaults and sentenced to the workhouse for those very crimes. Joe Galen sold prisoners with money on file tobacco and pipes at predatory prices that fleeced many prisoners of their deposits.

Fights were commonplace while guards remained nowhere in sight or looked the other way. Weaker prisoners received no protection from the violent criminals who bullied and badgered them in the cells and elsewhere on the grounds. Trusties, too, sometimes bullied fellow prisoners to strip them of their tobacco. In the reporter's diary, part of which was published in "Work-House Woes," he recorded canings by guards in the quarry. He also noted that guards assigned epileptics and those who suffered from vertigo to work on the steep ledges of the quarry. When Galen overheard a Black prisoner complain about his piece of meat at dinner, he beat the prisoner's head and shoulders with a cane. Galen then warned that he would bull ring any prisoner who complained about the meat.[20]

Despite harsh conditions, a few able-bodied inmates who enjoyed favored status as trusties preferred the workhouse to life on the outside. To see such cases baffled the undercover reporter. He singled out two repeat offenders who were favorites of officers in May 1886: Sweet Water (Henry Nolte, discussed earlier) and Billy Fisher (alias Ed Cunningham). The reporter described Fisher, a former newsboy and bootblack, as a "brawny, broad-shouldered man now but so weak in ambition that he aspires no higher than to be a trusty cart-driver at the Work-house." Fisher was sad when officers released him at the end of his sentence on May 20, but two days later, he was all smiles when he was hauled back to the workhouse, where he resumed his job as a trusty cart-driver in the quarry.[21]

In a meeting at city hall on March 5, 1888, Superintendent Kunz complained about the burgeoning workhouse population. Now numbering 450 prisoners, the institution was stretched far beyond capacity. Kunz attributed the spike to the policies of Judges J. C. Normile and Edward A. Noonan (soon to be mayor) in the Court of Criminal Correction. A recent legislative act granted judges discretionary sentencing power to send prisoners to the workhouse instead of the city jail, even if juries specified jail time in their verdicts. Judge Normile used the discretionary power to send prisoners to the workhouse, where the public would reap the benefit of their labor, instead of the jail, where prisoners would do nothing but drain taxpayers.[22]

Workhouse superintendents typically shielded cruel, corrupt guards against public outrage. Galen's severe punishment of prisoners went unchecked throughout the scandalous tenure of Superintendent Carroll and that of his successor, John C. Lohrum. On November 17, 1889, the *Post-Dispatch* published a story based on the revelations of Michael Walsh, an ex-guard fired by Carroll. Walsh, who gave specifics and named names, acknowledged that Carroll had fired him, but he insisted that an investigation and other named witnesses would back up his allegations. Walsh accused Carroll and other workhouse officers of neglect of duty and disgraceful conduct. According to Walsh, Carroll, who was often absent from the grounds for days at a time on drunken sprees, tolerated alcohol abuse among guards, some of whom were the superintendent's relatives. In one case, Walsh charged, a prisoner escaped when a drunk guard fell asleep on duty in the sentry shack. Guards allowed "gross immoralities" between male and female prisoners, and they profited from the sale of cigarettes, cigars, gum, and chewing tobacco to inmates. Padded payrolls, frequent escapes, arbitrary prisoner releases, and misappropriation of funds, as well as Galen's ongoing brutality, were among the practices singled out by Walsh.

According to Walsh's statement in the *Post-Dispatch,* punishment of prisoners depended on whether they had money in their office accounts to buy tobacco, cigarettes, and gum from guards. Walsh cited two prisoners whose escape was the result of the partiality shown to them because they had money in the office. When John Spray struck Gus Draber, a guard, Draber reported it to the superintendent's office, but no irons were put on Spray, who had money on file. Shortly afterward, Spray and another prisoner, Rudolph Wetzel, stole a cart and mule and drove away from the workhouse. Although the mule and cart were later recovered, the escaped prisoners remained at large.[23]

Walsh reported that guards, too, were miserably fed and housed at the workhouse. He complained of tainted meat, rancid butter, and bugs in the shucks of guard beds that had not been changed in more than twelve years. Beef, bread, and potatoes made up the standard daily fare, but added on Fridays was fish that was barely fit to eat. Eggs, regarded as a delicacy, rarely were available to guards, although the workhouse often requisitioned a large supply of them. "The quarterly report of the Commissioner of Supplies shows that 300 dozen eggs were used at the Work-house in March and early April," Walsh pointed out. "Now, the guards never saw more than twelve dozen of those eggs. There may have been some given to the trusties, but if they were it was not right, as the prisoners are not allowed any delicacies. Where the remainder of those 300 eggs went is a question."[24]

Amid reports of "sumptuous dinners" at Superintendent Carroll's Point Breeze residence a few months later, the superintendent's monthly report revealed expenditures of more than twenty-five dollars in bread for the table at his own home. In contrast, the report indicated a total of only $433.30 in expenditures to feed five hundred prisoners. Despite hopes that the workhouse might become self-sustaining, it went in the hole more than $1,000 for the month. What particularly raised eyebrows in the offices of the *Post-Dispatch* was the money spent on ammunition. "Judging from the report as to the amount of powder and ball used," a reporter observed, "last month the Work House must have been undergoing a state of siege, as $41.53 worth of ammunition was consumed."[25]

The Board of Public Improvements appointed a committee consisting of harbor and wharf commissioner M. J. Murphy, park commissioner Richard Klemm, and Colonel Henry Flad, president of the BPI, to investigate charges of drunkenness, neglect of duty, financial improprieties, and other accusations against Carroll. Flad did not show up for the hearing, at which Carroll, ex-guard Walsh, and a few others were questioned. The committee presented its findings to Mayor Edward A. Noonan, who refused to fire Carroll. The mayor emphasized that the accusations were not sworn statements. Tensions between Carroll and the board increased. The lackluster financial performance of the workhouse led him to make an unusual request of the BPI in November 1890. He asked not to be required to submit a report on the work of prisoners in upcoming months, citing the closing of the brush factory. With cold weather on the way, he pointed out that quarrying operations would be drastically curtailed if not stopped altogether until spring. The BPI denied his request.[26]

On June 25, 1890, the suspicious death of Nathan Clark put an even more critical spotlight on abuse of inmates. Clark was a thirty-two-year-old homeless Black coach driver born in Mississippi who was fined twenty-five dollars for trespassing and had been sentenced to the workhouse the day before. Superintendent Carroll, on the night of June 24, summoned Dr. David Nowlin of the city hospital to examine serious wounds on the back of Clark's head. When Nowlin arrived at the workhouse, Clark was sitting in a chair, bleeding profusely from wounds on the back of his head. "I've been clubbed down here," Clark replied, when Nowlin asked what had happened. A guard standing nearby spoke up: "No, he's crazy; he don't know what he's talking about." An ambulance took Clark to the city hospital, where he arrived conscious and able to answer questions. Later that day, he sank into a coma and died of a brain concussion.[27]

At first, police arrested Edward Farndell, an English professional nurse previously employed at the Protestant hospital on Eighteenth Street. Farndell had given Clark a beating with his fists on the evening of June 22, when Clark cursed and threatened a group of young girls and struck Farndell behind a saloon at the corner of Thirty-Second and Olive Streets. Farndell, who denied he hit Clark with an object or with such force that would have killed him, dismissed as preposterous the notion that his blows were responsible for Clark's death. The incident behind the saloon had led to the trespassing charges against Clark that landed him in the workhouse. According to Farndell, Clark suffered only a cut lip from his punches. After a coroner's investigation ruled that Clark died of blunt force to the back of his head by parties unknown, however, fingers of suspicion pointed directly to workhouse guards.[28]

At the inquest, Dr. Nowlin testified under oath that Clark's wounds were fresh when he examined him at the workhouse. Prior to Nowlin's arrival, crude attempts were made to stop the hemorrhaging by using cobwebs and lampblack to fill the wound. Nowlin indicated that Clark was rational at the time of his examination. According to a *Globe-Democrat* reporter, at least twenty witnesses with sterling reputations claimed that after Dr. Nowlin testified, he made it clear, off the record, that Clark's claims of being clubbed at the workhouse likely were accurate. Nowlin politely told the reporter that out of deference to H. C. Dalton, superintendent of the city hospital, he would not comment further on the case.

John Kelley, an inmate released from the workhouse on July 2, furnished a statement implicating guards in the beating that killed Clark on his first night in the institution. According to Kelley, Clark bore no signs of a serious wound when prisoners gathered for supper in the dining room.

After the nine o'clock bell rang, Clark asked guard Pat Ryan for a bucket of water in the cell. Because it was the practice not to grant inmates' requests for water after the nine o'clock bell, Ryan refused and warned him not to ask again. When Clark asked again, Ryan went downstairs to get another guard. As Ryan unlocked the cell door, the other guard rushed into the cell and cracked Clark on the head. With blood splattered on the walls and floor of the cell, the guard continued to hit Clark time and again. As guards carried the injured prisoner down for medical care, Superintendent Carroll met them on the stairs, summoned Dr. Nowlin and an ambulance, and ordered a cleaning of the cell. According to Kelley, who named a couple of inmates as eyewitnesses, the guard, when asked by Carroll what happened, replied, "The black —— made a lunge at me."[29]

Superintendent Carroll dismissed Kelley's story, insisting that Clark suffered the mortal blow to his head before he entered the workhouse. Yard foreman Joseph Galen pointed out that Clark had a swollen upper lip and a cut on the left side of his forehead at the time he arrived. Carroll, who dismissed newspaper coverage as overblown, refused to grant the *Globe-Democrat* reporter a private interview with the eyewitnesses named by Kelley. When witnesses were asked about the incident within officers' earshot, they concealed the facts of the case, according to Kelley. In fact, the official workhouse version shifted a bit in a day or two. Kelley pointed out that "now they are saying that he [Clark] fell out of bed, and that they only struck him once with a raw-hide cane. It was a big club, loaded with lead in one end . . . and not a raw-hide cane." With Clark in Potter's Field and without vigorous investigation by law enforcement, Clark's murder remained an official mystery and his murderer(s) went unpunished. "It is believed that the Work House officials know more about the matter than they care to tell," concluded the *Globe-Democrat.*[30]

In May 1891, the city council unanimously approved Mayor Noonan's appointment of John C. Lohrum to replace Superintendent Carroll. A "lieutenant" of the Noonan "push," or agrarian, wing of the city's Democratic Party, "Big John" was a city contractor whose limestone quarries next to the workhouse in the Eleventh Ward produced crushed rock for St. Louis streets. Lohrum owned a two-story house and a large barn for stabling teams of mules and horses used in his quarrying operations. He was often referred to as the "mayor" of the waterfront shantyboat settlement of Chickentown, below the workhouse. In 1890, Lohrum was on the mayor's initial slate of nominees for street commissioner, but the BPI recommended against his appointment on account of a naked conflict of interest. In his most recent nomination for a patronage appointment, the city council overlooked a similar conflict of interest. When Lohrum's appointment as superintendent of the workhouse was confirmed, the *Post-Dispatch* noted that "he can now work his quarry, which adjoins the Work-house, to suit his pleasure."[31]

When Lohrum took the reins at the workhouse on June 1, 1891, he confronted an uproar over ongoing reports and charges of brutality behind the walls of the institution. In the final days of Superintendent Carroll's tenure, a workhouse guard gave inmate Michael O'Keefe a terrible beating. O'Keefe, who was in the workhouse on a charge of larceny, complained that he was sick and unable to work. The guard, suspecting him of shirking, tried to beat the laziness out of him. When O'Keefe's sentence expired on June 8, he was still suffering from injuries sustained in the beating. He was under the care of two doctors, but under the strain and agony of his injuries he lost his mind and was committed to the insane asylum. Mary O'Keefe, convinced that her son's condition was caused by the workhouse beating, went to the Four Courts Building in search of justice and swore out a warrant for the guard's arrest.

The *Post-Dispatch* put pressure on Mayor Noonan's administration to do something about abusive conditions in the workhouse, describing past investigations as a "wretched farce." Superintendent Carroll had once claimed that only a rubber hose was used to keep inmates in line, but recent beatings and killings during his tenure indicated otherwise. When George Roberts jumped a fence and tried to escape, he surrendered after guards caught up with him, but they used a baseball bat to beat him so badly that his head was a bloody pulp. The newspaper noted that recently a guard shot and killed William Bower in an alleged escape attempt, although no evidence of such an attempt was introduced before a handpicked coroner's jury. Neither was there a satisfactory explanation as to why it was necessary to shoot and kill him in what the jury ruled a "justifiable homicide."

On May 20, Thomas P. Duggan, an officer at the workhouse, killed Henry Trabue, a Black trusty who was often sent to the workhouse on account of drunkenness and petty offenses. There were no witnesses, but according to Duggan, he was on an electric car going home late at night when he saw Trabue board the car in a drunken state. Duggan, who recognized him as a trusty, followed him toward the workhouse when he stepped off the trolley at Meramec Street on the levee. Duggan allegedly ordered him back to the workhouse, but Trabue rushed him after reaching into his pocket as if to draw a revolver. Duggan claimed he fought him off with an umbrella, but then cracked him on the head with his revolver. In the confrontation, Duggan's pistol accidentally discharged, killing Trabue. At the coroner's inquest, workhouse officials emphasized what a dangerous character he was—even though they had granted Trabue special privileges as a trusty. The coroner's jury, consisting of a member of the House of Delegates and other politicos, turned over its findings to the assistant prosecuting attorney, who indicated that there was not enough evidence to prosecute Duggan, an Eleventh Ward delegate to the Democratic Central Committee. The jury's findings stirred considerable controversy. The *Post-Dispatch* suggested that Mayor Noonan consider making a personal investigation to put an end to the "barbarity that disgraced the last two administrations."[32]

The Trabue killing sparked a city council petition to form a joint committee with the House of Delegates to investigate the final three months of Superintendent Carroll's tenure. When a committee of the House of Delegates visited the workhouse on July 9, 1891, officers were expecting them. Everything was clean and neat, but after a noon meal with Superintendent Lohrum, members caught an earful from prisoners interviewed without the presence of a guard to eavesdrop. Committee members were embarrassed when several prisoners called them by their first names and recalled past friendships and favors. The prisoners complained about the brutality of guards who beat them routinely without provocation. The complainants singled out a couple of guards. When the committee later interviewed Joseph Galen, the chief guard and yard foreman, he defended the harsh treatment of inmates, arguing that they were dangerous, depraved criminals. Besides, he claimed, they were rarely hurt by the rubber hose beatings. Workhouse officers freely admitted that prisoners who were punished in the calaboose were tied up with their hands a bit high behind their backs, but they denied that they were hung up by their hands. Prisoners vigorously disagreed. They also complained unanimously about the food, describing the evening meal as "duff," nothing more than bread and warm water with a slight flavor of meat.[33]

Members of the investigative committee were appalled by the dilapidated shoes worn by the prisoners, who complained bitterly. Several prisoners, in fact, were working barefooted on the sharp rocks in the quarry.

Some complained they had been without shoes for three weeks. Workhouse officers indicated that on June 22 they requisitioned shoes from John Gilbert, the city's supply commissioner. Later, Gilbert protested that it was not his fault, pointing out that on June 30, he awarded a contract to Joel Swope & Company to deliver the shoes within ten days. After a *Post-Dispatch* reporter applied public pressure, Swope & Company delivered the shoes immediately to the workhouse.

Commissioner Gilbert blamed the fiasco on outgoing workhouse superintendent Carroll, who purportedly let things slide in the final days of his tenure, but the shoe contract dramatized a larger problem of corruption and delivery of inferior goods to city institutions by private contractors. In a mild crackdown on corruption that targeted ice and coal companies, Superintendent Lohrum set up scales at the gates to weigh provisions delivered by city contractors instead of relying on their verbal assurances. It was the first use of such scales in the workhouse's history.[34]

An investigation by Simon S. Bass, president of the Board of Charity Commissioners; William Cullinane, city councilman and fellow board member; and city councilman Charles James took place at the workhouse the very next day. They interviewed prisoners but allowed the intimidating presence of guards. As a result, the prisoners changed their stories or softened their previous charges and complaints. James suggested to Superintendent Lohrum that the two of them sit down and draw up a clear set of rules and guidelines for the workhouse. Bass added, "I am down on chains and shackles and many other things at the Work-house, and do believe that something should be done and done right away. St. Louis is far behind the times in this respect and needs a little modernizing."[35]

Like the second investigation, the third seemed more like an attempt at damage control. On the following day, a committee interviewed both male and female prisoners, but spent most of its time lecturing workhouse inmates about the behavior and criminal conduct that had led to their confinement. The committee, composed of chairman Julius Lehman, S. P. Keyes, Peter O'Brien, James Rauer, and John Courney, summoned a few of the women to interview. When they did so, a *Post-Dispatch* reporter noted, "In a joking way somebody advised the committee to go easy, as they might run across some embarrassing acquaintances." After drinks at the superintendent's house, the committee apologized to Lohrum for the baseless charges against him, assuring that, other than perhaps a few new guidelines, no fundamental changes would be required at the workhouse. The reporter described the investigation as a "farce comedy."[36]

The special committee continued to investigate, however, holding hearings in the committee room of the House of Delegates. At the center of the hearings was the brutality of guards. Yard foreman Galen's brutality and personal financial operations at the workhouse drew sharp criticism. As custodian of the prisoners' funds, he sold cigarettes and tobacco to inmates from his own store inside the workhouse at twice the market rate while prohibiting them from using their funds to buy from outside sources. Former superintendent Carroll had extended greater powers and privileges to Galen, who also raised hogs for private profit on the slopes of the workhouse, feeding them with offal and slop from the kitchen.[37]

The far-ranging hearings included the testimony of clerk John H. Stansbury, recently fired by Lohrum for reasons that had to do with Eleventh Ward politics. Stansbury, hired in 1882 and promoted to chief clerk and bookkeeper, noted that at one time under Superintendent Kunz's tenure, an apparatus was used to string up disobedient prisoners by the thumbs, but it was abandoned in favor of stringing them up with their arms tied behind their backs. Stansbury criticized ex-superintendent Carroll for giving too much authority to Galen, employed at the workhouse since 1880. In fact, Stansbury complained that Galen exercised nearly full management of the workhouse, and he agreed that Galen's harsh treatment of prisoners was excessive. Stanbury pointed out that until Carroll took over the workhouse, it was a custom not to punish prisoners without the superintendent's authorization, but Carroll conceded to Galen the unilateral power to inflict punishment. When asked by the committee whether Galen kept his own hogs at the workplace, Stansbury confirmed that ever since the beginning of Carroll's tenure, Galen had raised between fifteen and twenty hogs there for the market: "Yes, he buys young hogs or shoats, feeds them until they grow up, then sells them."

When quizzed about spending and costs at the workhouse, Stansbury replied that the average cost of keeping a prisoner under Carroll's management was thirty-three cents per day but that the daily cost after Lohrum took charge increased to forty-five cents. Lohrum spent a considerable sum fixing up his house. During the final year of Carroll's superintendency, the workhouse was self-sustaining, but Stansbury noted that in the current year the institution would likely operate in the red. Finally, Stansbury mentioned that when Galen was showing Lohrum around at the beginning of his superintendency, they barged in on three or four women prisoners bathing. Shocked, Lohrum regarded the routine invasion of the women's privacy as improper, but Galen did not see anything wrong with it.[38]

On September 11, 1891, the committee issued its report, which called for Galen's firing and an end to his tobacco store and stock raising at the workhouse for private profit. The committee urged the creation of a hospital for the sick on the premises, higher wages for the workhouse doctor, and the hiring of six additional guards and a matron with disciplinary authority and the necessary skills to help rehabilitate "fallen women." The report called for an end to stringing up inmates with pulleys and ropes, recommending further that punishment be carried out only by orders of the superintendent and in his presence. Members of the committee also called attention to the outrageous bathing arrangements that forced healthy men into large bathing tanks with men who carried infectious diseases.[39]

The investigative committee's report was the most damning official indictment of the workhouse to date, but if members hoped the committee's recommended reforms would quiet things down, satisfy critics, and meet with the new superintendent's approval, they were sorely disappointed. The findings of the committee were leaked to Superintendent Lohrum before the report was read in the House of Delegates. Angry, he hopped into his buggy and off he went to the mayor's office. A *Post-Dispatch* reporter caught up with him in city hall to get his reaction to the committee's report. Lohrum dismissed the recommendations out of hand and criticized meddling by outsiders. He scoffed at hiring a matron: "Well, they can't put a nice woman down there. The only kind of matron that could handle a woman would be a degraded woman like themselves. A nice woman manage those people! Why a man can't do it." He also insisted that no additional guards need be hired.

> We can manage those prisoners if they will let us alone with the guards we have now, but ever since this investigation commenced the prisoners have been so encouraged that they would just stand up and look us in the face and refuse to work. What can we do? We can't whip them. All we can do is to starve it out of 'em, and we've had to put 'em in the bull pen and say: "All right, if you don't want to work, you don't have to eat," and let them stay down there for awhile [*sic*]. That fetches them generally, but not always.

Lohrum, indicating he enjoyed Mayor Noonan's full support, refused to fire Galen: "Galen is the best man I've got and I'm not going to get rid of him . . . He's not a cruel man. He's good to those people down there, too good by a — sight. He's got a heart in him bigger than you or I ever dared to have."[40]

An editorial in the *Post-Dispatch* blasted Lohrum's rejection of the committee's report and called for his removal: "Mr. Lohrum's methods are not in harmony with sound and humane principles of prison government. His ideas fit the Russian better than the American system of criminal punishment."[41] When asked about Lohrum's response to the recommended reforms, Julius Lehman, chairman of the House of Delegates workhouse committee, shrugged. "Those recommendations were for the Mayor. If he will not act on them what can we do? We can only recommend. Superintendent Lohrum wants to keep Galen at the Work-house because he has been running the place for those fellows and allowing them to leave their duties and attend to private business. If Galen was discharged they couldn't go off to horse races and theaters as they have been doing, but they would have to stick to their work. It's an outrage."[42]

With Mayor Noonan's backing, Superintendent Lohrum had little to fear from the BPI or the investigative committee of the House of Delegates. The official oversight boards and special committee reports may have annoyed workhouse officers, but they were little more than a nuisance when it came to the internal methods and daily practices of the institution. The workhouse was the superintendent's de facto fiefdom, an entity nearly unto itself, unrestrained by oversight in any fundamental way. Critical reports and newspaper exposés came and went. They kicked up a momentary storm of outrage and controversy but the storm soon blew over and the pressure on workhouse officers abated. The same dismal conditions and brutality plagued the workhouse from one superintendent to the next.

3

THE FIEFDOM OF "BIG JOHN" LOHRUM

While Superintendent Lohrum was still fuming over the report of the investigative committee of the House of Delegates, his use of workhouse gangs for his own private quarrying interests and his authoritarian methods stirred further controversy. He and Henry Rucking, whose quarry lay just south of Lohrum's on the riverfront at Osage Street, were engaged in a bitter dispute. The workhouse quarries were nearby, just a little farther down the riverfront. Both private quarries were hemmed in by high bluffs to the west, and to the east lay the Iron Mountain Railway tracks and a crude road sometimes referred to as First Street. When Rucking erected a rock crusher on the edge of his property and arranged with the railroad company to put in a switch to the main tracks so he could easily dump crushed rock directly from the crusher into freight cars, it threatened Lohrum's access to the only economically feasible outlet for his rock. Rucking allowed Lohrum's wagons to use the roadway across his property, but Lohrum stormed into the office of M. J. Murphy, head of the city street department, to protest. Commissioner Murphy ordered the Iron Mountain Railway company to halt the laying of tracks for a switch to Rucking's crusher. At Murphy's behest, a police officer was stationed there to guard Lohrum's interests in the dispute by making sure no further track laying took place.[1]

Earlier, Lohrum had used a workhouse gang, carts, and guards to grade and fix things in a way that benefited his interests in the area. Rucking was furious that his rival profited by using workhouse labor and city resources while he had to pay out of his own pocket to improve his operations. He complained that Lohrum used the same crew to move his office, and that he was now quarrying city-owned rock to build a new office. Murphy defended Lohrum's use of city resources for his own financial interests, arguing that his road improvements helped both quarries to enjoy better access to the city's business district. Murphy's defense of Lohrum did not mollify Rucking, who blasted his rival: "Lohrum wants to shut us out here . . . and we won't have it, we will have our track in to our crusher and can put it on our own property. Lohrum thinks because he has the city behind him he can walk over us as he has over the small fry, but he is mistaken."[2]

This was not the last time Lohrum was embroiled in controversy over the use of workhouse labor and resources for private benefit. In a letter to the editor of the *Post-Dispatch,* dated December 2, 1892, and signed "One Who Knows," a citizen called public attention to the conflict of interests. The anonymous complainant and opponent of the Noonan "push" faction of the Democratic Party's agrarian free silver wing pointed out that Lohrum started using a gang of workhouse convicts on Thanksgiving Day to cut down a large embankment on the southwest corner of Broadway and Neosho Streets. The lot where the embankment was located belonged to William Lohrum, a saloon keeper and brother of the superintendent. William's saloon was just south of the lot. Street commissioner Murphy dismissed the complaint, arguing that the Lohrum lot was the closest place to get fill dirt for nearby street grading. The author of the letter to the editor complained, "I think this is an outrage on tax-payers to allow convicts, maintained at public expense, to be used for the private gain of John C. Lohrum and the push."[3]

The high-handed way in which Lohrum operated the workhouse often put him in hot water. After the embarrassing escape of a trusty shortly after he took command as superintendent of the workhouse in 1891, Lohrum began to open inmates' mail. He quickly received a scolding letter from George A. Dice, an inspector from the United States Post Office, who had received complaints. Dice ordered him to stop the practice: "You have no right to open a letter addressed to a prisoner in your charge without you have his free consent to do so." When Lohrum sought legal advice, city counselor W. C. Marshall advised him to comply with the law, but Mayor Noonan stood behind Lohrum. The mayor suggested that Marshall contact the postmaster general because "it is of the greatest importance that the officials should know the contents of the letters before they go out; with their letters as sacred as those of unconvicted citizens the prisoners could fix up all sorts of schemes with their friends outside and do a great deal toward making it dangerous for the officers. I certainly advise against submitting to the decree, even though it is technically right."[4]

Although the Board of Public Improvements exercised oversight of the workhouse, Superintendent Lohrum disregarded the need to consult the commissioners. He expected them to rubber-stamp his requisitions and actions. The BPI, upon receiving notice of his appointment of John Kearney as a workhouse guard without prior consultation, at first approved the appointment on the assumption it was fast-tracked because Mayor Noonan was behind it. On November 3, 1891, however, the BPI reconsidered its pro forma approval. The BPI tabled Kearney's nomination until the commissioners had time to examine his credentials more thoroughly.

In the meantime, Lohrum added Kearney and Larry Kiernan, a political operative and former post office official, to the payroll as guards. Despite a reprimand from the BPI, Lohrum rammed the appointments through. President George Burnett, who complained that Lohrum thumbed his nose at the board's authority, favored firing the two employees, but the rest of the board felt it would be unfair to do so.

Lohrum's disregard for oversight of his authority became further apparent when inmate George Sundlin escaped on May 16, 1892. The city ordinance required superintendents to notify the mayor and chief of police within twenty-four hours when a prisoner escaped from the workhouse, but Lohrum failed to do so. Instead, he sent his own workhouse guards to track Sundlin down.[5]

Brutality at the workhouse would not get one fired, but being on the wrong side of factional political squabbles would. Superintendent Lohrum, who refused to get rid of Joseph Galen for cruelty, did not hesitate to fire John H. Stansbury, the chief clerk of the workhouse for the previous eight years. Stansbury was the Democratic central committeeman from the Eleventh Ward who had opposed Mayor Noonan in the primary two years earlier. Lohrum headed the Noonan wing of the Democratic Party's Eleventh Ward delegation to the Central Committee. Two of his new workhouse guards, Kiernan and Thomas F. Mahrer, were alternates on the delegation. Lohrum denied that the firings and hirings were politically motivated, but he also removed Patrick McNamara, a blacksmith at the workhouse. McNamara was the Democratic central committeeman from the Fifteenth Ward, whose sin was being on the wrong side of the Noonan factional divide. In April 1892, Superintendent Lohrum fired Anton "Tony" Neiser for alleged "neglect of duty," but anti-Noonan forces in the Democratic Party attributed the firing to his brother's politics. Martin Neiser, a former city marshal and central committeeman from the Seventh Ward, had opposed Noonan in the primary.[6]

Mayor Noonan's appointees felt vulnerable when his bid for reelection failed in 1893. There was newspaper speculation that the new Republican mayor, Cyrus P. Walbridge, former president of the city council, would fire Lohrum, but Lohrum remained as superintendent of the workhouse. Confident of Mayor Walbridge's support, Lohrum continued to do things his way. On May 10, 1894, he arbitrarily released Patrick McNichols, Martin Spellman, and John Hardy, who had been arrested as pickpockets, fined $500, and sent to the workhouse on January 31, 1894. Each was serving a six-month sentence to work off the fine. Police chief Laurence Harrigan, upset by Lohrum's release of the prisoners, complained to Mayor Walbridge. When asked by the mayor's office to justify his actions, Lohrum explained that he had granted them ninety days of overtime for exceeding the normal daily quota of fifty cubic feet of macadam in the quarry. He claimed he did so in keeping with an order from the BPI, but the BPI president, Robert McMath, denied that the order allowed for granting overtime.[7]

While padded payrolls, political cronyism, nepotism, and corruption continued, the problems of overcrowding and a rotting infrastructure worsened in the workhouse. The daily average number of prisoners in 1892–1893 was 402 (329 men and 73 women). Lohrum, who complained to no avail about overcrowding, observed to a reporter that the dog pound offered better accommodations than the workhouse, especially in the male quarters. On July 21, 1893, he emphasized to members of the BPI that more than half of the four hundred inmates housed in the workhouse came from criminal courts. Commissioner Murphy added that the criminal courts, to avoid major prosecutorial expenses and other costs of a criminal trial, accepted guilty pleas to lesser felonies in many cases. As a result, state courts often slapped felons with two or three sentences, each less than a year, to comply with the law, but the bottom line was that they were imprisoned in the workhouse continuously for two years or longer.[8]

In late August 1894, a mysterious epidemic broke out in the workhouse. On September 20, an eighteen-year-old Black inmate, John Ray, died, followed by Edward Kelly on the twenty-fourth and Henry Harris on the twenty-fifth. By the following month, approximately thirty additional prisoners had fallen ill with high fever, nausea, and severe pain in swollen joints, feet, hands, and knees—symptoms resembling inflammatory rheumatism, or dropsy (congestive heart failure). The puzzling sickness, confined solely to the male quarters, hit Black male prisoners particularly hard, but it was not contagious. By late October, the epidemic that had claimed four lives subsided considerably, with only three remaining cases in the workhouse.[9]

Superintendent Lohrum and other officials were at a loss to explain the source of the epidemic. Speculation centered around the diet of inmates, especially a lack of vegetables and possibly contaminated food supplied to city institutions by corrupt contractors. Dr. Arnold Sellner, the workhouse physician, believed the cause of the outbreak to be malaria that led to a form of kidney disease. At a meeting of the BPI the city health commissioner, George Homan, argued that it was not his job to launch an investigation unless the BPI requested him to do so. Finally, nearly six weeks after the outbreak, the BPI gave Homan the authorization. He then asked Warren G. Priest, chief physician at the city dispensary, to investigate. The investigation by Homan and Priest included taking samples of earth from under the cells for chemical and bacteriological analysis.[10]

On November 7, 1894, Homan submitted the results of the investigation to BPI president McMath. The devastating report, which focused mainly on sanitary issues and matters of drainage and ventilation in the men's quarters, laid bare the horrible, unsanitary conditions that grew out of overcrowding and years of neglect of the rotting infrastructure of the workhouse. "Ten prisoners are required to sleep in a cell . . . the air space at night for each prisoner is about the size of an ordinary grave," reported Homan. "That conditions dangerous to health and life develop there is not surprising." He pointed out that there were twice as many prisoners than the quarters could house under reasonably hygienic conditions. "The authority that commits to prison," he continued, "has no moral rights to impair the prisoner's health or subject him to conditions liable to cause disease."[11]

Homan found decay, mold, and refuse that collected in confined spaces under the floors of the lower cells. He also called attention to unventilated spaces between the lower cells and the floors above them, where "very objectionable matter" gathered. Many of the cells that housed the sick inmates had no sunlight whatsoever. Homan recommended that all wooden flooring be torn out of lower-tier cells and replaced with broken stone or concrete, topped with cement or asphalt. He also called for lime washing of cells, the elimination of plaster ceilings, subjecting all bedding to sulfur fumes, and replacing the old drainage system that led sewage from yard toilets to a sinkhole. Homan urged a new drainage plan that piped the sewage directly to the Mississippi River. Without these desperately needed reforms, Homan warned that "outbreaks of disease must be looked for, with a high mortality rate in those affected in spite of all possible care on the part of those in charge."[12]

Two days after Homan's report became public, BPI commissioners met with Superintendent Lohrum at the workhouse. They ordered him to prepare a new stone yard and to make recommendations for building a new addition to the workhouse. The dimensions of the addition remained unspecified at the time, pending Lohrum's recommendations. During the discussions between the BPI and workhouse officers, Dr. Sellner urged the creation of an on-site hospital. In response to Homan's recommendations, Lohrum ordered repairs to the cell house floors, but little more. Due to the cynicism and contempt of officers for the inmates, the stinginess of public officials, and foot dragging by the municipal assembly, it took many more years before construction work began on a new addition to the workhouse. In the meantime, the final days of Superintendent Lohrum's tenure were marked by revelations of high-profile escapes, lax discipline, ongoing corruption and brutality of guards, and growing pressures to hire a matron for the women's quarters of the workhouse.[13]

A round of carefully planned escapes followed on the heels of the workhouse epidemic. On January 2, 1895, four prisoners, led by John (alias Jan) Hardy, escaped on their way back from a day's work in the stone quarry. Hardy, a thief serving a sentence of six months, was in line with about 250 prisoners as they marched up the steep, winding hill to the workhouse for the evening meal. William A. Muehlhausen, a guard at the top of the climb, looked down upon the slow, rhythmic procession. When the younger prisoners who led the procession reached the guard, they stopped to wait for the older, slower inmates to catch up with them. As the guard watched the stragglers come up the hill and those in the vanguard milled around to await them at the top, Hardy and three other inmates made their break, right under the nose of the guard. Hardy quickly bent down, loosened a board on a ten-foot-high stockade fence, and off he went, followed by sixteen-year-old Carl Lohrman, nineteen-year-old Joe Downey, and Tom Cummings, age twenty-six. All four wore shackles, but Hardy managed to free one of his legs.

Muehlhausen pointed a double-barreled shotgun at the remaining prisoners and threatened to fill with buckshot the next prisoner who tried to follow the escapees. Guards Andrew Schweigler, Dan Sweeney, Tim Denehy, and John A. Lohrum, the superintendent's son, pursued the escaped prisoners. Schweigler fired four shots from his revolver at the escapees, but the shots only made them run faster. Three of the escapees, worn out by the chase, soon surrendered, but Hardy jumped into a buggy that was waiting for him at the end of the workhouse grounds. After pursuing him down Broadway for nearly seven hours, two guards in a buggy gave up. Upon investigation, it became clear that an accomplice on the outside had loosened the board on the stockade fence and had marked it so that Hardy knew which one was loose.[14]

On January 8, a *Post-Dispatch* reporter was in Superintendent Lohrum's office, discussing with Lohrum and chief clerk John Denehy the mysterious disappearance of inmate John Wilson (alias A. J. Walsh or C. B. Smith) earlier that morning. "I can't, for the life of me, see how that fellow escaped," Lohrum said. "He slipped out of the prisoners' ranks while they were marching out from breakfast, but how he got away without being detected by the guards, is more than I can imagine . . . Every other time that a prisoner has escaped, the method of his flight was known to us as soon as he had gone. But the earth seems to have opened right up and swallowed that fellow, as we can find no trace of him anywhere."

While the reporter was there, guards captured Wilson in the stable and shoved him into the superintendent's office. Wilson, a jewelry thief also wanted by Chicago authorities, had crawled into a small space of a private carriage owned by the superintendent's daughter and had covered himself with a rubber storm flap. A member of the superintendent's family discovered him crouched in the buggy. A few minutes later, guards captured another prisoner, who had escaped while coming back from the quarry. They found him hiding in the stable, too. Later, clerk Denehy explained to the reporter how prisoners sometimes removed their shackles in the quarry. Superintendent Lohrum, expressing satisfaction that Wilson had been found and brought back, touted the capture as a vindication of his guards:

> Every one who heard of his escape today, seemed to think or suspect that it might be due to complicity on the part of a guard. His capture just now shows the suspicion to have been unfounded. I am very well satisfied with

> the work of our guards. We only have seventeen here. Three are on duty at night, leaving us fourteen for day service. And they have to keep both eyes open all day, because they have to watch over 200 desperate criminals who are planning every hour some new scheme by which they may elude the vigilance of the armed watchmen and regain their liberty.[15]

When Wilson appeared before Chief Harrigan at the Four Courts Building on January 9, 1895, he recounted several escapes that occurred while he was an inmate. He boasted that he could easily have escaped if he had money to pay off the guards. "I have been in the Work-house about nine weeks," he said, "and in that time eleven men have escaped to my knowledge. In the case of one man, Clayton, who escaped a couple of days ago, I was told that money was used in order that he might make his escape." According to Smith, two additional convicts whose names he did not know had escaped in the week after Hardy fled. A *Post-Dispatch* reporter who went to the workhouse to verify Smith's claims discovered that Ed Rohlfing, an inmate serving a one-year sentence, had escaped on January 5 under what workhouse officers termed mysterious circumstances.[16]

Perhaps the most embarrassing escape for Superintendent Lohrum was that of Maggie Seifforth, a mature-looking fifteen-year-old. Admitted to the workhouse on charges of petit larceny on November 10, 1893, she toed the mark and was made a trusty assigned to Lohrum's personal home. She escaped one day, wearing a dress belonging to one of the superintendent's daughters. Lohrum, who took it upon himself to search for her, found her "streetwalking" downtown and took her back to the workhouse.

The final months of the beleaguered superintendent's tenure were a disaster. In February 1895, an outbreak of smallpox in the city spread to the workhouse. The outbreak hit Black neighborhoods along the levee. In mid-February, the *Post-Dispatch* reported that all forty-one victims of smallpox to date were Black. On January 29, health commissioner Homan notified the BPI, which at once ordered Superintendent Lohrum to vaccinate workhouse prisoners. When BPI president McMath visited the workhouse on February 8, he learned that Lohrum had not complied. Lohrum claimed he had requisitioned the vaccine points but did not receive them. However, records in the office of the Commissioner of Supplies showed that he did not requisition the vaccine points until the day McMath and members of the BPI visited the workhouse. Three days later, the requisition was filled and five hundred vaccine points were received at the workhouse. Nonetheless, when chief dispensary physician Priest inspected the workhouse on the February 17, no vaccinations had been administered. He took charge immediately, and with the assistance of workhouse physician Sellner and Dr. Gustav Fuchs of the city's dispensary corps, began the vaccinations. Only one prisoner had come down with smallpox at that point, but Dr. Priest emphasized the need for vaccinations and fumigation of the cells, given the overcrowded conditions. Superintendent Lohrum, when pressed by the BPI to explain the delay in administering the vaccinations, blamed it on bureaucratic inefficiency and misunderstandings.[17]

Against the backdrop of the smallpox vaccinations, three members of the Board of Charity Commissioners inspected the workhouse on February 18, 1895, in preparation for the board's annual report to the mayor. In its report, the board criticized the workhouse medical system, its disciplinary methods and nepotism, and the quantity and quality of the food served to prisoners. The report noted that Dr. Sellner, the workhouse physician, visited the institution only three times a week to examine prisoners who were sick. Rarely, if ever, did he examine the other prisoners or inspect the facilities. The charity commissioners pointed out that incoming prisoners did not receive a medical examination to determine whether they carried contagious diseases. Instead, the workhouse used a trusty to check them in. All the new men were forced into the same segregated baths upon arrival, even if they were infected.[18]

The Board of Charity Commissioners urged the hiring of a matron for the women's quarters, condemned the food served to prisoners, and criticized the brutal methods of guards. Galen, the assistant superintendent, admitted that he whipped unruly prisoners in violation of the city ordinance, which called only for solitary confinement and a diet of bread and water as punishment. On the assumption that it would impress the commissioners, he boasted that he often clubbed newly arrived Black women prisoners as a matter of routine practice.

The commissioners, after interviewing every guard as well as several prisoners, confirmed the use of torture at the workhouse. A guard admitted that drunkenness was a problem among fellow guards, who often were intoxicated when they beat prisoners. The board's report called for Galen's immediate firing, and it severely censured Superintendent Lohrum for allowing the use of ropes and pulleys to pinion victims' hands behind their backs and to raise them up until their feet no longer touched the floor. As a *Post-Dispatch* reporter noted, "Prisoners have been allowed to hang by their wrists until their arms were swollen almost to their shoulders and they were so stiff in body and limb that they could scarcely stand."[19]

The report called attention to a leaky roof that had gone unrepaired, and it warned that large chunks of plaster falling from fifteen-foot-high ceilings posed a hazard to prisoners in some of the cells. In addition, the investigation noted irregularities in contracts with meat vendors and other city suppliers. Finally, the charity commissioners criticized nepotism on the part of Lohrum, whose wife, although on the payroll as a cook, paid little attention to her job. Their son was also on the payroll, as a hostler, but he did no work. Each received forty dollars per month in salary. The report called for the hiring of a good cook.[20]

Lohrum was absent from the workhouse at the time of the charity board's investigation, but the release of the board's report and recommendations for reforms infuriated him. A *Post-Dispatch* reporter who called upon him at his office shortly after Mayor Walbridge's reelection in April found him combative over outside meddling in the institution's internal matters. The reporter was there to ascertain details of a fresh attempted escape in which three prisoners were shot by a guard. Two of them had recovered from minor buckshot wounds but the third was in the city hospital with painful but not dangerous wounds in the arm. According to the reporter, "this functionary [Lohrum]" gave him a "characteristically pompous reception," proclaiming that it was none of the public's business what went on at the workhouse, including methods of punishment by the guards.

At first Lohrum refused to reveal any details about the attempted escape or to allow the reporter to see the two injured prisoners: "I tell you, it's none of your business or that of anyone, who tried to escape or who was shot. My guard only did his duty . . . I wish he had blown the heads off all three. They are getting altogether too fresh down here, and an example ought to be made of some of them." When the reporter interjected that the workhouse was a public institution and that the public had a right to know how it was being conducted, the imposing superintendent, who weighed nearly three hundred pounds, moved toward him in a threatening manner. "See here, young fellow," Lohrum warned, "don't you give me any of your sass, or I'll put a head on you. I'll do it quick, too. I am big enough to do it, and don't you forget it."

At that point, an elderly man in the office who was listening carefully to the conversation interrupted Lohrum, called him outside the office, and whispered something in his ear. Upon returning, Lohrum's irate demeanor changed markedly. He sent for G. W. Craig, the guard who had shot the prisoners as they tried to escape from a quarry gang in the clay pit on Chippewa Street. Lohrum added that several prisoners had given them considerable trouble recently. He blamed their surly attitudes and refusal to work or obey orders on the visit by the Board of Charity Commissioners in February. "These people came down here to investigate certain rumors of brutality on the part of the guards and to institute a sort of reform," he complained. "I was away at the time, or you can rest assured they would never have gotten inside the place. They went about among the prisoners, filling their heads with silly notions, saying they were worked too hard, etc., and wound up by giving them their names and addresses and asking them to communicate with them in case they were imposed upon. The result is the prisoners think they are imposed upon if made to work at all."[21]

Shortly after Lohrum's disastrous interview, Mayor Walbridge announced that he would not reappoint him. Of course, the damning report of the Board of Charity Commissioners went unheeded. Its recommendations echoed those made in a similar report by an investigative committee of the House of Delegates five years earlier. No matter how many times abuses in the workhouse were exposed, the institution's practices and methods remained unchanged. Lohrum's authoritarianism and abrasive use of the superintendency as a political plum might have raised hackles in a few municipal circles, but political patronage was the name of the game. The drunkenness and brutality of guards went unchecked. Superintendents protected guards if they were loyal partisans in ward politics who delivered votes. With cynicism and contempt for workhouse inmates prevailing, it mattered little whether Democrats or Republicans controlled municipal politics. There was little political support for increasing expenditures to benefit the inmates of Point Breeze, and little political will to challenge the internal practices of the workhouse or to improve its rapidly rotting infrastructure.

4

KARR'S GANG OF GUARDS

When Mayor Walbridge announced his slate of new appointees to city departments and institutions in 1895, the building teemed with disgruntled Republican office seekers who did not receive appointments. The *Post-Dispatch* noted that the appointments were based solely on patronage, not qualifications. The newspaper singled out German-born Nicholas Karr, appointee to head the workhouse, as a primary example. Karr, who joined the Union Army as a drummer boy at age eleven or twelve and fought in the battle of Vicksburg, was a Ninth Ward Republican stalwart. For the previous twenty years he had operated a saloon at 604 Walnut. A group of political friends, including Judge John A. Talty, surprised Karr and his family at their private residence at 2640 Ann Avenue to fete him in song and speeches with plenty of good cheer. The revelers toasted him for his loyal political work, presented him and his family with a silver tea service, and congratulated him on his new appointment as superintendent of the workhouse.[1]

As soon as Karr took office, he announced the resignation of longtime guard Joseph Galen, notorious for his abuse of inmates. Guards Benjamin Wiethuchter and L. B. Gabard resigned, and Karr fired four other guards in a housecleaning. Karr hired six new guards to fill the vacancies. Many were former policemen with stained records. In an article, "Karr's Gang of Guards," a *Post-Dispatch* reporter called attention to the practice of hiring ex-police officers with questionable records, and he named a few names. Chief among them was Gus Krueger, "a low-browed, bull-necked fellow" fired from the police force for drunkenness on April 15, 1895. Previously, he was fined ten dollars for abusing a citizen of the city he was sworn to protect. Harry Jones, assistant superintendent of the workhouse, was fired from the police force on September 4, 1894, when he was found away from his post with an "immoral woman." Edward Saxey was fired on November 1, 1887, for conduct unbecoming an officer, and guard Isaac Ketchum had resigned as a police officer five days after being demoted to a janitorial position on August 3, 1886. The reporter noted, "It looks a little from this as though the Work-house Superintendent had gathered up all the broken policemen he could find just to give them an opportunity to once more swing their clubs free from the restricting discipline of a Board of Police Commissioners."[2]

It did not take long for Karr to get mired in controversy over the brutality of his own guards. In the afternoon of October 14, 1895, the Black Maria hauled fifty-two-year-old Thomas Malone to the workhouse after a public drunken spree that led to his arrest and a fine of twenty-five dollars. Too sick and unfit to work in the quarry the next day, Malone was taken to the workhouse physician. Dr. Ludwig Brewer examined him but could not determine what was wrong with him. On the morning of October 16, workhouse officers sent Malone to the city hospital in a state of unconsciousness. Other than Malone's name, workhouse officers provided no further information or explanation when they sent him to the hospital. A hospital doctor called the workhouse for information to determine the best line of treatment, but he was told only that Dr. Brewer was not there. Malone died shortly before midnight.

At a coroner's inquest, the examining physician at the city hospital testified that there were bruises and marks of violence on Malone's body, including a severe abrasion on the bridge of his nose. The doctor concluded that the victim died of a cerebral hemorrhage as the result of long-term alcoholism, the violent blows, or a combination of both. The testimony of Henry Eberhard, the workhouse clerk, yielded little additional information other than the date Malone was admitted to the workhouse in a drunken state and the physician's examination of Malone upon arrival. A postmortem examination at the morgue by Dr. Louis Wolfert confirmed cerebral hemorrhage as the cause of death but noted that there was no indication of violent blows to Malone's head or body. Without calling any other witnesses except the police sergeant who had arrested Malone, the coroner closed the investigation, stating he did not believe Malone was beaten in the workhouse.[3]

Eyewitnesses in the workhouse and a *Post-Dispatch* investigative reporter revealed a different story. Inmate Joseph Marcus, a peddler of spectacles, claimed that upon entering the workhouse on October 15 on a charge of disturbing the peace, he was put into a cell with Malone. At that time,

Malone was crouched down in a corner, evidently sick. Assistant Superintendent Jones ordered Marcus to bring Malone out of the cell to the doctor, who gave Malone some bromide and whiskey. About a half hour later, Malone sat on a bench, apparently feeling a bit better, but when prisoners lined up in the yard to go to the dining room for the evening meal, he could not walk without Marcus's assistance. As Marcus told the reporter, "A guard they called 'Gus,' whose other name I didn't know, came up and ordered me to 'let that man go.' I let go, and the man fell down." While Malone was on the floor, Krueger beat him with a hard rawhide whip that had a steel ferrule on the end of it, striking him on the face, back, neck, head, and hands. Krueger even unleashed his big dog on Malone, according to Marcus, who did not see his cellmate again but heard he was taken to the hospital the next day.[4]

When the *Post-Dispatch* reporter went to the workhouse to look further into Malone's death, Assistant Superintendent Jones told him that Superintendent Karr was too sick to be bothered. Clerk Eberhard refused to talk about the Malone case, insisting that the coroner's inquest was closed. The reporter asked to speak to Krueger, but Eberhard at first refused. Jones claimed that Krueger never saw Malone, who was too sick to work in the quarry. After ten minutes or so of trying to assure the reporter there was nothing more to be learned in the matter, Jones relented and directed him to the quarry, where Krueger was overseeing a work gang. "This whole thing is a conspiracy to do me up," Krueger complained to the reporter. "These 'Kerry Patch' hoodlums have got it in for me because I make them work." Krueger denied that he gave Malone a beating. He said that when he and Superintendent Karr tried to get Malone's name from him after he failed to answer roll call, "We slapped him and pinched him a little, but he wouldn't wake up, and Mr. Karr said to let him alone until he sobered up." Krueger insisted that he merely poked Malone with his stick and asked what was wrong with him when he stumbled in line for the evening meal. He denied that his dog was even with him at the time.[5]

Two additional prisoners stepped forward to substantiate Joseph Marcus's version of the beating of Malone at the workhouse. Conrad Knab, who was sent to the workhouse on September 17 and was released on October 18, added that Krueger was drunk when he beat Malone. J. R. Cheek, upon release from the workhouse, recalled, "He [Krueger] was so drunk all afternoon in the quarry that he could not walk straight. When we were lined up for supper we saw this man [Malone] sitting helpless in the gangway. Krueger was beating him with a heavy cane . . . I was well treated for the few days I was in the Work-house, but I can't say as much for others. The guards are drunken brutes."[6]

Marcus, Knab, and Cheek named several other witnesses to the beating, but the coroner remained steadfast in his determination not to reopen the investigation. When Louis J. Singer, W. H. Lee, and George C. Hitchcock—members of the Board of Charity Commissioners—visited the workhouse on October 25, Singer asked the clerk, Eberhard, if the accusations against Krueger were true. Eberhard conceded that Krueger might have prodded Malone a little with his stick but denied that a beating took place. When the *Post-Dispatch* reporter reminded Singer that three witnesses had corroborated Marcus's charges, Singer replied that workhouse prisoners, if questioned, would lie or say nothing at all. Hitchcock emphasized that the charity commissioners had no authority to fire workhouse officers. "After the statement we secured from Mr. Eberhard this afternoon," he said, "I think we can pursue the matter no further and that it rests with others than ourselves to proceed."[7]

The *Post-Dispatch* reporter persisted in efforts to talk to Superintendent Karr, who earlier was unavailable to discuss the Malone case. The reporter caught up with Karr at the workhouse on October 24. Karr, when asked whether he intended to investigate allegations against Krueger, summarily dismissed the need for further investigation. "There's no use of it at all," he insisted. "There's nothing in it at all. I do not permit any brutality on the part of my guards. I do not allow them to strike the prisoners save in self-defense." Karr stressed that he saw Malone in his cell on the first night after Malone failed to answer roll call. When the reporter asked Karr if he could shed light on what happened to Malone on the following day, he replied, "No. I have been away on leave of absence and am not informed as to that. Krueger may have prodded the fellow a little with his stick, but that's all. He certainly did not beat him any. That is not permitted."[8]

Karr's bland assertion that Krueger did not beat Malone because rules did not permit it prompted an editorial from Charles H. Jones, editor and manager of the *Post-Dispatch.* Jones demanded that the coroner reopen the investigation into Malone's death: "The inmates of the Work-house are vicious characters and sometimes require rough treatment, but this fact does not justify the brutal and wanton killing of a sick man. No matter how degraded the man, he was entitled to the kind of treatment dictated by common humanity."[9]

On the heels of Malone's suspicious death, the mutilation of inmate Jim Smith in a dynamite explosion on November 2, 1895, further dramatized the reckless disregard for life on the part of workhouse guards. Smith, an eighteen-year-old Black inmate who had served between four and five months for petty larceny, was working as a powder monkey, or blaster, in a quarry gang under the supervision of a guard in the afternoon when a charge of blasting powder failed to explode. The guard ordered Smith to dig out the charge and put in a new fuse, insisting that there was no danger. Smith protested that the hole should be wetted first, but the guard ordered him to proceed. Smith nervously picked at the charge with a crowbar until a flash of sparks froze him in his tracks. Once again, he asked for water to wet the hole, but a guard ordered him to perform the task without it. Smith's crowbar struck flint, and the spark from it set off the dynamite charge. He was blown about ten feet into the air, along with two or three tons of rock. Afterward, his left hand and arm dangled from his shoulder and his face was horribly mutilated. He lost his sight and the blast tore away his upper lip. At the city hospital, doctors amputated what was left of his shredded left arm. Somehow, he managed with great difficulty to give his account of what had happened, making it clear he had asked for the hole to be wetted. According to police reports, it was Gus Krueger who ordered Smith to dig out the charge. A *Post-Dispatch* reporter linked the mutilation of Smith and the death of Malone to the criminal carelessness of "Karr's Gang of Guards": "Nick Karr himself is none too good but his staff of assistants are such as to cause surprise."[10]

The relationship between workhouse officers and the *Post-Dispatch* grew stormier as reports of whippings and beatings continued. On July 23, 1896, the newspaper published a narrative by John C. Cameron, who had been released from the workhouse two days earlier. Cameron, a wagon maker who served a one-year sentence for assault with intent to kill, called attention to a handful of prisoners, including himself, who were tortured by guards. John Lawler, a new inmate unaccustomed to hard labor, was put to work on the rock pile in the quarry. "Each man has to crush five loads of stone," Cameron said, "a task impossible for a new man to accomplish." After Lawler developed painful blisters that made it impossible to hold a hammer, guards took him to a toolshed, "where they tied the end of a rope about his wrists and then strung him up to the rafters in the roof. While his feet were off of the stone floor, one of the guards beat him over the back with a cane, drawing blood at each blow."

After mentioning other prisoners who had suffered the same fate because they failed to meet the quota of crushed stone in the quarry, Cameron told his own story. "My cell mate was dirty and slovenly and would not clean up the cell. He slept on a cot above mine, and during the night he would spit and cough, and the refuse would come down on me. One night I could stand it no longer, and I got up and licked the old man. I didn't hurt him much and left no bruises on him." Guards Ike Hamilton and Will Peters dragged Cameron out of his cell and threw him into solitary confinement. They beat him all the way down the hall, and Hamilton hit him in the mouth with his fist and split his lip wide open as they put him into the dungeon. "Of course, I swore at him," Cameron conceded. "I could not help it. There is not much man in a fellow if he would not resent such treatment. Then they got a heavy cane with a steel rod running through it and, after one of them had bared my back, the other applied the club."

Cameron lost consciousness. When he awoke, he found himself in a dark, damp cell without light. For two weeks, the bullring was his home. He was fed nothing but a crust of bread twice a day and a cupful of warm water. "My back was bleeding in a dozen places, and I was used up. I thought I was dying," he recalled. With the scars still visible on his back, he added, "The place is the dirtiest on earth. Nothing could be worse. We could not sleep for the vermin which covered the walls of the cells and infested the beds. No effort is made to abate the pest and the numbers are increasing each day. If I thought I had to serve another year in that place I would commit suicide." When a reporter went to the workhouse to check out Cameron's stories, he was barred from seeing Superintendent Karr or any of the officers. The guard to the entrance said he would never allow a reporter into the workhouse unless he was a prisoner.[11]

Karr banned reporters from the workhouse even if they had a pass from Mayor Walbridge's secretary. City officials and the friends and family of inmates were allowed to visit the workhouse if they went through the mayor's office, but reporters were required to obtain a permit with the mayor's personal signature. This requirement marked a departure from the practices of previous workhouse administrations. If reporters did get the mayor's personal approval to interview a prisoner, they had to conduct the interview in the superintendent's workhouse office in the presence of Karr or one of his guards.[12]

About a week after Cameron's revelations, a recently released inmate provided a detailed firsthand account of abuse he and others had suffered in Karr's workhouse. Harry Henney, an employee in the pressroom of the Price Bros. *Advertising Bulletin* before he was sent to the workhouse on March 16 for disturbing the peace, kept a diary while he worked off a fifty-dollar fine. Upon his release on July 30, he gave a statement to the *Post-Dispatch* in which he outlined incidents of brutality. Gus Krueger was often responsible for the cruelties. On June 30, according to Henney's record, guards took a Black prisoner known as "Jamaica" to a toolshed, where they strung him up with ropes and pulleys until his feet barely touched the ground. Then Krueger beat him so badly with a cane that had a steel rod running through it that Jamaica collapsed, bleeding from the head when they let him down. Krueger kicked him to make him get up. When Jamaica staggered to his feet, he collapsed again and was left to lie there.

Krueger's sadistic cruelty and use of torture knew few boundaries. In the quarry, he rigged up a "whipping barrel," which he kept in a large shed with other equipment. To inflict punishment on a prisoner working in the quarry, he forced him to lie across the barrel with a leather strap fastened around his neck to prevent him from moving it. The guard then flogged him in front of the other quarry prisoners. Krueger's brutality was not limited to inmates. On June 23, he was drunk when he spotted three boys in a peddler's wagon coming down a steep road to the quarry. The road was off-limits to outsiders and open only for use by city contractors delivering supplies. Krueger ordered two of the boys off the wagon and sent them back up the road. He allowed the boy who was driving to continue down the road to turn around at the bottom of the incline, but when the boy reached the bottom, Krueger grabbed the horses and beat the boy with a cane as the youngster sat on the wagon. When the victim got halfway back up the road in the wagon, he yelled an angry remark at Krueger, who caught up with him, pulled him off the wagon, and beat him with the cane again. A blow to the head knocked the youngster out temporarily. When he regained consciousness, he tried to climb back onto the wagon, but Krueger beat him yet again. When the wagon finally reached the top of the road, a sentry, in response to a signal from Krueger, arrested the boy and locked him in the sick cell of the workhouse. He lay there until Superintendent Karr found out what had happened and released him.[13]

Henney's record detailed several other cases, including his own, in which guards abused inmates. Krueger beat Henney and threatened to shoot him, stopped only by the intervention of other workhouse officers. According to Henney's revelations, guards, especially Krueger, often ignored Karr's orders and did whatever they wanted to do to the prisoners. Karr seemed ineffectual at best. Henney, who spent three days in the bull pen, pointed out that Krueger, "Long-Haired Willie" Peters, and two other guards teamed up to beat him when he objected to their overloading him with extra-large carts of stone to break up each day. According to Henney, Ike Hamilton in the workhouse office "never gives the men any shoes unless Karr makes him, and the men have to walk on the sharp rocks barefooted, cutting their feet horribly." When Karr tried to extend Henney's stint in the workhouse for three days beyond his sentenced time, Henney protested and threatened to sue Karr, reminding him that such action would be in violation of the ordinance. Only then did Karr release him.[14]

George Lamar, a middle-aged first-time inmate released on April 8, 1896, after serving a thirty-five-day sentence, contradicted a recent grand jury report that praised the cleanliness of the workhouse. He noted that the only clean place was the superintendent's quarters. But, he added,

> while it is hard enough for men to be confined in cells reeking with vermin and dirt, they could tough it out much more composedly if in many instances their tired frames did not bear gashes and great black whelps inflicted by the raw cowhide and stiff rubber hose clubs of the guards. These clubs of old hose are about three feet long and two inches thick and raise the skin at every lick. I was struck on the head three times with one of them by a guard and the bump it raised was black for a week. Guards use their clubs on the slightest provocation, and often for none at all.

Lamar, who noted that there were daily beatings in the workhouse, named several other prisoners who were beaten, one of them almost to death. Although Lamar indicated he had never seen Superintendent Karr or Assistant Superintendent Jones beat anyone, he emphasized they were well aware of the practice. "A prisoner dare not complain to the principal for the few who have tried it have had their punishment doubled by the guard so reported."[15]

A mutiny broke out in the quarry on April 15, 1896, when thirty-two prisoners defied guards by refusing to work. Karr used the bullring and corporal punishment to punish the ringleaders and quell the rebellion, which was followed by several attempted prisoner escapes. To downplay the mutiny in the newspapers, Karr blamed the trouble on the customary rebelliousness of prisoners upon the arrival of spring weather. On the night of the mutiny, he garrisoned the workhouse from sundown to sunrise, even pressing citizens into service to join the guards with shotguns and rifles. Karr claimed he received a tip that a major prison breakout was being planned by friends of prisoners on the outside. The alleged scheme purportedly involved the use of dynamite, but James Sullivan, one of the leaders of the mutiny, blamed guard Krueger, who routinely beat prisoners while he was under the influence of alcohol. "He [Krueger] beat a negro named Calhoun with a club until the fellow shouted for mercy," Sullivan said. "Then Calhoun's friends declared they could not work for such a brute."[16]

There seemed to be no end to the outrageous actions by Karr's guards. Without provocation, Krueger attacked John Gehres, a regular Sunday visitor to the workhouse, on August 30, 1896. On nearly every previous allotted ten-minute visit with Gehres's brother, Henry, in the workhouse, Krueger had stood near them, insulting them with derogatory remarks. On this occasion, when Henry asked John to bring him some underwear next Sunday, Krueger blew a gasket, accusing John of spreading rumors to reporters about abuse at the workhouse. John, a man of slight build who was still recovering from a recent illness, strenuously denied the accusation, but Krueger cussed at him and punched him in the face, knocked him to the floor, and kicked him repeatedly. Gehres swore out a warrant for Krueger's arrest, but he got nowhere. The assistant prosecutor told him to go complain to Mayor Walbridge, since it was up to the mayor to remove Krueger.[17]

On the evening of September 3, 1896, trolley car number 100 of the Southern Electric Railway Company was crossing Osage Street at the intersection of Broadway when a line of fifteen slow-moving workhouse carts under the supervision of guard Leopold "Loophole" Matt began to cross the track, impeding the trolley's progress. The carts and crew were on their way back to the workhouse after a day of work on city streets. The trolley conductor slowed his speed and stopped. After three or four of the workhouse carts crossed the track, he called to the next one to stop and let the trolley pass. On the assumption that the driver of the mule-drawn cart would stop, the conductor resumed speed and collided with the cart, knocking it over on its side. Traffic on the street and the tracks was blocked at a busy time.

Workhouse guards Matt and "Long-Haired Willie" Peters cursed the conductor, who returned the favor. Matt stuck a double-barreled shotgun in the conductor's face, ordered him off the trolley, and commanded him to follow him to the workhouse. When the conductor asked by whose authority, Matt said by his own and grabbed him and continued to curse. A street brawl broke out when men from the nearby powerhouse, including a few conductors who saw what happened, rushed to the aid of the trolley conductor. Matt let go of the conductor and poked his shotgun into the side of an onrushing conductor from the powerhouse, knocking him down. Peters and the workhouse guards charged into the melee. A large crowd of people gathered to watch the fight, which the men from the powerhouse won. There were injuries, and the superintendent of the railway company threatened to prosecute guard Matt. When Karr's office was contacted for a response, Karr was out of town in St. Paul, but one of his officers retorted that workhouse carts would not stop for streetcars, funerals, or any kind of traffic. When Karr returned from St. Paul on September 5, he defended his guards and pointed the finger at the railway employees. He even charged that the interference with workhouse carts was an intentional ploy to allow prisoners to escape.[18]

Public criticism of Karr's guards also surfaced when workhouse crews graded and repaired city streets. In March 1897, when a workhouse gang was repairing California Avenue, nearby residents complained about the gang's lack of concern for public decency. According to the complaints, the guards encouraged loud cursing by prisoners within earshot of women and children in the neighborhood. A resident complained about the salty language to guard Matt, who cursed and told him to go to hell, daring him to try to do something about it. The resident revealed to a reporter that guards used a crippled inmate to make beer runs to Kramer's Saloon for the work crew inmates and guards alike.[19]

Six weeks earlier, police had arrested one of Karr's guards, identified as Joseph Gallis, who went on a Saturday night drunken spree after attending a theater. He fired bullets from his revolver into the air near "Tin Cup Row." When nearby police heard the shots, they came running. Gallis, who had already thrown away his revolver, was uncooperative and belligerent. He invited the officers to fight. They arrested him and found a set of brass knuckles in his pocket. Judge Thomas Peabody fined him five dollars on each charge for carrying a concealed weapon and discharging a firearm. Amid public rumors that workhouse guards used brass knuckles on prisoners, Peabody told him he was unfit to be a guard.[20]

As in the case of Superintendent Lohrum and his predecessors, Karr used the labor of inmates, including work gangs, maids, and other household servants, for private benefit. After the devastating tornado of 1896 damaged Karr's personal residence, he sent work gangs under the supervision of his son, Jake, who was on the payroll as a guard, to repair damage to the Karr house on Ann Avenue. Instead of employing skilled union laborers, Karr tapped the pool of skilled prisoners to do the repair work. When two prisoners assigned to the work gang escaped, they were recaptured, but Karr did not report their escape. His neighbors confirmed that he also used city carts and teams of mules to haul dirt and stone for a new foundation fence at his private residence. Neighbors who had to pay to repair or rebuild their own homes damaged or destroyed by the tornado confirmed the details of how the two prisoners escaped. On the day after the public found out about Karr's use of workhouse labor and taxpayers' money to repair his private residence, the city auditor balked when Karr submitted a requisition in the amount of eighty-five dollars for a buggy horse. The workhouse appropriation specified mules, not buggy horses.[21]

Corruption flourished during the superintendency of Karr. Jake Karr ran the store formerly operated by guard Joseph Galen for many years. Jake, who held all money belonging to inmates, sold cigarettes, tobacco, and other items to them at a profit. For a two-dollar bribe of a guard, a prisoner might get an easier work assignment. Five dollars would cancel court costs associated with a prisoner's case and guarantee a prisoner's release immediately after he worked off his fine.

While overseeing a workhouse grading gang at the House of Refuge, a guard ordered prisoner Frank Crosby, who was sentenced to the workhouse for burglary, and another prisoner to steal sheet copper and lead being stored for future use by William Nolte, superintendent of the House of Refuge. At the behest of the guard, the two prisoners sold the stolen items to a nearby junk dealer for $3.75. The guard pocketed three dollars and sent Crosby on a beer run with the remaining seventy-five cents.

Sexual abuse of prisoners by fellow prisoners went on in the workhouse with the full knowledge of guards, who joked about it. Much of the brutality by guards took place without Superintendent Karr's knowledge, but prisoner Crosby later insisted that Karr took part in one of the beatings he witnessed.[22]

As the economic depression of 1893 deepened over the next five years, overcrowding in the workhouse worsened. Suicides, attempted suicides, escapes, and attempted escapes were the result. In what a *Post-Dispatch* reporter called "an epidemic of the dumps," three young women serving sentences in the workhouse for hanging out in wine rooms tried to kill themselves on May 3, 1898, by swallowing laudanum. Belle Dugan, age nineteen, Jessie Lawson, age twenty-three, and Lucy Williams, age twenty-two shared the same workhouse cell. At first, Lawson and Williams tried to talk Dugan out of drinking the laudanum. Reportedly, Dugan grew ever more despondent when a letter she expected from her sweetheart did not arrive. She paced the floor of her cell until around midnight, sinking deeper into depression. The more depressed she became, the more despondent Lawson and Williams grew. They fought briefly over the bottle of laudanum, which Dugan later claimed she found on the ledge of her cell window. In the end, they decided to share the drug in equal amounts. Workhouse authorities pumped coffee down them, forced them to walk up and down the corridor, and sent them to the South Side dispensary, where a doctor pumped their stomachs and sent them to the city hospital.[23]

Later that year, a twenty-four-year-old woman from Cuba, Missouri, with a self-confessed morphine habit swallowed ground glass in a workhouse suicide attempt. She survived the ordeal and told the first version of her story to a *Post-Dispatch* reporter. Her name on the city hospital books was "Daisy" Cook, also known as Alice, but when she came to St. Louis more than two years earlier she claimed she gave her name as Jessie Cook. Formerly a night telegraph station agent for the Frisco Railway in Cuba, Missouri, she had met a railway company employee from St. Louis whose train stopped regularly in Cuba. They gradually developed an intimate relationship, but when her father, a merchant, found out her suitor was married, he ordered her to stop seeing him. She and her father had a bitter falling out. Afterward, she resigned her position, moved to St. Louis, and went to work in the glove department of a dry goods store, where she was employed until about seven months before she attempted suicide in the workhouse.

According to Cook's first account of what led to her arrest and workhouse sentence, she went out lightly clad one night to get something to eat for her suitor, whose train had come in late. A police officer arrested her for walking the streets. Cook insisted she had broken no laws. She was confident she would be exonerated in court after establishing her good character, but Judge Peabody banished her to the workhouse. "My only misdeed," she confessed to the reporter at the hospital, "is that I have acquired the morphine habit. I was sick when I came here, unused to city ways and thought that morphine was a good thing to take when I was in the slightest pain. When they sent me to the Workhouse I was overcome with shame. In the four days I have been down there I had nothing to eat but bread and water. They made me work, weak as I was. Friday night I became desperate." Cook explained how she obtained the powdered glass: "After going into my cell I saw an empty soda water bottle on my windowsill. I pulled the heel off my shoe and then secured a scrub brush. By laying the head of the bottle on my heel I was able to break it off with the brush without making too much noise. Then I pounded the glass into powder. When I had a good dose of it I put in my mouth and then swallowed water until it was all down. Pretty soon I became deathly sick." A prisoner alerted workhouse authorities, who sent Cook to the hospital. Cook vowed to kill herself if they sent her back to the workhouse, and she refused to contact her family for help. "The only crime I committed was to get lunch at night for a hungry man. I will not send for my folks. When I left home my father said he did not want to see me again unless I was dying. If they send me to the Workhouse again he will have an opportunity of looking upon his dying or dead daughter. Not before."[24]

About ten days after she swallowed the ground-up glass, the woman, whose condition was still precarious, revealed her legal identity to a city hospital physician. Her name was Florence Lee Jones, daughter of Newton Jones, of Cuba. Her father was not only a prominent, well-to-do merchant but also Crawford County's representative in the Missouri legislature from 1874 to 1878. From her hospital bed, she claimed a young physician on Olive Street had lured her to St. Louis two years earlier and supported her for about a year. Afterward, she lived with a railroad employee until he ran out on her. Her life then went downhill.

At the time of her arrest, she roomed at Fifteenth and Chestnut Streets in the heart of a tenderloin district of saloons and bordellos. She asked her father if she could move back home, but he refused to let her return to the family household. Ashamed and cut off from morphine, she had decided to take her own life. In critical condition at the hospital, she asked the attending physician to send for the minister of the Centenary Methodist Episcopal Church. The minister visited her and afterward indicated that she had asked for and received divine forgiveness for her sins. An aunt in Cuba who visited her in the hospital brought word that Florence's father had relented and agreed to let her come home.[25]

What Florence failed to reveal was that she had married William James Wallace in Steelville, near Cuba, on May 18, 1895. They moved to East St. Louis, where Florence gave birth to their daughter, Ruth Lee Wallace, on April 14, 1896. Florence's son, Lloyd Newton Wallace, was born on September 18, 1898, a mere two months before she tried to kill herself in the workhouse. It is not clear who had custody of two-year-old Ruth and baby Lloyd while Florence was in the workhouse and hospital. Newspaper reports did not mention either child. Afterward, Florence and William reconciled and built an enduring marriage in East St. Louis that lasted until the death of her husband, a streetcar conductor for twenty-one years, in 1927. Florence, who likely never returned to the workhouse after she recovered from the attempted suicide and morphine withdrawal, lived until the end of 1955.[26]

For inmate Nellie Woods, also known as May Willard, drug addiction, lying, and thievery went hand in hand. They were at the root of a life of crime that sent her repeatedly to the workhouse. According to her, she came from a respectable family in Chicago but began to steal as a young teenager. After an arrest for shoplifting, she was sent to the Good Shepherd's Home in Chicago. When she left, she did not return home. According to a Chicago newspaper, she and her sister, Julia Lowe, had come to Chicago from Toledo around 1884. She was about thirteen. In Chicago, they ran a longtime "disreputable resort," where they stole money from clients, many of whom were too embarrassed to pursue charges or show up in court. A noted thief, Willard was arrested countless times, but through repeated delays, payoffs, and subterfuges, she evaded convictions in the criminal courts. In 1896, however, a jury convicted her of stealing thirty dollars from a Colorado mine owner in Chicago, and she did time in the Illinois State Penitentiary at Joliet.[27]

Upon release, Willard met a Chicago traveling salesman who took an active interest in her, urging her to turn her life around. By her own account, she, too, wanted to reform, and she convinced him of her sincerity. They married and moved to St. Louis, where they lived comfortably. Then, as she explained to a *Post-Dispatch* reporter, "I became a morphine fiend. My husband was away from home a good part of the time and he knew not of my downfall. When I realized that I could no longer conceal my condition from him I sold out all our pretty furniture."

A prisoner to her drug habit, Woods moved out while her husband was away. When he came looking for her, she was so ashamed and in such despair that she tried to kill herself by jumping out a third-floor window at Fourteenth Street and Clark Avenue. She was in the city hospital for a month. The attempted suicide left her with a disfigured broken nose. As she later explained, "I wanted to die. I almost succeeded, for when they picked me up I was unconscious and many bones were broken. My nose was broken and my face so badly disfigured that any claims I may ever have made to personal beauty were gone for all time."[28]

The police in St. Louis knew Willard better as Nellie Woods. She insisted that she used aliases to avoid tarnishing the reputation of her family, but Chicago newspapers indicated that she and her sister were in cahoots, and that Willard's mother lied for her and once hid her in the icebox when police searched for her after she jumped bond. Woods claimed she chose the surname of Willard because her mother was a temperance advocate who admired Frances Willard, president of the Woman's Christian Temperance Union. In November 1897, Woods was arrested in St. Louis for petty larceny after stealing a cape from a woman with whom she was boarding. She was sentenced to twenty days in Karr's workhouse, and again for sixty days in June 1898. While in the holding cell at Four Courts, Woods tried to kill herself. She tore apron strips, tied them together, fastened one end to the bars on the top of her cell, put the other end around her neck, climbed on a bench, and jumped. She dangled by the neck, but a woman in the holding cell yelled for the jailer, who cut Woods down. Unconscious, Woods was taken to the city hospital, where she recovered.[29]

For five years, Woods was in and out of the workhouse for burglary and petty larceny. When thieving at night, she wore men's clothing. She became well known as a mysterious, vivacious, and attractive thief and addict in her late twenties who readily confessed to crimes as soon as she was arrested. Cooperative with police officers, she led them voluntarily to pawn shops where she sold stolen items. A self-described kleptomaniac and morphine addict, she evoked sympathy among those convinced of her sincerity and drawn to her story. During one of Woods's stints in the workhouse, Catherine Haynes, a member of Willing Workers who operated the Door of Hope, took an interest in her case. At the end of Woods's sentence, Haynes invited her to move into the home for women who sought rehabilitation and reform. Within an hour after Woods arrived, she fled with valuable items that belonged to Haynes. By the time Woods was arrested and sent back to the workhouse, she was physically devastated from the ravages of drugs. She became ill and was taken to a cell in the observation ward of the city hospital, where Dr. H. L. Nietert treated her for morphine addiction in summer and fall 1900. By Thanksgiving, she was much improved and in cheerful, hopeful spirits. Dubbed "Angel of the Cells" by a woman in the hospital, Woods developed a reputation for helpfulness among those around her. A reporter who visited her observed, "She is good looking, but above all her cheerful nature and kind disposition stands forth as her most beautiful characteristic."[30]

While in the city hospital, Woods intervened heroically when a male insane patient, Joseph Dunn, attacked matron Sarah Woodruff. Dunn clubbed Woodruff with a board, knocked her down, and beat her with a padlock from an open cell. Then he tried to strangle her. Woods and another inmate rushed to Woodruff's aid, grabbing the board and beating Dunn with it to force him to loosen the stranglehold on Woodruff's neck. When Dunn's grip proved too strong, Woods used her fist to break through a window so that attendants outside the cell area might hear the cries for help. Other attendants and a guard came to subdue Dunn. Woodruff suffered a brush with death, and Woods suffered a badly lacerated hand from breaking the window. To reward Woods for likely saving the matron's life, authorities released her from the workhouse, but a few months later she was back again on a sixty-day sentence. Judge Ben F. Clark revoked her parole after she pleaded guilty to two charges of stealing clothing.[31]

The pattern repeated itself until Woods was arrested and sentenced to five years in the Missouri State Penitentiary. A wealthy man whose stolen clothing she was wearing at the time of her arrest felt sorry for her and visited her in jail before she was taken to Jefferson City. At her request, he brought her stationery and a few dollars for postage so she could write to her friends. Contrite, she expressed regret for having disappointed those who tried to help her. "A term in the penitentiary will do me good," she told a *Globe-Democrat* reporter. "It will break me of the drug habit at least. I hope they will send me there, but I would rather hang than go back to the workhouse. I've been there several times, and it is the worst place imaginable."[32]

On July 12, 1902, at age twenty-nine, Woods entered the Missouri State Penitentiary as May Willard. She soon gained the trust of the matron, who made her a trusty in the women's wing of the prison. One of sixty-four incarcerated women in the penitentiary, Woods was entrusted with the keys to answer the doorbell when visitors or other prison officers wished to enter the women's ward. Each night, she locked the outside door before returning the keys to the matron. At roll call on the morning of January 14, 1904, however, Willard was missing. She had closed the door but left it unlocked the night before. She did not let other inmates know, but shortly after returning the keys to the matron, she entered the matron's room, stole one of her dresses, a hat, and other apparel, and walked out the front door into the night. Nearly two weeks later, a St. Louis detective spotted her on a streetcar and took her into custody. "I came to St. Louis at once," Willard noted. "I knew I would get caught, but I like the town." She was released from the penitentiary on April 6, 1906, in accordance with Missouri's three-fourths sentencing law.[33]

In some cases, inmates gained mysterious access to morphine and laudanum in their cells to commit suicide. Such was the case of Henry Cole, a photographer from Cincinnati who had fallen on hard times. He took his own life with a large dose of morphine on July 5, 1898. Sentenced to the workhouse on January 4 to serve a sentence of nine months, he despaired of receiving a pardon for stealing photography materials from a St. Louis gallery. The authorities rushed him to the city hospital, where his stomach was pumped, but to no avail.[34]

On October 2, 1897, Judge David Murphy sentenced Jerry Reynolds, a morphine addict and hotel cook, to twenty days in the workhouse for stealing a pair of shoes. Reynolds collapsed on the floor from withdrawal spasms as a deputy sheriff led him from the courtroom. On October 10, Reynolds slit his own throat with a razor in a workhouse cell crowded with ten other prisoners. Fellow cellmates stopped him after he made the first gash, which was about four inches long but not deep enough to kill him. Rushed to the South Side dispensary, where fourteen stitches stopped the bleeding, Reynolds was taken to the city hospital and put under suicide observation. Thirty-two years old with a degree of education, he warned that he would try to kill himself again if he had to endure withdrawal cravings, hallucinations, and the harsh compulsory labor regime of the workhouse. In a bedside interview, he showed a reporter the little blue needle marks that covered both arms. While in the hospital, he contracted pneumonia from his wound, died on October 20, and was buried in Potter's Field.[35]

A couple of days later, Superintendent Karr asked the mayor's permission to release one hundred inmates to relieve overcrowding. Karr also asked the police court's Judge Peabody to suspend sentencing temporarily, urging him instead to order those who were hauled into court out of the city within a specified number of hours. At the time, there were 589 prisoners in the workhouse, among them 110 women. There were only forty-five cells (twelve by eighteen feet) to hold 479 male inmates. Max Starkloff, the city's health commissioner, blasted the male quarters as "an outrage on civilization."[36] The women's quarters were just as crowded as the men's cell house. Karr, concerned that women in the workhouse had too much idle time, recommended the creation of a sock factory to employ them, but he also complained that it was nearly impossible to run the institution under such crowded conditions.[37]

To discourage a growing number of prisoner escapes, Karr hired Joe Golish as a new guard to be stationed at the top of the quarry hill. Known as a deadly shot, Golish was to be armed with a sixteen-shot Winchester repeating rifle. Karr also added a new restriction on unruly prisoners who worked in the quarry. From now on, instead of wearing leg irons, they would be chained to a huge boulder that weighed several tons. The chain, about six feet long, would confine them to a single place all day as they broke rock. Frank Crosby, a workhouse inmate, explained, "The heavy chain is fastened around the prisoner's neck and the other end is fastened to a ring in the rock. The victim is compelled to stand all day, and he is lucky if, in addition to the chain, he doesn't have to carry on his shoulders a couple of heavy weights."[38]

Suicides and attempted suicides under Karr's tenure became so commonplace that when the guard Loophole Matt fired a shotgun blast at escaped inmate James Clark in the Mississippi River on July 21, 1898, the *Post-Dispatch* at first described Clark's death as a suicide. Clark, who was about sixty years old and a bit frail, was in waist-deep water and wearing a ball and chain at the time. Numerous shantyboat eyewitnesses in Chickentown insisted that Clark was murdered by Matt. They saw Clark drop in the water when Matt fired at him. According to them, Superintendent Karr threatened to have them evicted from the waterfront if they told reporters what they had seen. Further investigative reporting raised suspicions when a badly decomposed body was fished from the river a couple of days later and sent to the city morgue by workhouse officers who claimed it was Clark's. The coroner ruled that the cause of death was accidental drowning, but a

Post-Dispatch reporter caught city officers in the morgue and the coroner's office in a web of contradictions. Under pressure, a deputy coroner held an inquest, but not a single eyewitness from Chickentown was called to testify. The coroner's initial ruling stood.[39]

When Mary Morgan, a young Black woman, was sent to the workhouse on a misdemeanor charge in late 1897, she was physically robust. Upon her release in the spring, she was a shadow of her former self, unable to walk. After she got into a fight with another inmate, workhouse officers banished her to the bull pen on a diet of bread and water during the coldest of winter. Thinly clad, sockless, and wearing worn-out shoes, she begged for warmer clothing and a fire. After two days of horrible suffering in the bitter cold, she received a visit from Superintendent Karr, who ignored her pleas for help and confined her to the bull pen for several more days. In the meantime, she endured frostbitten feet, ears, nose, and hands and contracted tuberculosis. Upon release from the bull pen in a suffering condition, she was forced to serve her remaining sentence.

At the end of her sentence in April 1898, a friend picked her up at the workhouse and called an ambulance to take her to the city dispensary, where Morgan next was sent to the city hospital. A *Post-Dispatch* reporter who visited her in the hospital described her condition: "She was one of the most pitiable objects seen there for a long time. Her feet were rotting masses of flesh, wrapped in cloths, and she was so emaciated and weak that she could scarcely whisper." The reporter noted that her feet would require amputation, but he also pointed out she was likely to die soon from tuberculosis. Morgan told the reporter: "When my feet were frozen stiff I begged to be taken to a fire, if only long enough to thaw them, but my begging was met with curses and threats of beating. My ears, nose and hands were badly frost-bitten, and while Mr. Karr saw the condition I was in and how I was suffering after two days in the bull pen, he kept me there for a whole week." She pointed out that others were sent to the bull pen while she was in the workhouse, but none of them were kept there for as long as she was. "It would have been less cruel for them to have killed me with an ax," she bitterly complained, "than to murder me by such slow degrees as this."[40]

From the standpoint of municipal politics, public revelations of such cruelties, suicides, and outrageous conditions in city institutions put embarrassing pressure on the Republican administration of Mayor Henry Ziegenhein. A week after the Democratic *Post-Dispatch* described the workhouse as "one of the moral pest-holes of St. Louis," the Republican *Globe-Democrat* published an article that was much more favorable toward the institution. The *Globe-Democrat* reporter noted that Julius Romer, a guard, only recently returned to his duties after recovering from injuries suffered in an attack about a year ago. Six Black prisoners had jumped Romer as he turned to step into a guard shack. He suffered a gunshot wound in the shoulder and was badly beaten. The reporter noted that guards had to be watchful every minute, calling attention to amputees in the workhouse's "one-legged brigade" who would not hesitate to crack a guard with a crutch. In the case of Sunday visitors, guards could not trust even the most innocent-looking. While the reporter was at the workhouse, a guard searched a food basket and discovered at the bottom cocaine for inmate William Johnson. The demur young woman who brought the food and cocaine turned coarse and combative, threatening the guard and warning about what she would do to him if she ever encountered him on the streets.

The reporter emphasized that many inmates formed lifetime friendships in the workhouse, pointing to a considerable number of interracial relationships observable during Sunday visits to the institution. Many Black women brought food to white male prisoners, and many Black men visited young white women confined to the workhouse for public drunkenness or other minor offenses. The *Globe-Democrat* pointed to a specific relationship between William Melton, a Black trusty, and a young blonde woman who visited him with a beautiful fair-skinned child with kinky hair. According to Superintendent Karr, the woman was from a wealthy southern family and Melton had been the family's coach driver. Melton was her only friend in the world, now that she lived as an outcast. For Karr, the interracial relationships in the workhouse were an indication of just how degraded and devoid of self-respect the inmates were.[41]

Growing political activism of women's organizations and clubs over the plight of women in St. Louis's penal institutions spelled trouble for Karr's regime at the workhouse. At the Conference on Charitable and Philanthropic Institutions held in St. Louis in February 1892, the Christian Willing Workers organization urged petitions to the appropriate authorities to hire a matron at the workhouse. In 1884, thanks to lobbying by the Woman's Christian Temperance Union, the police department added the position of police matron and hired Louisa Harris, a member and delegate to state and local WCTU conventions, to fill it. The WCTU, which sought to ensure that women who were arrested would receive dignified treatment at the police department's central station, paid part of her salary and furnished her quarters at the Four Courts Building. Part of Harris's job was to help "rescue" "fallen women" who wanted to change their life of self-degradation. She was also president of the Hephzibah Home, president of the Society for the Protection of Women and Children, and a guiding force in several charitable organizations. Her death on January 20, 1897, helped to set in motion developments that brought women activists into growing conflict with workhouse superintendent Karr.[42]

At the time of Harris's death, leading women's organizations in the city were outraged over an incident that had occurred one month earlier in which two white prostitutes were sexually assaulted by two Black burglary suspects while in custody and in transit from the Chestnut Street station to the city jail in the Black Maria. Officer Michael Lynam, the guard who rode on the back of the police wagon, did nothing to intervene as the screams of the women pierced the night.

The incident was layered with racial implications. Eighteen-year-old Daisy Daly and nineteen-year-old Blanche Reeves were prostitutes in keeper Etta Mason's house at 2031 Chestnut. They were arrested for "roping," or standing at a door or window to entice men off the street. Daily and Reeves fought off the attackers with the help of two Black women and a young white man inside the wagon, but neither Officer Lynam nor the driver offered to help. According to Daily and Reeves, Lynam told them they deserved what they got as prostitutes. By the time the police wagon reached the Four Courts Building, both women had sustained injuries, but no doctor was summoned to treat them. The women filed charges of assault and battery against the attackers, but in the Court of Criminal Correction, Judge Murphy released the attackers on grounds of insufficient evidence. The prosecutor complained that the police department made only a halfhearted effort to gather evidence in the case.

The WCTU, the Woman's Political Economy Club, and other women's organizations were furious at the judge and the dismissive attitudes of the police department. Similar sexual assaults had occurred in the police wagon previously. In each case, officer Lynam was the guard. Eliza B. Ingalls, president of the St. Louis WCTU and vice president of the Missouri organization, called for Lynam's firing. Representatives of several women's organizations asked questions at a hearing held by the Board of Police Commissioners at which Lynam was removed from the police force. Without political pressure from the organizations, the matter likely would have been swept under the rug, and the underlying attitudes of Captain Peter Joyce and others in the police department toward prostitutes would have gone unchallenged.[43]

Against this backdrop of women's activism and concern over treatment of women in city institutions, further controversy erupted when police chief Harrigan appointed Louisa Breen as acting police matron at the Four Courts Building after Louisa Harris's death. Ingalls, unhappy with Harrigan for breaking a promise to appoint the WCTU's candidate, claimed that Harrigan's reversal was connected to the firing of officer Lynam in the previous case. The WCTU pushed the candidacy of Catherine A. Gilbert, who, along with Laura C. Shepherd, had recently been hired by Superintendent Karr as a guard at the workhouse. The St. Louis Central WCTU submitted a petition endorsing Gilbert to the Board of Police Commissioners, whose approval was necessary to finalize the appointment. The commissioners approved Gilbert, who resigned from her workhouse position. Before she could start her new duties on May 1, however, they withdrew her appointment. After countless delays, they finalized the appointment of Breen on July 7, 1897.

To appease the WCTU, the commissioners dismissed Rosetta Hainsworth and replaced her with Gilbert at the Fourth District station. Breen's tenure at the Four Courts Building did not last long. She and Gilbert soon traded places, but the Board of Police Commissioners fired Breen for neglect of duty in early November and restored Hainsworth to her former position at the Fourth District station. Karr, refusing to follow the recommendation of women's organizations, hired Minnie Gammeter to replace Gilbert as a workhouse matron.[44]

The following case provides a poignant example of why the WCTU and other women's clubs felt it important to have a woman with their stamp of approval in the position of workhouse matron. It also demonstrates how easily an early teenage girl might end up incarcerated for the crime of homelessness. In late 1897, itinerant Holiness preacher the Reverend A. S. Orne and his wife, Clara, conducted religious services in the workhouse during a stay in the heart of the St. Louis slums. The Ornes, advocates of juvenile courts and industrial homes, were devoted to social uplift and sociological research while spreading Holiness doctrines wherever their wagons and boats took them. Influenced by the Social Gospel movement, they took an active interest in delinquent children of the poor. When the Ornes toured the workhouse, Reverend Orne asked matron Gammeter if there were any juveniles incarcerated in the institution. Gammeter singled out Jessie Wilson, a thirteen-year-old girl confined without a specific charge on an indefinite sentence.

Sympathetic to Wilson's plight, Gammeter told Reverend Orne that Wilson would be better off if the Humane Society looked after her. In a conversation with Wilson, Reverend Orne learned that her mother was in the insane asylum and that her drunken father was "no good." After living with an aunt who did not want her, Wilson took to the streets with her dog. When a police officer asked her where she lived, she answered, "I have been staying with my aunt, but she don't want me anymore." Wilson hoped the officer might find her a better place to live, but instead she was taken to police court, where a judge sent her to the workhouse. Orne spoke to an agent of the Humane Society of Missouri, who promised to try to place her in a better environment outside the workhouse. Whether Gammeter, although sympathetic, had the commitment or the necessary contacts to intervene on Wilson's behalf is doubtful. Had it not been for intervention by the Ornes, the Humane Society's attention might never have been brought to bear on Wilson's outrageous confinement in the workhouse under Karr.[45]

When Karr left the workhouse in 1899, he left behind a mess for the city and for the new superintendent. Conrad Kempf, approved by the city council as Karr's successor on May 26, 1899, complained that the storehouse was empty when he took over on June 1. Karr's most recent requisition, a rather large one involving several hundred dollars' worth of supplies, was delivered to the workhouse on May 15. In less than two weeks, the goods vanished. To protect himself, Kempf notified the Board of Public Improvements, which investigated but maintained public silence about the missing supplies. However, an investigation by a *Post-Dispatch* reporter revealed that a young man recently released from the workhouse claimed that in late May he helped another man and a Black cook to move storehouse goods to a private residence in the city at two o'clock in the morning. The job took several nights.

Superintendent Kempf complained that everything in the workhouse was in bad shape, and he raised the question of what had happened to the vegetables grown on the grounds. He noted to the reporter that prisoners never got to eat them. The reporter observed that the missing supplies included coal, bacon, flour, hams, oatmeal, sugar, tea, lemons, potatoes, crackers, coffee, dried fruits, canned goods, vinegar, syrup, hay, bran, corn, lumber, office chairs, china ware, glassware, horse blankets, sponges, wash linen, spool cotton, thimbles, and needles. "In fact," wrote the reporter, "everything was included that was needed to stock a home." Superintendent Kempf pointed out that even the rose bushes and young trees furnished to the workhouse by the Park Department had vanished overnight.[46]

At the time of Karr's departure, he was embattled and embittered. For most of his tenure, in fact, he was embroiled in public controversy. The city charity commissioners preferred charges of mismanagement against him, but they were not sustained. Earlier, Judge Murphy in the Court of Criminal Correction had held Karr in contempt for failure to comply with a habeas corpus order. The *Post-Dispatch* singled him out as one of Mayor Walbridge's worst appointments. The BPI had its own management frustrations with him, too, but the controversy that brought him down in the end was his treatment of a woman in the workhouse, whose remarkable case came to the attention of the WCTU and the Humanity Club.[47]

5

THE LITTLE PINE STREET ANARCHIST

The torture of tiny Mary Duff, held long past her sentenced time by cruel overseers in the Karr regime, was shocking, sadistic, and flat-out barbaric. Seven weeks of solitary confinement on bread and water in the bullring nearly blinded and killed her, but she remained defiant. Her case dramatized more than a half century of countless abuses by appointed workhouse officers. At worst, Duff was a quarrelsome nuisance to police and other authorities, who branded her "the little Pine Street anarchist" after she protested the execution of the Chicago Haymarket anarchists in 1887. She never backed down in an argument, whether political or otherwise. Often single and homeless, she was locked up repeatedly as a squatter for disturbing the peace and occupying vacant rooms in the tenement slums of St. Louis. Police court judges slapped her with fines they knew she could not pay, banishing her to the workhouse time and again to work off the fines. As she languished in solitary confinement, the intervention of prominent women's activists in St. Louis brought public scrutiny to her mistreatment and perhaps saved her life. A well-to-do clubwoman from the city's West End hired attorney Daisy Barbee to represent Duff, who fought back and gained at least partial vindication in the courts.

Duff's intellect and controversial views on politics, economy, and medicine marginalized her in St. Louis. She was a former teacher, writer, Spiritualist lecturer, trance medium, and anarchist sympathizer. An allopathic "doctor" with a specialty in "nervous diseases" and a physician's diploma of some sort, she was also a police character with at least eight confinements in the workhouse. A self-described "mental science healer," metaphysician, and freethinker, Duff advocated common-law marriage and spoke her mind to even the burliest of police officers and workhouse guards. Because of her alternative political views and scrappy determination to defend them, she was often harassed and embroiled in public disturbances. In 1876, when she arrived in St. Louis at age twenty-five with her epileptic younger sister, Sophronia, she had a promising future and ample savings from previous teaching jobs in southern Illinois. The repeated abuse she suffered in the dungeons of the workhouse took its toll on her and punctuated the tragic descent of her life in the city.

Born in 1851, Mary Duff was one of seven children born to John and Lucinda D. (Smith) Duff, of Franklin County, Illinois. Her father, a highly successful farmer and county judge, died when Mary was six years old, and her mother died when Mary was fourteen. Her uncle, Andrew D. Duff, was a prominent judge in southern Illinois who trained young lawyers, and her brother, Alfred C. Duff, oldest of the children, was a lawyer. Mary graduated from Ewing College, which began as a Baptist high school and received its charter as a college in 1874. Critical of low teacher salaries in Benton, Du Quoin, and other southern Illinois towns near Carbondale, where she taught, she moved to St. Louis with Sophronia. As she later explained to a reporter, "When I got here I found that a teacher was expected to teach for one year for nothing on trial. With my experience I did not feel that this should be expected of me, so I abandoned the educational field."[1]

When Mary first arrived in St. Louis, she stayed at the Presbyterian Home on Sixteenth Street, near Chestnut, but soon ran afoul of police authorities. She entered a romantic living arrangement with Harris Baldwin, a well-respected attorney for whom she also worked, but the common-law relationship ended acrimoniously. On February 10, 1879, Baldwin secured a warrant for her arrest, charging that she had burglarized his home and law office at 514 Olive Street on January 15, 1879. The items she allegedly stole consisted of a life insurance policy, two promissory notes, and two letters worth about $320. When the case came up for trial a week later, Mary was surprised when Baldwin dropped part of the charges against her. The prosecuting attorney reportedly claimed she belonged in an insane asylum.

In 1880, however, Baldwin revived the charges of petty larceny and she was rearrested. When the judge asked her name, she insisted it was Baldwin, not Duff, and argued that it was her right to use the Baldwin name. Unable to raise a bond set at $1,000, she went to jail. Years later, she downplayed the dispute: "I took our household goods and he got out a warrant charging me with larceny. The case was not sustained. Baldwin disappeared and I heard he was dead."[2]

By the time of Mary's jailing, she and Sophronia ("Sophia") were well known among police court judges, police officers, and newspaper reporters. The *Globe-Democrat,* a week after Mary was arrested, referred to her as "the lady who has been 'raising Cain' in jail for the last week."[3] Reporters poked fun at the sisters and revised their surnames to Tough or Tuff. Sophronia sometimes used "Carrie Adams" as an alias. She, too, became involved in scraps that landed her in the workhouse.

Shortly after the Baldwin affair, Mary entered a stormy short-term relationship with Henry Jackson, who operated a plumbing business at 218 Locust Street. He filed trespassing charges that resulted in her arrest. She acknowledged they were not formally married but emphasized that they lived together. On March 4, 1879, she and Sophronia showed up at his place to ask for money to buy cheap meal tickets at the What Cheer Restaurant, 625 Morgan Street. Jackson customarily complied, but on this occasion he refused. A ruckus ensued. According to Mary, Jackson hit her on the head with a large pair of tongs. When Sophronia tried to put herself between them, he struck her in the right eye. She retaliated by hitting him with a piece of pipe while Mary beat him from behind with a large bucket. When Jackson yelled for help, the sisters headed to the city dispensary for treatment of injuries, but not before Sophronia hurled a brick through the window of Jackson's office. When they later returned, he demanded forty-nine dollars in damages and filed charges against Sophronia. He ordered Mary out of his apartment, but she locked herself in a room. Finally, she consented to leave, kicking the door off its hinges as she left.[4]

An amused reporter described Mary when she appeared before Judge John Jecko in the First District Police Court on March 7, 1879: "She is little but holds her head high and struts like a bantam rooster, while her little pug nose is always turned sky high, and a smile of contempt is perpetually stealing over her face." When the court recorder asked whether she was guilty or not, "she eyed him from top to toe, counted the hairs in his flowing beard, took two paces to the left and four feet to the rear, then, folding her arms, she stood like Ajax defying the lightning, and commanding the admiration of about three score of her bosom friends who had come along to see her through the mill." Judge Jecko granted a continuance to Mary, who assured him that "in twenty-four hours, I can furnish witnesses to prove that my soul is as pure as the driven snow, and that the man who calls me a trespasser is a fabricator of the darkest hue."[5]

On March 14, 1879, Mary filed a suit against Jackson, charging him with slander, false imprisonment, and assaulting her. Jackson denied the charges, insisting he was the one who was beaten. When the trial began in May, Sophronia was still in jail, but police officers took her to court to testify. Several officers made it clear that Mary had given them a lot of trouble in the past. The jury failed to reach a verdict in her lawsuit.[6]

Sophronia was sick with a fever and chills when police brought her into court to face charges of criminal trespass for smashing Jackson's window. Angry, Mary showed up in the Court of Criminal Correction with a copy of *Chitty's Treatise on Pleadings and Parties to Actions* to guide her legal defense of Sophronia. As her sister's attorney, Mary requested a trial by a small jury. When the judge asked if a six-man jury would suffice, the sisters consented and asked for a delay so they could round up witnesses. The court found Sophronia guilty of malicious trespass and sentenced her to three months in the workhouse.[7]

Sophronia's epilepsy, poorly understood by medical authorities or the public at the time, no doubt intensified Mary's sisterly protectiveness in a world that was cruel and cold to epileptics. The public often shunned those who were afflicted with "fits." To attend school or sustain employment was nearly impossible for socially isolated epileptics. In some cases, they languished in workhouses or insane asylums.[8] Sophronia at times worked as a domestic servant under the Carrie Adams alias, but epilepsy made it difficult to sustain a job. At times, she became depressed and suicidal.

In 1884, Mary began a marital relationship with Ivory Brittain Watts, a professor at a business college in St. Louis. She described him as "an educated and cultured gentleman." According to her, they got along well for about a year, but then he accepted a new position in Denver. She claimed he disappeared en route to Denver. She tried to locate him but never found a trace, and she never heard from him again.[9]

Mary's radical political views are unclear, but like many middle-class women at the time, she was drawn to Spiritualism, metaphysics, magnetic and mental science healing, and alternative politics and medicine as sources of empowerment. Opposed to conventional thinking, she joined the journalist staff of what she termed a "socialistic" newspaper around 1878 and found the work "pleasant and exciting." She also contributed regularly to a New

York newspaper that expressed interest in her writings. After the Spiritual Association was incorporated in St. Louis in 1882, she wrote for Spiritualist publications, including the Cincinnati-based *Light of Truth* and St. Louis's first Spiritualist newspaper, *Light in the West,* in 1886.[10]

Duff was drawn to St. Louis's small community of political anarchists. In 1883, Austrian-born Joseph Reifgraber was a member of the committee that drafted the Pittsburgh Manifesto of the International Working Peoples' Association, a world anarchist political organization founded in London in 1881. He and his brother, Frank Reifgraber, opened a German-language newspaper, *Die Parole,* in St. Louis, which reportedly was home to about 150 anarchists. In November 1887, when four Chicago anarchists were convicted on flimsy evidence and hanged for the bombing at a labor demonstration in Haymarket Square on May 4, 1896, the Reifgraber brothers hung out an American flag in mourning. An angry mob backed by St. Louis police stormed the newspaper office and forced them to take down the flag.[11]

Duff, to show solidarity with the "Haymarket Martyrs," decorated the windows of her first-floor tenement rooms at 1503 Pine Street with pictures of the executed anarchists, draped in red bunting. In the center of the pictures was one of John A. Logan, a deceased Union Army general and U.S. senator from Illinois. She also wrapped an American flag in crape and hung it outside to mourn the executions. Below the pictures was a picture of Duff and an advertisement for her services. After a few days of brewing anger, a mob of more than one hundred led by a couple of representatives of the Grand Army of the Republic, formed outside.

Members of the mob were particularly indignant that she included Logan's photo among those of the revolutionaries. Spokesmen for the crowd entered the house and asked Duff to remove Logan's picture. Duff, who once taught school in Logan's hometown of Murphysboro, Illinois, refused. She insisted that he had been a friend of hers and that she was aware of what his sentiments would be in the matter. George Thomas, who lived across the street, told Charles P. Field that if he threw a rock through her window, Thomas would quickly snatch the photo of Logan. When Field heaved a rock through Duff's window, Thomas grabbed the photo but didn't get far with it. Duff, described as "a little, thin, shriveled woman, who probably does not weigh over eighty-five pounds,"[12] picked up a hatchet and threw it at him. When he dropped the picture, she recovered it and began to hurl fire clay bricks at the street mob, cursing as she threw. Arriving on the scene, police officer James Tyson assessed the situation and concluded that the only way to restore order was to arrest Duff. Rather than arresting Field, Thomas, and other members of the crowd, Officer Tyson charged Duff with disturbing the peace of Field and others by using profane language.[13]

To what extent is not clear, but Duff did have contacts with left-wing groups in the city. While in lockup at the Four Courts, she missed an anarchist demonstration that she had planned to attend. An unidentified "long-haired Socialist" who taught at a commercial college in the city stopped by the Four Courts for a long talk with her while she awaited trial.[14] Duff's attorney, Jeff D. Storts, tried but failed to have the case dismissed on the grounds the statute pertaining to disturbing the peace was not applicable in her case. At a trial by jury in Judge Charles F. Cady's First District Police Court, Duff defended her decision to include a photo of General Logan. She asserted her right to protest the hangings of the Haymarket Martyrs for their unpopular political views, pointing out that her American flag draped in crape was "sorry that men should die for expressing an opinion."[15] It took jurors only a few minutes of deliberation to acquit Duff, but the incident increased antagonism between her and the police, who in years ahead continued to tag her as an anarchist sympathizer.

Duff lived in the slums, where she offered services as a trance medium and clairvoyant at various addresses. She held séances and ran newspaper advertisements using the name of Dr. Mary Duff to advertise services to cure nervous diseases and hysterics. She also publicized her lectures on insanity, its causes, and cures. A sign outside her window on Pine Street read "Cures fits," but her sister continued to suffer from epilepsy. On November 24, 1884, Sophronia ended up in the city dispensary after suffering a major seizure at the corner of Tenth and Morgan Streets. Homeless, despondent, and friendless, she tried to kill herself ten years later by jumping into the Mississippi River at the foot of Lucas Street, but a night watchman intervened. The thirty-two-year-old servant, known also as Carrie Adams, was sent first to the city dispensary and then to the city hospital.[16]

In September 1889, Mary Duff engaged in the first of multiple neighborhood conflicts with practitioners of voodoo. Ed McFarland, a white follower of Black voodoo "doctoress" Hattie Johnson, sought her cures and charms, but he later sought treatment from Duff, a mental science healer. When McFarland improved after consulting with Duff, Johnson fell ill. Johnson's followers believed that by deserting her for Duff, he broke the charms and spells conjured by the voodoo priestess. Blaming McFarland for Johnson's illness, her disciples hovered outside Duff's building. One of them sneaked into her apartment and stole a shoe, but later returned it. Convinced that the shoe was "hoodooed," Duff refused to wear it, but a visiting niece wore her shoes and became so sick that she returned to her home in Illinois. Fearful that Johnson had put a spell on her, Duff consulted a friend knowledgeable about voodoo, who sold her a charm to break the spell.[17]

Late at night, Duff slipped over to Johnson's building and placed a line of salt around the place and spread a light dusting of yellow powder on the porch and steps while reciting incantations to hoodoo Johnson. A Black neighbor screamed when he spotted Duff and dashed inside to tell Johnson, who rushed outside, called Duff a witch devil, and jumped on her. During the hullabaloo, a crowd gathered, and the two women were arrested and hauled into police court for disturbing the peace.

Shortly after they were released, Duff found a mysterious bundle on her porch. She did not touch it or look inside to see what it was, but a neighbor did. He found a calf's head wrapped in a new towel. In the nose were pins and needles, and inside the mouth were hieroglyphic symbols and pieces of paper that contained thirty-five cents. The neighbor helped himself to the thirty-five cents, but Duff sank into depression, which she blamed on the calf's head placed on her porch. To keep Johnson's followers away from her apartment, she hired a woman to watch her house when she was away. Duff claimed that McFarland's mental faculties were compromised due to the overpowering influence of drugs and powders that Johnson gave him: "I hate to believe in hoodoos, but . . . well, I have seen some very strange things, about which I don't know just what to think."[18] Fearful for her life, Duff pressed charges against Johnson on October 1, 1889. As evidence in the case, she gathered a collection of powders and drugs allegedly used by voodooists in violation of the law. Johnson, backed by McFarland, denied knowing anything about the calf's head or having any association with voodoo. They insisted that Duff was delusional.[19]

Duff's campaign against voodooists continued for a couple of years. In an anonymous letter in February 1892, she warned Chief Harrigan about what she believed was a voodoo society, the Fraternal Order of the Eagles, a Black Republican club that met in a rear-alley craps house in her neighborhood, between Sixth and Seventh Streets and Clark and Spruce. Eph Houston, who headed the club, was trying to unify many of the city's poorest elements to vote for Republican candidates. Duff urged an investigation into the fate of members who tried to leave the society. Although Duff did not reveal her name in the letter, Harrigan identified her as its author. She named King ("Prince") Alexander, of New Orleans, as the high priest of the national voodoo society, pointing out that she once maintained correspondence with him. She complained of the use of drug compounds by voodooists to silence their enemies.[20]

Soon afterward, Duff was sentenced to the workhouse to work off a fine of ten dollars for throwing a rock at the apartment of a Black neighbor identified as Gypsy Vernon. On June 20, 1892, Duff was rearrested and fined ten dollars for disturbing the peace. The judge remitted the fine, but a week later Ed McFarland knocked on Duff's door late at night and disturbed her sleep. She believed he did so at the instigation of Hattie Johnson and other voodooists, to torment her. On other occasions, she alleged, McFarland had sneaked into her apartment and stolen items of clothing and a picture, presumably for hoodoo purposes. In mental anguish, Duff asked police "for protection from these agents of the devil."[21]

Duff's scrapes with the law became more serious on July 13, 1894, when she shot and nearly killed twenty-three-year-old Thomas Boyle, whose mother sought Duff's eviction as an undesirable tenant from her building on Locust Street. Boyle and A. H. St. Clair, a real estate agent, went to police headquarters the day before the shooting to file peace disturbance charges against Duff, who roomed in the building for about six weeks. Duff reportedly brandished a revolver when they ordered her to vacate the premises. On the following morning, Boyle took matters into his own hands. First he clubbed Duff's cat to death, and then he smashed the shutters on a window to her room, demanding that she let him in. After she fired a warning shot into the ceiling, Boyle went around to the door and chopped through it with a hatchet. Frightened, Duff shot him in the right side as he forcibly entered her room.[22]

In an interview at the police station, Duff showed no remorse, insisting that her rent was paid up until the end of the month. "Those people have disliked me during the whole time that I boarded there," she noted. "They wanted to run me out and because I wouldn't go, Mrs. Boyle tried to force me to leave before my month had expired. This I refused to do; hence the quarrel." She added:

> When young Boyle came to put me out of the room with his hatchet, after having so cruelly treated my cat, I was angry enough to do anything, and his outlandish advance in chopping the shutters of my window out and destroying the door to my room thoroughly aroused every bit of temper there was in me. I knew enough after having fired one shot into the ceiling to scare him that if he gained an entrance to the room he would brain me with his hatchet, consequently when he chopped the panels of my door out there was nothing left for me to do but shoot.

Duly acknowledging the unpopularity of her political views, Duff continued, "I am known from Boston to San Francisco. Of course, a great many people don't like me because my views of marriage and economy do not tally with those entertained by this Government. The Chicago anarchists were hanged. I sympathized with them and displayed the pictures of the men in front of my house in St. Louis, draped with red bunting. The police arrested me for this, but they did not shatter my sympathy with the anarchists."[23]

When asked about her views on marriage, Duff explained that she had been married twice under common law. To eliminate the role of religious authorities in the traditional marriage ceremony would put more money into the hands of the poor people instead of ministers, she argued. Described by a reporter as "quite a versatile and interesting woman," Duff favored taxation of Catholic Church property. Reportedly, she held strong anti-Catholic views as secretary of the American Protective Association. In keeping with the conspiratorial bent of the organization that blossomed in the Midwest in the 1890s, Duff blamed Catholic police officers and the push faction of the Democratic Party for her ongoing persecution. According to her, Captain William Lee tried to have her declared insane in 1883, and Chief Harrigan was now trying to put her into an asylum. After Boyle recovered from his wounds, Duff was arraigned in the Court of Criminal Correction on charges of assault and battery, but no charges were filed against Boyle.[24]

Apparently, the criminal case against Duff was dropped, but she was in and out of the workhouse for the next three years on minor charges of trespassing, disturbing the peace, and "lounging." In late April 1897, she was arrested for taking unauthorized possession of a vacant room on the third floor of a tenement building on Locust Street owned by the Noonan Real Estate Company. It was the third time in the past year she had tried to occupy the room without paying rent. After she nailed the door shut and refused to come out of the room, the real estate agent summoned police officers, who in the face of resistance from Duff, broke into the room and carried her off to the Four Courts for lockup. First District Police Court judge Thomas H. Peabody denied Duff's request for a jury trial where she could summon witnesses, tell her side of things, and plead her case. "I don't want to hear all that old story," he snapped. "You have been in this court a dozen times on the same charge. I sent you to the Work-house a few months ago for forcibly entering the same house. I believe you would try and break in there if a regiment with bayonets was guarding the premises."[25]

Back to the workhouse went Duff, homeless, without money to pay the stiff fine of fifty dollars levied by Judge Peabody. At a time when the workhouse was under increasing public scrutiny, her abuse at the hands of its officers soon hit the newspapers, thanks to the intervention of club women concerned about the treatment of women and children in the city's penal institutions. On October 5, 1897, workhouse superintendent Karr complained to Mayor Henry Ziegenhein and Wharf Commissioner C. H. Stone, who headed the workhouse committee of the Board of Public Improvements, about meddling by the WCTU and the Humanity Club. Karr urged the mayor to restrict visits to the workhouse by members of the Humanity Club and Eliza B. Ingalls, a women's suffrage activist and vice president of the Missouri WCTU. Specifically, Karr complained that they were trying to get a female guard fired and replaced by a woman with their stamp of approval. "I've always treated those ladies with utmost respect," he protested, "but they come down and propose to dictate to me just what I shall do, and how I shall do it. The prisoners see all this and it has a demoralizing effect so far as discipline is concerned." Karr complained about how hard it was to manage the overcrowded workhouse while under attack by outsiders. "A lot of women are the worst meddlers," he complained. "The 'regulars'—prisoners who divide their time between the hospital, Poor-house and Work-house—tell their tales to these women and a needless hubbub is raised. They can always find imaginary tales of persecution and these women investigators will believe them."[26]

Ingalls, appointed by Democratic governor Lon Stephens to the Missouri Board of Charities and Corrections earlier in the year, received a telephone message from a social worker calling attention to the abuse of Duff in the workhouse. In her capacity as a member of the Board of Charities and Corrections, Ingalls visited the workhouse to check on Duff's condition and to discuss her case with Karr. As she explained, "I set out at once and alone, and what I found was worse than I could possibly have imagined."[27]

Ingalls learned that Duff had spent seven consecutive weeks in solitary confinement on a diet of bread and water as added punishment for refusing to sew. At the time of Ingalls's visit, Duff had already served twelve days past her sentenced time. Without denying the facts of the case, Karr defended the treatment and continued detention of Duff, insisting that it was perfectly within his power as superintendent to hold her past the sentenced time as punishment and compensation for the days she refused to work. Ingalls, who emphasized that Duff was so sick and desperate that she had lost the will to live, pointed out that even in Duff's disheveled, weakened condition and workhouse garb, she had a look about her that suggested she may have been "a rich man's daughter or had been a more favored child of circumstances." Ingalls called attention to her intelligence, her beautiful blue eyes, and "high intellectual looking forehead."[28]

Immediately after Ingalls left the workhouse, Karr went on the offensive, blasting her, the WCTU, and the Humanity Club in a public statement. He complained that the organizations had no authority to conduct oversight of the workhouse, insisting that the institution would get along just fine without unnecessary meddling by women's groups. To counter his public comments and bring attention to the deplorable treatment of Duff, Ingalls went to the *Post-Dispatch.* In a statement released to the newspaper, Ingalls pointed out that she had investigated the workhouse not as president of the St. Louis district of the WCTU or on behalf of the Humanity Club but rather in her authorized capacity as a member of the state Board of Charities and Corrections. She did not challenge the validity of Duff's sentence, but instead focused on Duff's cruel treatment and confinement past her sentenced time: "Mary Duff is, perhaps, a hard character and an unruly prisoner. But it cannot be that her offense merited the punishment she received . . . When I saw the woman she was pale and sick. She had chills and was weak and emaciated. She said the physician had visited her in the dungeon, but had not given her any medicine. The wonder to me is that the punishment did not kill her."

Ingalls pointed out that since her appointment to the Board of Charities and Corrections in February, she had visited the workhouse only four times. She denied charges by Karr that she did not believe the "Dutch" to be capable of running a penal institution. She dismissed the allegation "as too ridiculous to entertain. Of course it is untrue and unfounded." While investigating the Duff case, "I took to look through the institution. The kitchen I found in bad condition. The sanitary condition of the entire institution is bad, but I realize that it cannot be helped until the city appropriates more money to remedy the evil."[29]

On October 7, an expanded investigation by a *Post-Dispatch* reporter led to a front-page story, "Torture of a Woman in a Dungeon at the Workhouse." Highly sympathetic to Duff, the article began, "Were Mary Duff any woman save a chronic police offender the howl of indignation over her treatment at the Work-house would be heard from one end of St. Louis to the other." In graphic detail, the article described the callousness of Karr and the horrors of the dungeon, where tiny amounts of air, bread, and water kept Duff barely alive for five days on the hard floor in the oppressive late August heat. "This air was so foul that the guard, on his bread and water visits to the cell," noted the reporter, "was forced to turn his head from the little hole in the door open for a brief second while he shoved in the bread and water for the poor wretch inside." A lesser woman, according to the exposé, would have died or ended up in the padded cell of a madhouse.

After Duff's first five days alone in perpetual darkness in the bullring, Karr ordered her removal to a cell in the women's quarters that was used to punish disobedient prisoners. On the way across the yard, her legs wobbled as she walked slowly and drew in fresh air, but the guard hurried her to the new dungeon that awaited her. The cell was a slight improvement, with a straw mattress on the floor, a bit more air, a three-legged stool, and tiny arc of light from a small opening above to let her know whether it was day or night. Nevertheless, the heat was suffocating. On the seventh week of solitary confinement in the dungeons, she still refused to sew. Had it not been for the intervention of Ingalls, the reporter noted, Duff might have died in solitary confinement.

Duff was on especially bad terms with police officer Barney Reagan. "She never stole anything that I know of," Reagan told a *Post-Dispatch* reporter. "She was just a kind of an anarchist and sort of 'daffy.' She would drink once in a while and fight anytime." Karr indicated that this was Duff's seventh confinement in the workhouse. On one occasion, she escaped by tearing men's overalls in two and sewing the ends together to make a cloth ladder to scale the wall. She was later apprehended and returned to the workhouse.

Karr complained that there was no punishment too severe for her, insisting that she deserved what she got.[30]

Karr released Duff after the investigation by Ingalls. Mayor Henry Ziegenhein promised officers of the Humanity Club that he would order Karr to allow them future access to the workhouse. The club women, whose earlier lobbying had secured ordinances requiring the hiring of matrons or female guards at city penal institutions, remained indignant at the disgraceful punishment meted out to Duff. They pushed for a greater role in the hiring of female guards. Unhappy with Karr's recent appointment of a guard without consulting them, Leonora B. Halsted, a writer and secretary-treasurer of the Humanity Club, fired a letter to Karr indicating withdrawal of support for his appointee. In an interview with a *Post-Dispatch* reporter, Mrs. Edwin Harrison, president of the club, insisted, "Were one of our women in charge of the female prisoners at the Work-house, that woman [Duff] would not have been tortured."[31]

A few days after Duff's release, Ingalls urged a full-scale investigation into the conditions of city institutions. She questioned whether they had deteriorated so much that they resembled the bastilles of France or "the black holes of Calcutta." She shed further light on Duff's case, pointing out that Judge Peabody had slapped her with a six-month sentence on charges of "lounging," which amounted to being without visible means of support or work. In Duff's statement in front of Ingalls and workhouse authorities, she made it clear she was denied a requested jury trial. According to Duff, she did not refuse to sew on all kinds of cloth, only on the dark blue cloth used to make the prison garb of male inmates. Her eyesight was very poor, and when reading and doing up-close work, she required an extra pair of glasses under her spectacles. She also claimed she was sick for several days before she was banished to the bullring. Duff acknowledged that a night matron did give her some medicine, and that on one occasion the matron had softened and slipped her some coffee when she refused the bread and water. Ingalls emphasized that Duff's mental condition, as some believed, may have been seriously damaged by her traumatic, extended solitary confinement in the workhouse.[32]

The city's Charity Commission defended Karr and blasted interference by Ingalls and the Humanity Club. Commissioner Gustav Cramer insisted that Duff had not been unduly punished, that she was a hardened police character deserving of the punishment. He claimed that Duff told him she would rather be in the workhouse than out of it. Cramer insisted that the city's penal institutions already were subject to adequate oversight and that they could get along just fine without meddling by the WCTU and the Humanity Club.[33]

In a front-page political cartoon and poem, the *Post-Dispatch* lampooned police court judge Thomas "Hairless" Peabody, an appointee of former mayor Walbridge. Peabody presided over the city's largest police court. The cartoon, "Now Mary Duff Has Threatened to Kill the Little Judge on Sight," called attention to Peabody's public statements supporting lynching and carrying concealed weapons, and it pointed out that when he sentenced Duff to the workhouse, she threatened "to have his heart's best blood." Now that she was free again and allegedly preparing to act on her threat, the cartoon mocked, "The only reason the Judge's hair does not stand on end at thought of her warlike attitude is because he hasn't any." Below the cartoon was a poem:

> The hairless Judge goes daily armed
> With pistol, gun and bowie knife,
> For, though as yet he's quite unharmed,
> A dame has sworn to have his life.
>
> "I'll kill you, sir, I will, on sight,"
> In baleful mood wrote Mary Duff.
> Such threats as these the Judge affright,
> For Mary vows it is no bluff.
>
> Across his windows slats are nailed,
> And Larry's minions guard his room,
> Lest he by Mary be assailed,
> And made to canter up the flume.
>
> A gun or two he takes along,
> And lays them close beside his docket,
> For Mary Duff might do him wrong,
> If they were hidden in his pocket.

At night he dreams of guns and knives
And women's faces, death and gore,
If Thomas had a dozen lives,
He still would wish he had one more.[34]

Less than a year later, a feud between Duff and Ferdinand Walz led to her confinement in the workhouse again. At the time, Duff lived in one half of a duplex at 4417 Clayton Avenue and Walz lived in the other half. They took their many quarrels to the city health department, where they argued and filed charges against each other for keeping unsanitary conditions. In Duff's backyard, she kept knickknacks and souvenirs that she scavenged from a nearby dump. After Walz complained to city officers about the weeds and condition of her yard, Arthur Becker, head of the health department's sanitary division, went to investigate. When Becker knocked on Duff's door, she greeted him with a revolver and ran him off, purportedly threatening to kill him. He swore out a warrant for her arrest and consulted with the mayor, who urged Duff's full prosecution.[35]

Judge Peabody, regarded by the *Post-Dispatch* as one of former mayor Walbridge's worst patronage appointees, hit Duff with a fine of $100 for disturbing the peace. When she could not pay it, he banished her yet again to the workhouse for six months, on June 8, 1898. Her sentence was to have expired on December 8, but in April 1899 she was still on bread and water in solitary confinement. A wealthy woman on the West End of St. Louis who chose to remain anonymous hired attorney Daisy M. Barbee on Duff's behalf. Barbee, who was admitted to the St. Louis bar in June 1895, was the first woman to gain membership in the St. Louis Law Library and to appear as counsel in the St. Louis Criminal Court, in 1897.[36]

On April 15, 1899, when Barbee went to the workhouse and demanded to see her client, the clerk refused, citing quarantine restrictions. Upon Barbee's request to see Duff's commitment papers, the clerk summoned Superintendent Karr, who, at the mere sound of Duff's name, lost his temper. Reporting on the case, the *Post-Dispatch* paraphrased Karr's angry response before he even bothered to find out who Barbee was: "You will never see Mary Duff. There was another woman down here not long ago bothering me about Mary Duff, and I told her I would never release her and that if she ever came back, I would throw her in the dungeon and keep her." Barbee firmly replied, "Mr. Karr, I demand to see the commitment papers." Karr snapped,

"Who the devil are you?" She responded, "I've been trying to tell you, but you would not listen. I am an attorney at law and I am making a lawful demand on you." Karr stammered an apology for getting irate, but he held fast to his refusal to produce the commitment papers: "Well, you can't get her out. You see the ordinance allows us to hold a prisoner under certain circumstances. There's no use in your trying to get her out." Barbee replied, "Well, Mr. Karr, you and I won't discuss that point here. We will let the courts pass on that."[37]

On April 17, Barbee filed a writ of habeas corpus in the criminal division of the St. Louis Circuit Court, presided over by Judge John A. Talty. Much of Duff's sentence was spent in the dungeons again, and reportedly the constant solitary confinement had damaged her eyesight further and rendered her nearly demented. Judge Talty granted the writ at once, and two days later, Karr brought Duff before the judge. Karr denied that Duff was mistreated in the workhouse, insisting that the ordinance authorized him to extend her sentence to punish her for refusing to work. "If the court rules that I can't hold a prisoner who refuses to work," argued Karr, "it simply does away with the Workhouse. I could not get a single prisoner to do any work if he knew he would get out just as soon without doing any labor."[38]

At a hearing on April 29, Talty ruled that the city ordinance invoked by Karr was unconstitutional. He conceded the right of municipalities to pass ordinances, but he upheld the courts' right to determine their constitutionality. In his opinion, Duff's confinement amounted to debt imprisonment, which was illegal in the state of Missouri. Her misdemeanor was an infraction of a city ordinance, not a state law. Talty acknowledged that Karr was simply following established practices at the institution, and likely the advice of city officers, but he ordered Duff's release from the workhouse.[39]

Karr faced political heat amid the controversy. On April 28, the city council followed the recommendation of the Committee on Municipal Affairs by voting not to affirm the reappointment of the former saloon keeper and Republican political boss of the Fifth Ward. After Duff left the workhouse on May 2, 1899, Barbee represented her in a lawsuit against Karr in the St. Louis Circuit Court, seeking $10,000 in damages for unlawfully detaining Duff past her sentenced time. Barbee also filed a suit in Justice F. A. Kline's court for $500 in damages against Karr for his refusal to furnish Duff's commitment papers when she requested them at the workhouse. Finally, she pursued a warrant charging Karr with a criminal misdemeanor in office. A *Post-Dispatch* reporter was impressed by the way Duff conducted herself in the courtroom: "Because Mary Duff's hand has been against the laws for nearly a quarter of a century it does not follow that she is rough. She is gentle in manner and speech and in conversation she displays a knowledge that one would not expect from one who has been long called a 'police character.'"[40]

On November 20, 1900, after a change of venue, appeals, and lengthy delays, the St. Louis Court of Appeals upheld the judgment of the circuit court, which granted Duff $200 as compensation for false imprisonment when she was held past her sentence. In a unanimous opinion written by appellate judge P. J. Bland, the appellate court was emphatic that Karr acted arbitrarily in violation of the city charter: "No state or city in this country has, or ever had the authority to confer upon any one the exercise of such an arbitrary and unheard of power, and it can no more be done under the guise of an ordinance prescribing a rule of prison discipline, than it can be conferred by a direct and positive act of the legislature."[41]

After two days of deliberations in the St. Louis Circuit Court, a jury also awarded Duff $500 on March 22, 1901, to compensate for Karr's refusal to furnish her commitment papers when attorney Barbee requested to see them. The Republican trial judge, Selden P. Spencer, set aside the judgment, however, ruling that the verdict was at odds with the evidence. Barbee appealed to the St. Louis Court of Appeals, which granted a new trial in the city's circuit court. On March 29, the municipal assembly authorized expenditures of $259.65 to cover Karr's legal expenses. In the final disposition of the case, on November 19, 1901, the St. Louis Court of Appeals affirmed Judge Spencer's decision to overturn the jury's verdict and to revoke Duff's $500 judgment. The appellate court agreed that the city ordinance required that the prisoner, not the prisoner's attorney, be furnished with the commitment papers upon request. Since it was Barbee, not Duff, who made the request, Karr was under no obligation to show the commitment order. In a game of legal semantics, Duff was stripped of $500 in compensation.[42]

As a result of the litigation, the controversial St. Louis ordinance that allowed Duff to be detained beyond her sentence at the workhouse was declared unconstitutional. The litigation was the most celebrated case in the career of Barbee, who stopped practicing law in St. Louis upon marrying in 1904 but later practiced in Nevada and Oregon. In the largest damages suit by Duff against Karr, for $10,000 and later reduced to $5,000, the court judgment was in favor of Karr, on April 23, 1902. When all the legal dust settled on the cases, Duff came away with $200.[43]

In a continuation of the long-running feud that had led to Duff's workhouse confinement, an altercation between her and Ferdinand Walz broke out in the 4400 block of Clayton Avenue on August 8, 1905. Some of the neighbors sided with Walz while others sympathized with Duff. On the day of the disturbance, Walz and his wife were moving to another house on the block. After he removed furniture and all but a few belongings, he returned to the duplex for the final time. The ensuing argument with Duff was over a pile of kindling and wood planks in front of her side of the duplex. Walz, a carpenter, claimed the lumber, and against her objections he began to remove it. Duff went into the house and came back with a revolver. When Walz tried to disarm her, Edward Green, a teamster, jumped from his wagon, picked up a small piece of lumber, and struck Walz a blow on the head that killed him. Duff, who testified at the inquest, insisted that Walz had threatened her and that she went for the revolver to protect herself.[44]

While Duff was detained as a witness in the Green case, an arsonist, on back-to-back nights, set fire to the frame house of the duplex where she lived. Not much burned on the first attempt, but on the second night, fire partially destroyed the house. Duff moved into a tent in the backyard, where she tended to her chickens. A gang of chicken thieves known as the Forty Thieves operated in the area known as Dogtown. In the previous year, chicken raisers in Dogtown took their case to the newspapers when about two hundred chickens were stolen in a single month. Duff complained about the ongoing lack of police protection and made it clear that as soon as her shotgun was ready at a repair shop, she would sit up at night to prevent theft of her chickens. "The police won't give us any protection, so we have decided to take the law into our own hands. We make a living by raising chickens for the market and we are not going to let the 'Forty Thieves' take the bread from our mouths."[45]

Vulnerable, Duff soon moved to a new location, but harassment and thievery followed her. With a lease signed by A. D. Cunningham, secretary of the Missouri Botanical Garden Association, she built a wooden shanty in 1908 at 3103 Watson Avenue, where she tended approximately sixty chickens. In an article on October 23, 1908, "Fire Follows Warning to Woman of Mystery," the *Globe-Democrat* reported that Duff's shanty burned shortly after she returned from mailing a letter to police chief Edmund P. Creecy to complain about threats against her. She claimed that for the past two weeks a couple of menacing men, who showed up to hunt in the vicinity, insisted that she had no right to occupy the premises. An empty saucepan, believed to have contained gasoline, was found near the ruins of her shanty. According to the newspaper, it was the fourth time she had been burned out in the past year. Duff broke down and cried over the loss of her chickens.[46]

Duff continued to warn about the "Whangdoodlers" and a "triple alliance of red, white, and black" that terrorized her and others in the area. Organized bands of chicken thieves operated widely in nearby Maplewood, Kirkwood, and Webster Groves at the time. Vigilance committees formed in response. Duff insisted that she knew the names of a dozen chicken thieves she hoped to present to a grand jury, but she linked the "brutes" to area police officers who protected them: "They are many of them police officers who only direct the dirty work of the black hand workers whom they control . . . They burned my chicken coops and many of my chickens. They tore down my houses and burned them and two of the black hand police hid their horses in the woods and searched the lot for chickens that had been fortunate enough to escape the fire. They thought I had left home but I had only gone on an errand and returned to find them searching the lot, to see them with my eyes."[47]

As arsonists and organized bands of chicken thieves continued a campaign of harassment against Duff, she narrowly avoided the workhouse yet again. A minister in Clifton Heights paid her ten-dollar fine when she was hauled into police court for shooting at a group of boys trying to steal her chickens. On January 26, 1910, her tiny hut burned again. The fire killed two dozen chickens. Sarah Jansen, a friend, had urged her to build a sturdy log cabin to protect herself from the elements, but Duff told her that she preferred to live out in the open air because several of her kinfolk had died of tuberculosis. She continued to scratch out a living as a ragpicker who tended her fast-dwindling flock of chickens, and she offered services as a trance medium and lecturer on topics related to mental science healing, nervous diseases, and psychotherapy.[48]

On March 17, 1912, John Jansen, a truck gardener, discovered the body of Duff, age sixty-one, facedown in a field south of Arsenal Street near Watson Road. For the final three years of her life, she had squatted in a tent and nearby rickety shack built of sticks, rocks, and carpets on land owned by the

Missouri Botanical Garden Association. Jansen told police she was barefooted and fully clothed, but her garters were cut and her stockings were pulled down at the time he found her body. When police investigated, they found her scant belongings scattered inside the hut, which appeared to have been ransacked. A report by the *Post-Dispatch* claimed that police found the bodies of a dead dog and cat, and fourteen decapitated chickens wrapped in bundles inside the shack, but the *Globe-Democrat* reported merely that police found fifteen nearly starved chickens when they searched her living quarters.[49]

Based on conversations with residents in the vicinity, officers at first suspected that robbers had murdered Duff, but the coroner's report ruled that a brain hemorrhage caused her death. Was the coroner's ruling correct or was this just another case of an underfunded, understaffed coroner's office less than eager to devote time and resources to a case in which the victim was poor and had been a thorn in the side of city authorities for decades? It is likely we will never know the answer, but for the previous several years Duff had suffered constant harassment from chicken thieves, hoodlums, and police. For a woman known for her eccentric ways and intellectual combativeness, to live as a squatter in the open air at her age made her dangerously vulnerable. Whatever the cause of death or condition of the chickens when Jansen found her body, Duff was buried three weeks later in Potter's Field.

6

REMIT SCANDALS AND A SINGLE TAX PRISONER

In the aftermath of the Duff debacle and the scandalous tenure of Superintendent Karr, Republican officers in the administration of Mayor Henry Ziegenhein were bent on damage control. Ziegenhein tapped Conrad Kempf to replace Karr, who was up to his neck in Duff's lawsuits. The new workhouse superintendent distanced himself from Karr and called public attention to the sad disarray at the workhouse. He complained that Karr had emptied the entire supply house and even stole the shrubbery outside the superintendent's house. With Duff's lawsuits pending, the *Globe-Democrat* sent Jane Frances Winn, its literary editor and a writer of children's plays, to the workhouse for a feature article in its Sunday edition. Allowed to take photos on the grounds, Winn published the article, "A Woman's Visit to the City Work House," on April 22, 1900. Superintendent Kempf and Edward Saxey, the yard foreman, escorted her on a tour of the institution. "We are glad to have the public know what we're doing here," Superintendent Kempf assured her, "and we have nothing to be ashamed of."[1]

Winn painted a favorable description of the workhouse. "Under the new regime at the institution cleanliness is the order of the day," she wrote, "and, besides, the desire is to bring a little color into the sordid lives in the way of grass and flowers, and pretty green lawns are beginning to take the place of the unsightly spaces, and flowers are being planted in the borders and beds." She acknowledged that the dungeon "must be a pretty dismal place with the door closed," but she emphasized that it was "freshly whitewashed within." In anecdotal fashion, Winn called attention to several "regulars" who preferred life in the workhouse, including "Sweet Water Henry." In the case of sixteen-year-old Morris Ross, who was raised in the House of Refuge and who previously did time in Boonville, she expressed sympathy for his plight and criticized the judicial system for throwing him into the workhouse on a one-year sentence, among thieves and hardened criminals, without any effort to rehabilitate him or teach him a trade. Winn identified about a dozen women as notorious drunken criminals in the workhouse. Unlike the men, who came from different social backgrounds, she emphasized that "the women belong unmistakably to the lowest stratum of society." After talking to the matron, Winn concluded they were hopelessly condemned to a life of degradation. In a final assessment of the institution, she wrote, "After all, the officers at the work house are doing the best that could be done under the circumstances for these unfortunate wretches, and deserve all the help the public can give them."[2]

No matter the efforts at damage control on the part of Superintendent Kempf, the workhouse posed a political problem for Mayor Ziegenhein's administration. The imprisonment of John J. McCann, a popular, principled tax protester, grabbed newspaper headlines in St. Louis and far beyond. In 1900, the sentencing of McCann to the workhouse stirred enormous public opposition. Held at arm's length by both political parties, he was a well-respected attorney for the St. Louis Single Tax League and an antimonopoly reformer. He had a history of pressing the city and state boards of equalization to tax franchise corporations that enjoyed monopolistic privileges. McCann emphasized that the failure to tax franchise corporations deprived the city of revenue. As a result, the city preyed on the poor and middle class for revenue.

McCann was highly critical of the St. Louis Transit Company, which argued before the Missouri Board of Equalization that the government had no right to tax corporate entities with monopoly franchises. When transit workers went on strike against the company in May 1900, McCann backed the strikers, championing the rights of the people over privileged corporations. To call attention to inequities in the tax structure, he refused to pay a twenty-five-dollar fee to operate as a real estate agent in 1896-1897. Judge Thomas H. Peabody, of the First District Police Court, slapped him with a $100 fine, but McCann challenged the constitutional authority of the licensing fee. He appealed the conviction to the Court of Criminal Correction and then to the Missouri Supreme Court, which ruled in favor of the City of St. Louis.

McCann refused to pay the fine, preferring instead to serve a six-month sentence in the workhouse as a matter of principle and an expression of protest. His friends offered to pay the fine, but he declined. Fifty-two years old and in declining health, he was taken from the city jail to the workhouse in the patrol wagon with eight other prisoners on July 17, 1900. "I am not degraded by this infamous prosecution," he told a *Post-Dispatch* reporter. "I am willing to undergo unjust punishment in defense of the rights given me by the constitution of my country if by so doing attention will be attracted to the principle for which I stand."[3]

As McCann served time in the workhouse, public outrage grew. Letters of support poured into the workhouse, urging him to hold fast to his principles. Supporters pointed out the sad irony that because of his persistent efforts before the board of equalization, city revenues from franchise corporations had increased by $237,000. "Think of it," blasted the *Post-Dispatch*. "The poor man must pay the State for the right to work; but the Transit Company should not be made to pay for the rich privilege of monopoly. The contrast is not likely to be forgotten."[4] A. B. Greene, a member of the St. Louis Board of Education, suggested McCann's nomination as city assessor. Richard Dalton, a Ralls County friend, commercial apple grower, and president of Missouri's Single Tax League who nearly captured the Democratic Party's gubernatorial nomination in 1892, wrote to McCann from his home in Saverton: "I sincerely trust the misery of your confinement may be softened by the conviction that you are a pioneer victim in the cause of a truer and more abiding liberty soon to dawn upon us." Dr. George Homan, who as city health commissioner in 1894 called attention to the atrocious unsanitary conditions of the workhouse, likewise sent McCann a letter of support on July 18: "As I had opportunity some years ago, in the course of official inspections, to learn a good deal about the interior of the workhouse, I beg to extend to you my sympathy in your deprivation and to express my feelings of admiration for the courage and self-sacrifice you have shown in the course pursued."[5]

At the time of McCann's imprisonment, there were 271 men and 81 women inmates in the workhouse. The *Post-Dispatch* noted the moral impact of his presence on fellow prisoners, who respected him and held him in high regard. Even cursing was toned down in his presence, and a few apologized when they cursed in front of him. When McCann lost some money in the form of prison scrip, a longtime convict wearing leg irons found and returned it to him. Among McCann's many visitors were women from the city's social work organizations and clubs. To supporters seeking his release, he made it clear he would not pay his fine or accept a pardon because of its implication of guilt. He stood firm in his resolve to call attention to the unjust tax system. In an interview with the city chaplain, the Reverend Thomas Harvey Hagerty, "who preaches industry, temperance and good association to the prisoners as the true guides to happiness," McCann told a reporter, "I asked him what he thought of my case in which I was fined and imprisoned for engaging in an innocent occupation. He seemed puzzled. I then asked him if he paid a license to preach the gospel. He said no. And I invited him to don the uniform and share my cell with me as one guilty as myself. He was called out by a visitor at this point and I have not yet heard his answer."

McCann described various features of life in the workhouse. Guards allowed him to walk in the yard after the other prisoners were in their cells in the evening. He regarded the discipline as "very rigid," the food as "not elegant," and the cells as clean, thanks to the women prisoners who scrubbed them. Noting the role of visiting ministers who conducted religious services in the workhouse, McCann observed that many, if not most, of the prisoners were "in the wild animal stage of human existence." After a moment of reflection, he conceded that his observation was harsh and perhaps unduly pessimistic. Among them he overheard promising conversations about the subject of taxation, which heartened him considerably. When it came to religious issues, however, he pointed out that although the prisoners sang "Nearer My God to Thee" and "Rock of Ages" during Sunday afternoon services, they quickly reverted to singing levee songs like "There Will Be a Hot Time in the Old Town Tonight," "Sally of the Alley," and similar refrains by evening. In McCann's letter to the editor of the Sunday *Post-Dispatch* on July 25, he offered this perspective as he looked out from the workhouse on Point Breeze:

> Looking through the alley, which divides the main buildings, you see two dim gas lamps burning and a guard pacing the eastern area. East, the silent waters of the Mississippi are seen pursuing their way to the gulf. The passing of the [excursion steamer] *City of Providence* is the event of the night. It passes too far from the prison to permit of its music being heard by the prisoners, but the brilliantly illuminated panorama of dancers and promenaders aboard is visible from the cell window and many of the young and middle-aged sigh for the time when they wore clothes other than these and were free men.[6]

McCann's imprisonment stirred antimonopoly and anticorporate sentiments in the city. Pressure mounted on Mayor Ziegenhein to release him from the workhouse. Richard Dalton went to St. Louis and called on the mayor in his office on Friday, August 24, 1900. If Ziegenhein did not release him, Dalton threatened to leave the next day to give stump speeches around the state to politicize McCann's imprisonment. It was an election year in state and national politics. Later that evening, Ziegenhein and the city attorney went to the workhouse to see McCann, who firmly rejected an offer to pardon him. Finally, Ziegenhein relented and informed McCann that he would remit the fine, an arrangement acceptable to McCann. Workhouse superintendent Kempf received the remit at about eleven o'clock that night. After forty days of confinement, McCann departed the workhouse. The mayor later indicated he did not think McCann was the type of man to lock up. "I also thought he had been sufficiently punished and that his health was such as to entitle him to relief. Richard Dalton did call on me Friday and put McCann's case before me. That is all I have got to say."[7]

Allegations and exposure of corruption and looseness in the longstanding policy of remitting workhouse fines likewise grabbed headlines in the second half of Ziegenhein's term in office. In what were often long lines outside the mayor's office, individuals customarily waited to request that the mayor, or his secretary, issue special permits or remit the fines of family members and friends sent to the workhouse. In other cases, ward political figures and influential friends arranged behind the scenes to have fines remitted. The practice was an open invitation to political favors and corruption at every level, from the workhouse all the way to the mayor's office.

On September 18, 1899, Mamie White appeared in the First District Police Court with a technical charge opposite her name on the docket, and her case was continued. A suspicious *Post-Dispatch* reporter dug up her history in police court and workhouse records. The investigation revealed that White had lived a charmed life in the St. Louis police court system. From November 13, 1897, to July 26, 1899, she was arrested twenty-eight times for streetwalking or for being an inmate or keeper of a house of prostitution. In a vast majority of the arrests, either the case was not prosecuted, or she was discharged. All the nolle prosequi cases were handled by Judge Thomas H. Peabody and attorney Harry Clover. In the few cases that were prosecuted, the fine was either remitted or cut in half. In the case of one of White's few convictions, she was fined and sentenced to the workhouse, but at a time when she was supposed to be in a workhouse cell under Superintendent Karr's charge, she was arrested again for streetwalking. "That Mamie White has been protected by someone betraying his official trust is borne out by the records," concluded the reporter.

On February 8, 1898, White and Maggie Raymond were convicted in Judge Talty's criminal court on charges of grand larceny after taking forty-five dollars from Mike Canivan in a panel game. One of the women sexually enticed Canivan into a room while the other sneaked into the room through a hidden panel and stole the preoccupied victim's valuables. Raymond, too, had lived a charmed life, with a police court record similar to White's. On at least two occasions she was sent to the workhouse but Mayor Ziegenhein's office remitted her fine and released her. The panel game conviction, however, took place in a criminal rather than a police court. On May 18, 1898, Raymond and White were sentenced to two years in the Missouri State Penitentiary. White appealed her case, but the Missouri Supreme Court upheld her conviction.[8]

On October 5, 1899, the murder of twenty-one-year-old Phrasia "Cora" Billups by her husband when she was supposed to be in the workhouse inadvertently drew further attention to how ward politics and prostitution shaped the mysterious remit system under Mayor Ziegenhein. Billups and Fannie English, both of whom were Black, were arrested on September 30 at 216 Valentine Street. English was charged with keeping a bawdy house and Billups was charged with being an inmate of the house. When the women appeared in police court, Judge William M. Kinsey fined English fifty dollars and fined Billups ten dollars plus costs. When English could not pay her fine, Judge Kinsey ordered her to the workhouse, but a funny thing happened on the way to Point Breeze. The city marshal, instead of taking English to the workhouse, released her. When Billups was unable to pay her fine, the judge sent her to the workhouse on October 3, but she too was quickly released. A *Post-Dispatch* reporter who investigated the case probed to find out who paid the fines and authorized the remits.

The investigative trail led the reporter to several city offices, where clever dodges were meant to disguise who remitted the fines of English and Billups. At the city marshal's office, the chief deputy acknowledged that in English's case, part of the fine was paid, and that only the balance was remitted. When the reporter asked to see the record of the full transaction, the deputy refused. The records of police sergeant James Dawson, who was on duty at the Central District police station the day Billups was sent to the workhouse, indicated that she was transported there on October 3, but the chief clerk at the workhouse insisted that no such person had been admitted. At Mayor Ziegenhein's office, the reporter asked Fred Ziegenhein, the mayor's private secretary and son, for the name(s) of whoever arranged for the fines of English and Billups to be remitted. Secretary Ziegenhein revealed the names, but they were fictitious. When asked who the fictitious names represented, Ziegenhein shrugged and said he didn't know. After pressing the secretary without success, the reporter asked, "Mr. Ziegenhein, are you sure that it was not Chris Schawacker who asked for and obtained these remits?"

Schawacker, a bondsman, was the city undertaker, an inspector in the street department, and a Republican kingpin in the Fifth Ward (the old First Ward) who built clientelist relationships with impoverished Black voters in the ward. Bud Bolin, a Black man who worked for him, was the one who carried a remit to the workhouse to secure Billups's release. Schawacker gave slippery answers to the reporter's pointed questions. When asked whether Bolin worked for him, Schawacker replied, "He used to, but he don't now." When the reporter went to the coroner's office, Fannie English was there. The reporter summoned a detective to listen to his interview with English, who confirmed Schawacker's role in getting the fines of both women remitted. When the reporter returned to the city marshal's office, Chief Deputy Marshal Fred Smith finally broke down and showed him the record book. "I knew that something would come of this and I didn't want to get mixed up in the affair," Smith confessed. "Now that is all out I don't care to keep still any longer. On the day that these women were fined Chris Schawaker [*sic*] came in in the afternoon and asked that they be held over until he could get a remit. He didn't insist on the Billups woman being held and she went down to the works. Afterwards the remit came and the English woman was released."[9]

Complicating the remit system was the relationship between the Democratic police department and the Republican administration of Mayor Ziegenhein. According to Schawacker, the Democratic police force routinely made wholesale arrests of Black men in his ward when it came time for voter registration and elections. Typically charged with idling and vagrancy, disenfranchised roustabouts and others were sentenced to the workhouse after their arrests. The Eagles' Nest, a political club of Black men with headquarters at Second and Valentine Streets, was often targeted as an appendage of Schawacker's ward political machine. Mary Duff had called attention to it as a voodoo society, and police charged it was a gambling den. When police officers raided the Eagles' Nest a month before the election in 1898 and arrested a dozen Black men, Judge Peabody, of the First District Police Court, criticized the arresting officers and ruled that the idling and vagrancy charges did not hold up to scrutiny. Indignant at the arrests, Schawacker put up bail for the men and provided an attorney to prove that the men were not shooting craps during the political meeting. Peabody, who insisted that they were being persecuted for racial reasons, argued that the arresting officers should be prosecuted for violating civil liberties guaranteed by the Constitution.[10]

On Sunday evening, November 25, 1900, the arrest of Frank Wedley, a Black workhouse trusty, in front of a saloon drew further attention to the "remit machine" in the mayor's office and the laxity at the workhouse. The police arrested Wedley as a suspect in several recent burglaries near the workhouse. After lying to the police at first about his address, Wedley, who was wearing a long, dark overcoat to hide his prison garb, admitted he was a workhouse trusty. The evidence against him in the burglaries was not strong enough to obtain a warrant. The police returned him to the workhouse. Superintendent Kempf was caught unawares when asked to explain how it was that Wedley, an inmate with a history of burglary, was out on the streets. The superintendent blandly replied that trusties were supposed to return to the workhouse before 8:00 p.m. Wedley was arrested at 8:30 p.m.[11]

Wedley's long criminal history illustrated the importance of having friends with important political connections. William Desmond, chief of detectives, emphasized that Wedley was particularly dangerous because of his ability to obtain political favors from city officials. Wedley escaped serious punishment on a burglary charge on March 17, 1898, and again on a highway robbery charge on May 18, 1898. After being arrested yet again three months later, he posted bond and fled to Cleveland, Ohio, but he was arrested and returned to St. Louis. When the grand jury indicted him, he pleaded guilty to a lesser charge and accepted a one-year sentence in the workhouse. Thanks to someone who obtained a remit from the mayor's office on his behalf, Wedley was released from the workhouse. Later, he was rearrested and sent back to the workhouse to serve another one-year sentence.

The Wedley case exposed tensions between workhouse officials and the police. Superintendent Kempf stormed into the Wyoming Street police station and demanded to speak to Captain Lorenz Schroeder, who was unavailable at the time. When Kempf asked why the police did not notify him immediately of Wedley's arrest, the lieutenant in charge demanded to know why Kempf failed to notify the police of Wedley's absence from the workhouse. Kempf left the station, angrily suggesting he might seek legal counsel to pursue a grievance against the police department. He emphasized that Wedley was a trusty because of his good behavior at the workhouse. According to Kempf, Wedley was so reliable that he was allowed to work around the Kempf house and to act as a coachman for Mrs. Kempf. The superintendent claimed that Wedley was in the saloon with his full permission to enjoy a beer.[12]

A revelation of corruption by Gus Cruse, a Black trusty of the workhouse, increased the spotlight on remits and corruption by guards at the time. According to Cruse, Wedley got word to Cruse's sweetheart, Emma Williams, that Assistant Superintendent Edward Saxey would get him out of the workhouse for ten dollars. Cruse, whose main duty as a trusty was to bring in beer for the guards, claimed he paid Saxey twenty dollars to secure his release through Judge Clark, of the Court of Criminal Correction. Williams and Mary Cruse, the trusty's mother, revealed that on October 22, they met Saxey at a side gate on Meramec Street, where Williams handed him a twenty-dollar bill. "Emma and I got the money and went to see Mr. Saxey," Mrs. Cruse explained. "He was in the office, but he made us go outside before he would talk to us. We offered him $10, but he refused it, and said that the man who was going to get a parole for Gus wanted $20. We told him we would get the rest of the money. He told us not to ask for him at the office the next time, but to go around to the side gate. We did so and paid him the $20."[13]

Superintendent Kempf insisted that Saxey told him that the twenty dollars was taken from Cruse at the time he entered the workhouse, but Saxey denied it. In the presence of a reporter for the *St. Louis Republic* and several witnesses, Mrs. Cruse confronted Saxey in the office of the workhouse on November 27. Saxey admitted he took the money from her, but he claimed that at Gus's request, he delivered it to a go-between who was supposed to arrange for his parole. Saxey, kicked off the police force thirteen years earlier for conduct unbecoming an officer, maintained he did not know the go-between's name. When the reporter asked him to bring prisoner Gus Cruse into the office so that he could give his version of events, Saxey refused. Superintendent Kempf, who was notified ahead of time that Mrs. Cruse would be at the workhouse to confront Saxey, promised to be there, but he was nowhere to be seen on the grounds.

According to Mrs. Cruse and Emma Williams, Saxey promised to arrange for Gus's release in about ten days. On October 31, after nine days had passed, Gus, who was serving a four-month sentence for petty larceny and for carrying a concealed weapon, escaped on the assumption that the transaction had been approved. Confident he was no longer subject to arrest, he enjoyed about three weeks of freedom in the city. He even went to the Four Courts Building and hung out in the corridors, where he was recognized and arrested. A reporter asked chief clerk Charles H. L. Groffman why he had violated the city charter by not reporting Cruse's workhouse escape to Mayor Ziegenhein and police chief Jack Campbell. Groffman replied that he refrained from doing so at guard Saxey's request. Saxey promised to track Cruse down and return him to the workhouse in a few days without notifying the police department. When the reporter asked Superintendent Kempf about it at the Four Courts Building, Kempf claimed that Saxey assured him that appropriate notifications were made.[14]

While details of the Wedley and Cruse cases were unfolding, another controversial case of workhouse remits directly involved Mayor Ziegenhein and his son, Fred, who served as his father's private secretary on the city payroll at a salary of $2,500 annually. On November 8, 1900, Henry Menges was arrested, fined $500 in the Dayton Street (Second District) Police Court, and sent to the workhouse for selling policy (lottery) tickets. His father, Jacob Menges, a grocer at Fifteenth and Carr Streets, sought his release. Accompanied by a former member of the House of Delegates, Jacob went to see the judge of the Second District Police Court who had fined his son. At their request, Judge Adolph Wislizenus mailed a letter to Mayor Ziegenhein stating that he had erred in fining Henry Menges so heavily. Upon the advice of Fred Ziegenhein, Jacob Menges drew up a petition with the signatures of representative citizens on his son's behalf. Jacob submitted a petition signed by seventy well-respected residents, including several who were close to the mayor, and mailed it to the mayor's office.

Jacob was confident his son would be released soon. Henry, age twenty-nine, had a good reputation with no previous run-ins with the law. Even the police downplayed the full extent of the lottery tickets he sold. When Henry did not come home, the elder Menges went to see Mayor Ziegenhein again to ask him to remit the fine, but the mayor refused: "The bucket is full now.

Everything that happens in this town, when there is no glory in it, is blamed on me, already. I have been a target enough already and I intend to turn the tables."[15] Then, according to Jacob Menges, both the mayor and Secretary Ziegenhein offered to cut the fine in half, to $250. When Menges refused, the secretary offered to lower the fine to $150 plus costs. "To this I made no answer," Menges maintained in a statement. "Knowing that I made no answer, young Ziegenhein said, 'Well, I will release your son this evening.' That was done. He came home."[16]

On November 15, Secretary Ziegenhein sent an order to the workhouse to release Henry Menges, but confusion ensued surrounding the details of the release. Jacob insisted that the release was unconditional, but the secretary claimed they had reached an understanding that the $500 fine would be reduced to $150 plus three dollars in costs, to be paid within thirty days. Secretary Ziegenhein made several visits to Jacob Menges to collect the fine, but Menges refused to pay. On December 5, Ziegenhein took Edward Saxey, chief guard of the workhouse, with him to put added pressure on Menges, to no avail.

On the morning of December 18, Ziegenhein and workhouse superintendent Kempf confronted Jacob Menges, threatening to put his son back in the workhouse unless he paid the fine of $150. According to Menges, Ziegenhein became abusive when Menges remained firm that he did not agree to pay any amount of money. Henry Menges, who was clerking behind the counter in his father's grocery store when Ziegenhein showed up, dashed out the back when he heard Ziegenhein's threat to return him to the workhouse. According to the elder Menges, his son went into hiding in East St. Louis to evade the authorities.

Angered by Fred Ziegenhein's persistent efforts to extort money from him, Mr. Menges went to see the mayor about it. "I told him the facts," Menges asserted, "but he said he could do nothing about it, as Fred was out of town. The mayor said he did not know about the remit business further than he had heard something about $25 and costs. I saw the mayor again, but Fred was still out of the city." Menges consulted a lawyer, who advised him that Ziegenhein had no right to lock up his son again. Upon his recommendation, Jacob returned home to his father. "If he [Henry] had done anything to break the law, I might have paid," Menges explained, "but all that he did was to sell policy tickets."[17]

Despite Fred Ziegenhein's threats to send police to capture Henry, no police officers came to arrest Henry after he returned home. The workhouse books indicated Henry's release on November 15 but did not show that a remit was received. When an investigative reporter for the *Post-Dispatch* asked Saxey about the affair, the guard was reluctant to say anything. "Well, I was just doing what my boss told me to do," Saxey said. In response to the reporter's question about what would have happened to the $150 if Menges had given it to Secretary Ziegenhein at the grocery store, he replied, "Mr. Ziegenhein told me, after we left, that if he had gotten the money, he would have had me bring it back to the workhouse." In June 1902, a grand jury investigating municipal corruption indicted Fred Ziegenhein on four counts of bribery and one count of obtaining money under false pretenses in the practice of issuing permits and remits.[18]

According to journalist Lincoln Steffens, the corruption that plagued St. Louis was at its worst during the Republican administration of Mayor Ziegenhein. As a mayoral candidate running against "Ziegenheinism," Rolla Wells promised business reform and more efficiency in government. The son of a former U.S. representative from St. Louis, he was a gold bug Democrat who had opposed his party's presidential nominee, William Jennings Bryan, in 1896. Wells steered the city's Democratic Party away from its push, or agrarian, wing and in a more pro-corporate direction. His pro-business philosophy made him palatable to many Republican voters.

Upon assuming office after a hard-fought mayoral campaign in April 1901, Wells announced that he would put an end to issuing remits through the mayor's office. The new policy, targeting corruption and Ziegenheinism, was consistent with his campaign message of operating municipal government in a more efficient, businesslike manner. Mayor Wells, who stressed that he had uncovered many irregularities in the issuing of permits and remits, remarked at the time of Fred Ziegenhein's indictment for bribery and extortion, "I have stopped the practice, and I propose to drive the petty grafter from the City Hall."[19]

Coinciding with Mayor Wells's promises of reform was the election of Joseph Wingate Folk as the circuit attorney in St. Louis. Formerly president of the Democratic Party's reform-minded Jefferson Club, "Holy Joe" drew praise from labor and antimonopoly elements for his role as the attorney for transit workers who mediated an end to the turbulent streetcar strike against the St. Louis Transit Company in 1900. As circuit attorney, he set out to prosecute boodlers and political bosses like Edward Butler for corruption. An Irish immigrant, "Boss Butler" had controlled city hall, ward politics, and elections for a quarter century, amassing enormous wealth in the process. The Big Cinch, the city's elites, paid him bribes to secure city contracts and franchises. He was a Democrat who was not averse to working with Republicans if the political moment called for it. In fact, his maneuvering in Democratic Party factional disputes in 1897 helped to elect "Uncle Henry" Ziegenhein, his favored candidate all along. Rarely in question was Butler's control over the House of Delegates. In 1902, he was convicted of bribery, but the Missouri Supreme Court overturned the conviction on a technicality two years later. Folk's prosecutorial efforts were only minimally effective, but in 1904 he rode the public wave of popularity into the Governor's Mansion in Jefferson City.[20]

Although the practice of remitting fines did not end under Mayor Wells, it was drastically curbed. For the workhouse, this meant no more long lines of people at the mayor's office seeking clemency and a fine remit. The drastic reduction in remits reduced chances for the corruption that had flourished in previous administrations. Thanks to the curtailment of remits in police courts and the mayor's office, city revenues increased sharply. During the final year of Mayor Ziegenhein's tenure, remittances totaled $33,600. Workhouse remittances constituted $24,760 of the total. The rest came from police courts. After Mayor Wells's first year in office, workhouse and police court remittances totaled only $3,965.[21]

The spirit of reform that accompanied Mayor Wells's election victory was quite limited in its sweep. He may have driven a few "petty grafters" from city hall, but most of the big-time boodlers escaped jail time. In the 1901 election campaign, Wells faced pressures from within his own Democratic Party and from the antimonopoly Public Ownership Party candidacy of Lee Meriwether, former Missouri labor commissioner. Wells emphasized that the workhouse, poorhouse, city hospital, jail, and other city institutions should be run more efficiently. The answer was not public ownership, nor was the solution to raise taxes to improve the facilities. Instead, Wells advocated trimming bloated payrolls and operating the institutions more prudently and economically. He complained that under Ziegenhein the institutions had damaged St. Louis's image. With planning well under way for the Louisiana Purchase Exposition (World's Fair) to be held in the city, he urged running the institutions in a way that drew praise, inspired pride, and improved St. Louis's image in the eyes of the world.

Workhouse stable and garden with Mississippi River in background. Photo by Helen Primavesi. Captain Frank J. Primavesi, "Prison Reform in America," *Herald of the Star,* January 11, 1916.

Edward A. Coleman, arrested in St. Louis for forging a money order on December 2, 1911, and sentenced on June 3, 1912, to two years in United States Penitentiary, Leavenworth. Released on January 10, 1914. Previously reported to have served one year in the St. Louis Workhouse for forging checks. United States Postal Inspection Service, *Photographs, Descriptions and Records of Persons Charged with Violation of the Postal Laws,* vol. 2 (Washington, D.C.: Government Printing Office, 1916), 446.

Workhouse fountain and grotto in the center, women's cell house on the left, and the original cell house (a monastery before 1850) on the right. The fountain and grotto were built at Superintendent Frank J. Primavesi's personal expense to beautify the workhouse surroundings. Photo by Helen Primavesi. Captain Frank J. Primavesi, "Prison Reform in America," *Herald of the Star,* January 11, 1916.

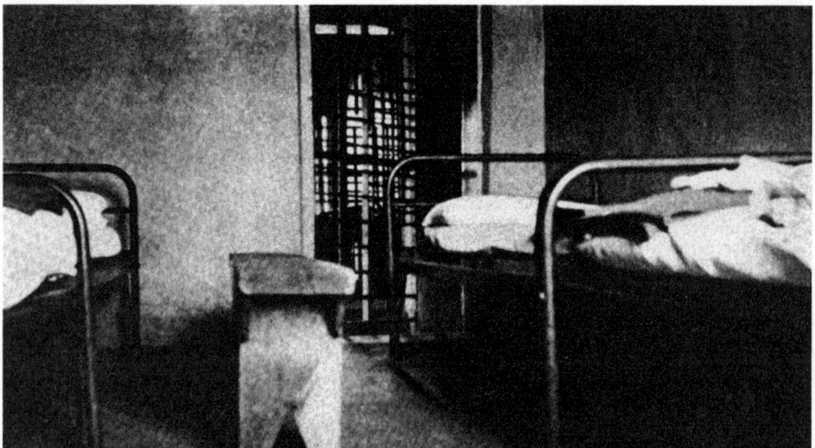

Interior cell in the original cell house. During Superintendent Primavesi's tenure, the old windows were replaced by French windows to allow for better ventilation, and inmates were provided with sheets, pillowcases, nightgowns, and underwear. Photo by Helen Primavesi. Captain Frank J. Primavesi, "Prison Reform in America," *Herald of the Star,* January 11, 1916.

A special newspaper feature by "A Friend of Prisoners" put the spotlight on the continued use of shackles at the workhouse. The feature, which included several photos and names of shackled prisoners, urged Mayor Rolla Wells to abolish the practice. *St. Louis Post-Dispatch,* April 16, 1905, 62.

City workhouse, 4200 South Broadway, 1946. Joseph Hampel Album. Missouri Historical Society, St. Louis.

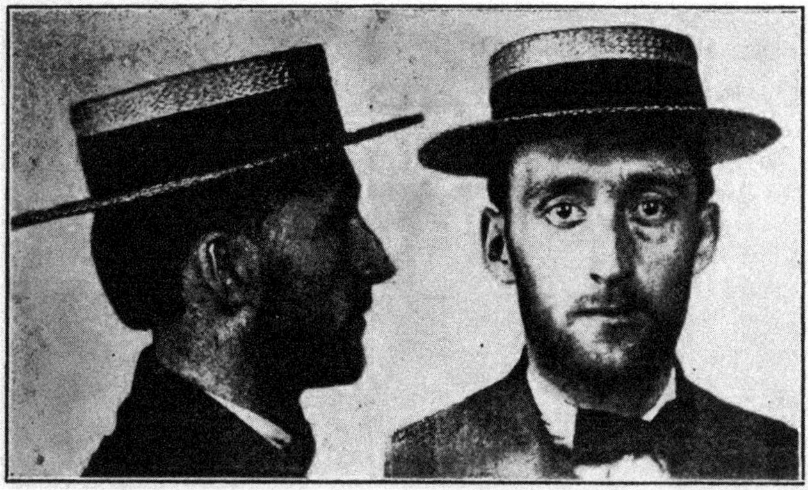

Sylvester J. Thomas, sentenced on November 6, 1911, to two years in the United States penitentiary at Leavenworth, for burglary of a post office in St. Louis on July 7, 1911. Released on June 15, 1913. Previous record included a one-year term in the St. Louis Workhouse for disposing of stolen property. United States Postal Inspection Service, *Photographs, Descriptions and Records of Persons Charged with Violation of the Postal Laws,* vol. 2 (Washington, D.C.: Government Printing Office, 1916), 274.

Women's cell block. Civic League of St. Louis, *Report on the St. Louis Workhouse,* 1911.

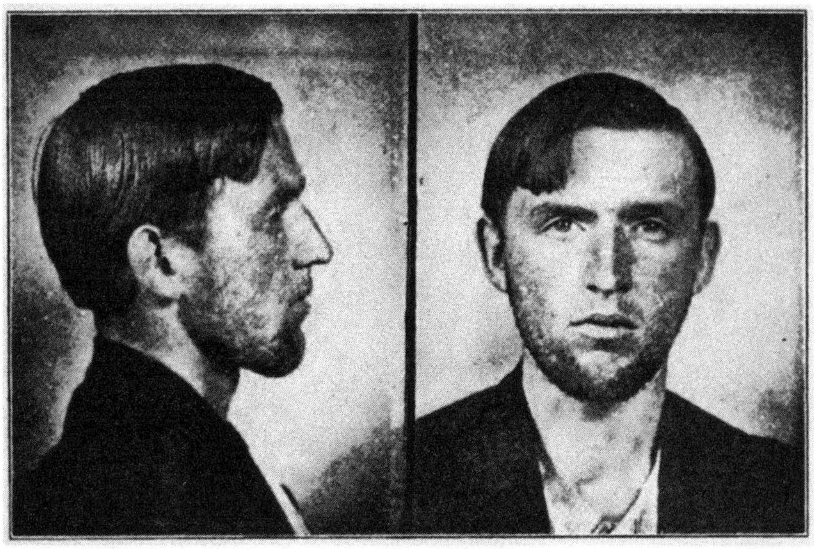

Matthew F. Woods, sentenced on November 6, 1911, to one year and eight months in the United States penitentiary at Leavenworth, for burglary of a post office in St. Louis on July 7, 1911. Released on March 11, 1913. Previous record included two terms in the St. Louis Workhouse for carrying concealed weapons. United States Postal Inspection Service, *Photographs, Descriptions and Records of Persons Charged with Violation of the Postal Laws,* vol. 2 (Washington, D.C.: Government Printing Office, 1916), 276.

Workhouse quarry, Mississippi River and South Broadway, with steamboat at Workhouse Landing and prisoners at work. *Cement Era* included this photo in its December 1912 issue to highlight the use of concrete in new building construction under way at the workhouse. William G. Swekosky Notre Dame College Collection: South St. Louis Civic Buildings. Missouri Historical Society, St. Louis.

A staff artist's courtroom sketch of Mary Duff when she filed a lawsuit against the workhouse superintendent, Nicholas Karr. *St. Louis Post-Dispatch,* May 17, 1899.

Artist's sketch of Sunday visitors in the women's section of the workhouse. The sketch highlights an interracial relationship, picturing a white man visiting a Black woman prisoner and holding a baby. *St. Louis Post-Dispatch,* February 4, 1894.

St. Louis Workhouse. Photo by Robert Benecke, circa 1870s–1880s. Penal Institutions Collection. Missouri Historical Society, St. Louis.

View of the Iron Mountain Railway tracks and Mississippi River from the St. Louis Workhouse, 1885. Three men sitting on a workhouse fence. New York Public Library, New York.

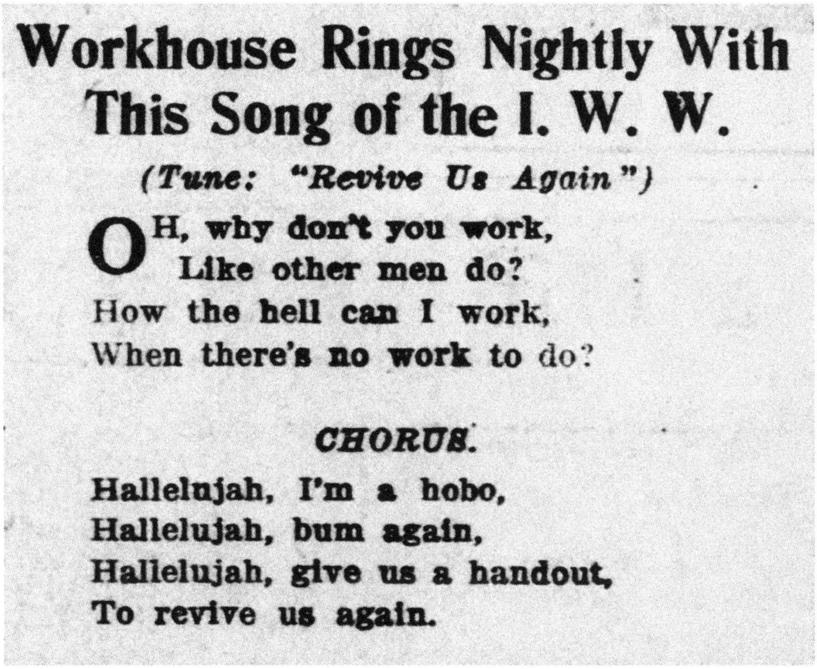

Workhouse Rings Nightly With This Song of the I. W. W.

(Tune: "Revive Us Again")

OH, why don't you work,
Like other men do?
How the hell can I work,
When there's no work to do?

CHORUS.

Hallelujah, I'm a hobo,
Hallelujah, bum again,
Hallelujah, give us a handout,
To revive us again.

First verse of an Industrial Workers of the World song sung in the St. Louis Workhouse. In winter 1914–1915, dozens of members of the radical IWW filled the St. Louis Workhouse. They were arrested for giving soapbox speeches on street corners, blasting capitalism, and charging restaurant meals to the mayor. *St. Louis Post-Dispatch,* January 3, 1915.

Captain Frank J. Primavesi, superintendent of the St. Louis Workhouse, 1912–1917. Captain Frank J. Primavesi, "Prison Reform in America," *Herald of the Star,* January 11, 1916.

Workhouse quarry at the Mississippi River and South Broadway, circa 1920s. William G. Swekosky Notre Dame College Collection: South St. Louis Civic Buildings. Missouri Historical Society, St. Louis.

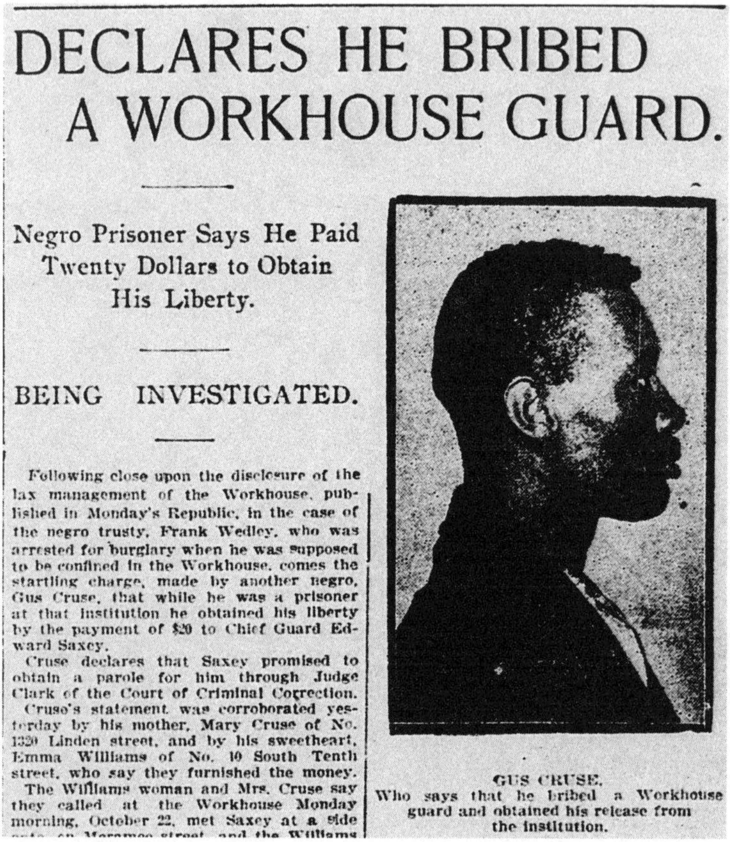

DECLARES HE BRIBED A WORKHOUSE GUARD.

Negro Prisoner Says He Paid Twenty Dollars to Obtain His Liberty.

BEING INVESTIGATED.

Following close upon the disclosure of the lax management of the Workhouse, published in Monday's Republic, in the case of the negro trusty, Frank Wedley, who was arrested for burglary when he was supposed to be confined in the Workhouse, comes the startling charge, made by another negro, Gus Cruse, that while he was a prisoner at that institution he obtained his liberty by the payment of $20 to Chief Guard Edward Saxey.

Cruse declares that Saxey promised to obtain a parole for him through Judge Clark of the Court of Criminal Correction.

Cruse's statement was corroborated yesterday by his mother, Mary Cruse of No. 1320 Linden street, and by his sweetheart, Emma Williams of No. 10 South Tenth street, who say they furnished the money.

The Williams woman and Mrs. Cruse say they called at the Workhouse Monday morning, October 22, met Saxey at a side [illegible]

GUS CRUSE.
Who says that he bribed a Workhouse guard and obtained his release from the institution.

Workhouse prisoner Gus Cruse, reportedly released after bribing a guard. *St. Louis Republic,* November 28, 1900.

Artist's sketch of the workhouse dungeon where Mary Duff was confined. *St. Louis Post-Dispatch,* October 7, 1897.

Oscar R. Bullard, an adulterous medical student, high-profile workhouse escapee, and physician whose case took many twists and turns over two decades. *St. Louis Globe-Democrat,* January 19, 1910.

Workhouse mules in the quarry, early 1900s.William G. Swekosky Notre Dame College Collection: South St. Louis Civic Buildings. Missouri Historical Society, St. Louis.

The workhouse bell being transferred from contractor Fred Weber Jr. to Charles A. Head, warden of the newly opened Medium Security Institution. *St. Louis Post-Dispatch,* July 9, 1966.

7

FAINT HEARTBEATS OF REFORM

Conrad Kempf, a Republican, continued as superintendent of the workhouse in Mayor Wells's first administration, but in 1903, Wells did not renominate him for the position. Instead, the mayor chose police sergeant William T. Dowdall. While Dowdall's nomination was pending approval by the city council, he sent a police detail to Kempf's workhouse home to make sure he did not cart away furniture or steal anything. Insulted and infuriated by Dowdall's action, Superintendent Kempf went to the mayor's office to complain. Afterward, Mayor Wells withdrew Dowdall's nomination and named Andrew Scully as his replacement. Scully, defeated earlier in a bid to become Democratic committeeman of the Twenty-Sixth Ward, was a grocer and supporter of St. Louis attorney Harry B. Hawes, who backed him for the appointment. Dowdall assured the mayor that his overzealous dispatch of police officers to the superintendent's house was not meant as a personal slap in the face but rather was aimed to prevent theft of city property. He remembered what had happened to the furniture and other items stripped from the house when outgoing Superintendent Karr vacated the office.[1]

Despite the usual problems of escapes, overcrowded conditions, lax discipline, and institutionalized corruption, Superintendent Kempf's record at the workhouse arguably had fewer blemishes than the tenure of his predecessors, especially Nicholas Karr's. Perhaps St. Louis newspapers lost some of their investigative zeal, but undercover reporters' horror stories of savage beatings and torture of prisoners diminished. Maybe the overall quality of guards improved. Kempf, who came into office determined to distance himself from Karr's policies, generally succeeded in avoiding major controversies. Certainly, he was better equipped than Karr to handle public relations.

When municipal authorities made it clear that no monies would be made available for a special Thanksgiving meal at the workhouse in 1900, Kempf paid for the special meal out of his own pocket, featuring roast pork.[2]

In the waning months of Kempf's tenure, perhaps the most mysterious confidence man in workhouse history entered by way of Judge Daniel O'Connell Tracy's police court. St. Louis police arrested "Lieutenant Colonel F. Seymour Barrington," alias George Seymour Barrington, alias Sir Frederick Syndenham Burgoyne, for assaulting and disturbing the peace of James F. Cochrane shortly after marrying Cochrane's sister, Wilhelmina Grace Cochrane, of Kansas City, Kansas.

Upon arriving in St. Louis, Barrington, whose real name was believed to be George Frederick Neville Barton, checked into the Southern Hotel as Lieutenant Colonel F. Seymour Barrington, an officer in King Edward's Horse Guards. He ran an advertisement in local newspapers as an English gentleman of high social rank seeking marriage to a refined, educated woman. After running out on an unpaid bill at the Southern Hotel, he rented a room at the fashionable boardinghouse of Mrs. Robert R. [Margaret Cochrane] Elliott on December 26, 1902, posing as an English gentleman and heir to a castle in Brighton. His Prince Albert jacket, silk hat and gloves, sophistication and charm, aristocratic affectations, tales of military adventure in South Africa and India, and command of German, French, Spanish, and other languages impressed Elliott. She urged her nineteen-year-old sister in Kansas City to hurry to St. Louis to meet him. Two weeks after the sister, Willa, met forty-two-year-old Barrington, he persuaded her to marry him without the consent of her father, Robert G. Cochrane, a widely known Scottish-born stockman who had founded and operated the Cochrane & Son Packing Company with his son, James.

The short-lived marital bliss and fantasy image of the Lord and Lady Barrington ended abruptly. The boasts of aristocratic heritage aroused James Cochrane's suspicions. He went to the British Embassy and learned that Barrington was a fraud. Cochrane confronted Barrington, thrashed him, and threw him out of his sister Margaret's home in St. Louis on February 3, 1903. The confrontation led to charges against Barrington in Judge Tracy's police court, where Tracy hit him with a steep fine of $500. Barrington, unable to pay the fine, entered the workhouse on a six-month sentence. Known to fellow inmates and officers as "the lord," Barrington went to work on the rock pile and impressed Superintendent Kempf as a model prisoner.[3]

In the meantime, investigations into Barrington's past revealed that he was George Frederick Neville Barton, with a long criminal history of fraud, embezzlement, forgery, and perhaps murder dating back to childhood. Well known among Scotland Yard detectives in London, Barton came to the United States in 1901 after being released from Dartmoor Prison in the Devon County village of Princetown. He quickly discerned a fondness among American elites for English aristocratic titles and linkages via marriage. By the time he arrived in St. Louis, he had honed his skills as a confidence man.

In Brooklyn, posing as Sir Frederick Syndenham Burgoyne, he married a woman in 1891, then persuaded her and her mother to sell all their property and accompany him to England to live with him in a wing of the family's six-hundred-room castle. After a few weeks of lies, delays, fraud, a princely lifestyle, and lavish spending of mother and daughter's fast-disappearing resources, he was rearrested by English police and sent back to prison on a ten-year sentence. Released from Dartmoor Prison on December 13, 1900, he soon returned to the United States. He reappeared in Brooklyn and tried unsuccessfully to reconcile with his wife, who in the meantime had given birth to a child. He drifted to Jersey City and Philadelphia, where he married and fleeced yet another wife after convincing her to go with him to Cincinnati. He deserted her in Cincinnati and stole some of her belongings. The next stop was St. Louis.[4]

Barrington's case in St. Louis generated phenomenal publicity. While "the lord" was breaking rock, his lawyer filed a suit against James Cochrane in Kansas City for $10,000, charging that Cochrane, not Barrington, had perpetrated the assault for which Barrington was arrested. The notion of an English gentleman breaking rock in the St. Louis Workhouse aroused sympathy for Barrington in the city. His lawyer, Colonel John I. Martin, emphasized that Barrington was not guilty of the crime that landed him in the workhouse. Martin took depositions from eyewitnesses to the altercation who swore that Barrington was the victim, not the perpetrator of the altercation. After gathering the depositions, Martin took them to Mayor Wells, who signed an order for Barrington's release from the workhouse on April 10, 1903.[5]

When Barrington left the workhouse, he sent a letter to his new bride, asking for a reconciliation, but she denounced him as a rogue and fraud, and she indicated she would seek a divorce. John W. L. Gillespie, a saloon owner who saw a chance to cash in on Barrington's notoriety, employed him to manage what became dubbed Lord Barrington's Saloon. With a walking cane and his characteristic Prince Albert jacket and silk hat, Barrington regaled throngs of patrons with story after story. There he met James P. McCann, a high roller who flashed money around and bet heavily on horse races. Attracted by Barrington's roguish reputation and style, McCann gave him fifty dollars as a gesture of friendship. Soon, McCann invited him to live in the Leland Hotel, a small boardinghouse owned by McCann and his wife, Jessie, who also ran a matrimonial agency with an office in downtown St. Louis. The McCanns had a history of looking for get-rich-quick schemes in Chicago before they came to St. Louis in 1902. Barrington often accompanied McCann to local saloons and placed bets on the horses for him.[6]

About two and a half months after Barrington left the workhouse, he was arrested for murdering McCann, whose decomposed body was found in an abandoned quarry along the Missouri River in St. Charles, near the Bonfils Station. When questioned by police, Barrington admitted he had gone to that part of the county with McCann that night, but he disavowed any role in the murder. He concocted fantastic but contradictory versions of what happened to McCann, insisting that the victim drove away in a carriage.

On March 5, 1904, a jury convicted Barrington based on circumstantial evidence. He was sentenced to hang for first degree murder. The Missouri Supreme Court upheld the verdict on June 20, 1906. With funding from the British government, Barrington took an appeal to the United States Supreme Court. Although the highest court in the land denied the appeal on April 22, 1907, Governor Folk used dissenting opinions on the state bench, public sympathy, reported sightings of McCann, and reigning confusion over Barrington's identity to justify commuting his sentence to life imprisonment on August 13, 1907.

After four years in the Clayton jail in St. Louis County, Barrington entered the Missouri State Penitentiary on August 28, 1907. Missouri governor Frederick D. Gardner further commuted his sentence and released him from the penitentiary on December 24, 1918, on the stipulation that he leave the country within sixty days. Gardner arranged for the St. George's Society of New York to fund Barrington's passage to England. Barrington sailed from New York aboard the *Mauretania* on January 7, 1919.[7]

When Mayor Wells picked Andrew Scully to be the superintendent of the workhouse, he insisted on the adoption of more humane practices and methods. With the World's Fair under way in 1904, the mayor suggested an end to the use of shackles and ball and chain at the workhouse, if practical. Scully warmly endorsed the mayor's suggestion, and so did Mary E. Perry, president of the Missouri Board of Charities and Corrections. Perry, of St. Louis, served as a member of the Charities and Corrections exhibit at the World's Fair. Scully informed the state board that at the beginning of his tenure, 115 of the 282 male prisoners were shackled, whereas only six prisoners were held in shackles at the time he wrote on November 11, 1904. After nearly a year of implementation, he pronounced the experiment a success in February 1905. When visitors to the World's Fair asked to see the "chain room" at the workhouse, Superintendent Scully showed them piles of shackles, irons, balls, and chains in the room, and he boasted that they were mere relics of a bygone era, now grown rusty from lack of use.[8]

Scully condemned the practice of beating, kicking, and shackling prisoners as unnecessarily cruel. "Such methods, with the practice of weighing down a poor wretch with anklets, chains and a huge ball, the whole weighing perhaps seventy pounds, are relics of barbarism," he insisted. The practice unfairly left prisoners with a permanent mark that made them recognizable. "The swinging shuffle, with the dragging step of the right foot," Scully pointed out, "will immediately spot out the ex-convict of the workhouse in the days of the chain gang. I know it wherever I see it, no matter how the man may be dressed or where I meet him, and more than once seeing a man in the city who has the walk and I have made inquiries and have ascertained that he had served his time."[9]

An end to the practice of shackling prisoners represented glimmers of a more progressive philosophy taking root at the workhouse, but it might have been designed more to improve the city's image during the World's Fair. "Putting St. Louisans into Chains," a feature article by "A Friend of Prisoners" in the Sunday edition of the *Post-Dispatch,* revealed the policy's limits on April 16, 1905. Noting that about a year previous "a great hullabaloo was made at the workhouse about a wonderful reform in abolishing shackles," the writer urged the mayor to take the next step by ending the practice entirely. The article likened workhouse prisoners in chains to Czarist Russian exiles in Siberia, pointing out that the Russian shackles weighed less than those worn by inmates in the workhouse. Among workhouse prisoners still wearing shackles was Charles Chrisen, a "frail" sixteen-year-old boy sentenced on a charge of trespass, who was put to work loading wagons in the quarry. The article included photographs and names of other shackled inmates at work in the quarry. Four of the other shackled inmates were imprisoned on charges of "idling," trespass, fighting, and assault. "Now I assert that the reason why these men are in chains in the St. Louis Workhouse is because they are poor," the writer protested. "Every lawyer in St. Louis knows this to be a fact. Probably many of them are innocent, but certainly every one of them is 'broke.' There would be no more chance of a man with money having chains put on him in the St. Louis Workhouse than there would be of a camel passing through the eye of a needle. Has it come to this—that poverty itself has become a crime?"[10]

Superintendent Scully did not mention the shackling or unshackling of prisoners in his 1904–1905 annual report in April. Instead, he emphasized that there was plenty of space due to the completion of a new addition to the workhouse. He touted the purchase of new beds, repair of the older ones, and the installation of new boilers. When the grand jury visited the workhouse a month later, there were no prisoners in irons or solitary confinement. Only a few guards carried firearms. The grand jury's report painted a highly positive picture of conditions in the institution, calling attention to its clean facilities and a newly installed bathing apparatus. Perhaps even more importantly, the grand jury emphasized the profitability of the workhouse, which was $10,000 in the black.[11]

The workhouse was one of many city institutions that Mayor Wells hoped to dress up as best he could during the Louisiana Purchase Exposition in 1904. The mayor hoped to showcase St. Louis as a modern city, avoid controversy, and promote the city's public image in the eyes of the world. Police court justice had an internal logic of its own, however, and the workhouse yet again found itself in the middle of controversy while the exposition was under way. By the time Mayor Wells tried to resolve the controversy, it was too late.

On August 18, 1904, police court justice led to the confinement and death of workhouse inmate Michael (Mike) C. Bennett in the Mississippi River. Bennett was a thirty-seven-year-old unmarried traveling insurance agent from Des Moines, Iowa, where he once was employed in the money order division of the United States Post Office. His brother Frank Bennett was the Democratic county supervisor in Des Moines, and his brothers Peter and Lewis had businesses there. With a sterling reputation at home, Bennett came to St. Louis to attend the Democratic National Convention and the exposition. He registered at the Jefferson Hotel. After a few days, the hotel clerk became uneasy and asked him to pay his bill. Bennett, who fell ill while attending the convention, gave him a draft on his brother in Des Moines, but when the hotel clerk sent Bennett's brother a telegram, no reply was forthcoming. Bennett was ordered to vacate the hotel, but he continued to hang around while he waited for his brother to approve the draft. On July 26, the clerk followed him to a second-floor hallway and demanded to know what he was doing there. Bennett replied that he hoped to meet William Randolph Hearst, whose campaign headquarters were on that floor. Suspicious, the clerk summoned a police officer, who arrested Bennett for loitering. When Bennett tried to explain at his arraignment in police court, Judge Tracy cut him off, fined him twenty-five dollars, and sent him to the workhouse.[12]

The workhouse rock pile wore Bennett down. Unaccustomed to hard manual labor and still not fully recovered from the illness he suffered while attending the convention, he lost a lot of weight as his condition weakened under the regimentation of workhouse life. In the meantime, the nightmare of confinement pushed Bennett to the edge of despair. On August 18, while working at the bottom of the quarry, he made a desperate break for freedom along the Iron Mountain Railway tracks. He ran north on the tracks, but guards on the northern rim of the quarry spotted him and scrambled down the steep embankment to head him off while other guards pursued him from the south.

Bennett made a hasty decision. The river, about fifty feet away, was the only option. He soon disappeared underwater and reappeared about fifty feet from shore. The guards pointed their guns at him and threatened to shoot him unless he returned to shore, but it seemed to them that he could not swim well, if at all. They claimed he yelled, "I can't make it. Send word to my folks" before he disappeared under the water for the final time. Later, dynamite blasts in the river brought the body to the surface, and his brother came to take the body to Des Moines for burial.[13]

What Bennett did not know at the time was that Mayor Wells had remitted the fine and issued an order for his release. The order was scheduled to arrive at the workhouse on the following day. As soon as J. V. Fry, of the Mechanics National Bank, found out that Bennett was in the workhouse, he had contacted Paul B. Grace to work to secure Bennett's release. Both Fry and Grace were formerly of Des Moines, and they knew the Bennett family. They sent a letter to Peter Bennett, a brother of the incarcerated, to make him aware of the confinement. He was out of town at the time they wrote to him, so his response was delayed considerably. In the meantime, Bennett's sister, Mary Swift, was notified of the letter, and she quickly asked what she could do to get her brother out of the workhouse. By that time, Grace knew that the mayor planned to send the release order to the workhouse the next day. Grace went to the workhouse to take Bennett some fruit and cigars and to let him know his release was imminent, but Bennett was in the quarry working and unavailable at the time. Superintendent Scully denied reports that guards had fired at Bennett, who, he insisted, did little work and spent most of his days in the city hospital.[14]

In 1905, a flurry of charges and accusations against Scully's workhouse regime hit the newspapers. When prisoners staged a "sick-out" and refused to work in the quarry in the bitter cold of mid-January, he revived a controversial punishment tool that had not been used at the workhouse in many years. For inmates who complained that they were too sick to work, he cut back on food rations to two meals a day to force them back to the rock pile. When charges of corruption were made by a prisoner who was pardoned by the mayor and released from the workhouse, acting mayor Joseph L. Hornsby called workhouse officers on the carpet. Henry Miller, sentenced for beating his wife, was released by Mayor Wells at the behest of Miller's wife, who needed his financial support for their destitute family. Upon release, Miller complained to the mayor that Michael Noonan, a workhouse guard, had offered to assign him easier work and to see to it that he did not have to wear shackles in exchange for payment of ten dollars. Hornsby summoned Superintendent Scully, Noonan, a few other workhouse employees, and a prisoner. After the workhouse officers denied Miller's accusations, Hornsby took the matter under advisement, and it is not clear whether he investigated further. Some of Superintendent Scully's friends attributed Miller's charges of corruption to factional Democratic Party disputes on the part of Scully's political enemies, who sought his ouster at the workhouse.[15]

The workhouse escape of Gonzola White, a sixteen-year-old Black woman, prompted an investigation not only into how she escaped but also into her charges that she was whipped. Her case drew public attention to whether workhouse women were still subjected to lashes at the whipping post under Scully's superintendency. During a grand jury inquiry in October 1905, suspicions increased when Patrick Bradley, a workhouse guard, refused to answer questions about whether guards used bullwhips to punish unruly women prisoners. The grand jury also asked him specifically whether Superintendent Scully used bullwhips to administer punishment. Bradley was sent to jail for refusing to answer the questions, but he was soon released and taken to the grand jury room after he agreed to tell all he knew about the matter. James G. McConkey, Mayor Wells's secretary, indicated that the mayor's office was investigating the matter, but the results of these investigations were not made public.[16]

When James L. Dawson replaced Scully as superintendent of the workhouse in 1907, he announced a philosophical shift in the treatment of prisoners. A retired police sergeant who had previously served as the city jailer, Dawson abolished the whipping post. Influenced by more progressive ideas of how to run penal institutions, he was a member of the National Association of Charities and Corrections and the chairman of the Committee on the Treatment of Criminals. National criminologists often commented favorably on papers he presented at conferences. As an advocate of the reformation and rehabilitation of prisoners, he was highly critical of the use of corporal punishment. "Corporal punishment or brutal intimidation of any kind has never brought a single criminal one step toward reformation," he remarked. "Since I have been here [at the workhouse] I have taken clubs away from the guards and have instructed them to treat the inmates with kindness and consideration, but to be firm." To use brutal methods and unnecessary roughness only hardened the inmates and increased their resentment against the officers who kept them imprisoned. "I never believed in punishment for punishment's sake," he told a *Post-Dispatch* reporter. "It has never accomplished anything in the way of uplifting an offender and it never will. I have seen 21 years of it and I know that my conclusions are right."[17]

Superintendent Dawson emphasized that the dark solitary confinement cells and a diet of bread and water would be used only in the most extreme cases of punishment, and never for more than twelve hours. In cases of unruly incorrigibles, his policy was to call the police to rearrest them and take them back to police court, where the judges could do what they wished to do with them in the way of added punishment. The practice of swinging clubs was too tempting for guards to use to brutalize prisoners. Only in cases of self-defense did Dawson endorse their use. He urged the establishment of manual training classes with an emphasis on educating and uplifting inmates so that they might become productive citizens.[18]

The *Globe-Democrat* praised the innovations under Dawson's more enlightened superintendency in October 1907, but at the very time of the article, a banking crisis unleashed a nationwide economic depression that worsened conditions and undercut reforms in the workhouse. In 1901, the average daily number of prisoners was 334, but by 1908 it skyrocketed to 697 and sometimes went as high as 900. The number of annual commitments to the workhouse shot up from 2,095 in 1901 to an all-time high of 3,724 in 1907.

A year after the *Globe-Democrat* praised Dawson, a devastating report by the October grand jury charged that prisoners in his overcrowded workhouse were treated "worse than cattle." Four pages of the grand jury's eight-page report submitted to Judge Claflin C. Allen in Criminal Division 12 were devoted to the workhouse. The report absolved Superintendent Dawson of responsibility, instead blaming the municipal assembly for not providing relief to the highly overcrowded workhouse. Dawson also complained that union labor refused to work alongside prison labor to construct a new addition. Toilers thrown out of work by the depression of 1907 now filled the institution as "vagrants." "Many of the men are not criminals," stated the report, "but are victims of the general financial depression in business for the past twelve months." For immediate relief, the report suggested parole for well-behaved prisoners and the relocation of some to the city jail. The grand jurors noted that Dawson had called repeatedly for funds to relieve the congested conditions and to give the workhouse a rehabilitative function.[19]

The jurors recommended wide distribution of their October report, calling on ministers and churches to prick the public's conscience against "penning up, worse than cattle, the prisoners in our workhouse." The report urged an investigation into the long delay in building new cells, for which money was already appropriated. Finally, the jurors called on the succeeding grand jury to continue investigating conditions in the workhouse, including the lack of medical care. The report revealed that each cell in the poorly ventilated men's quarters held from fifteen to eighteen prisoners locked up after supper until six o'clock in the morning with no recreational outlets. "When the weather will not permit the men to work," the report added, "they are compelled to stay in these overcrowded cells day and night . . . It is the opinion of the jury that these men are treated worse than cattle, owing to the congestion of the prison, and that this condition will be made worse during the winter months, as is usually the case. Owing to the congestion many prisoners must sleep on the cell floors after working all day in the quarry of the city."[20]

After the grand jury report, Superintendent Dawson found himself in the crosshairs of city politics. The House of Delegates, rather than acting to correct the problems outlined in the report, appointed a special committee to investigate Dawson and the possible abuse of his position. Chaired by James J. Gallagher, the committee held public hearings over allegations he used workhouse labor for his own personal benefit. Dawson admitted he had ordered Michael Finnigan, foreman of the workhouse carpenter shop, to put some prisoners to work finishing Dawson's yacht, the *Mary Dawson,* which was under construction. "I then permitted two guards to take the boat to Creve Coeur Lake one Saturday night," he explained. "They remained at the lake over Sunday, but no time was lost since, on account of the holiday, they would not have been employed even if they had been at the Workhouse."

Other charges included sending workhouse crews to grade a street embankment, purportedly for the benefit of his friend J. G. McConkey, the mayor's private secretary. On another occasion, Dawson allegedly took advantage of the services of a physician, who was a workhouse prisoner, to treat him. The committee also targeted the superintendent's practice of keeping his own hogs on the premises and feeding them offal from the workhouse kitchen and dining room. The hearings seemed more a political sideshow than an investigation, considering the critical issues highlighted in the October grand jury's report. The *Post-Dispatch* had a field day with the committee's investigation, satirizing "Dawson's Pigs" and deriding the hearings as a farce comedy.[21]

Plans to construct a new cell house to relieve overcrowding at the workhouse encountered delays rooted in city politics. On April 1, 1908, the city treasury held $19,000 appropriated for the construction of a new cell building, but the project required additional funds. On October 6, 1908, ground was broken for the new building, the workhouse's eighth, but a simmering conflict deepened over the employment of prison labor on the project. Mayor Wells backed the use of convict labor, but the Building Trades Council strenuously objected to using workhouse prisoners to work alongside skilled union laborers. Andrew J. O'Reilly, president of the Board of Public Improvements, also pointed the finger at labor unions for causing the delays. On October 30, 1908, the House of Delegates passed a resolution to postpone all work on the new cell building until the labor matter was resolved. Frustrated, Superintendent Dawson went to city hall to complain about severe overcrowding at the workhouse and to emphasize the urgent need for the new building.[22]

In January 1909, the House of Delegates passed a concurrent resolution calling on police judges and Mayor Wells to release fifty prisoners to relieve the severe congestion in the workhouse. Cells at the time held from twelve to fourteen prisoners, and some prisoners were sleeping in the corridors. Members of the city council opposed the resolution. Both houses of the municipal assembly called on BPI president O'Reilly to go forward with the construction of the new cell house, over the protests of union labor. For six weeks, an ordinance was pending in the House of Delegates for an additional appropriation of $6,000 to build the cell house without prison labor, but it was not expected to pass anytime soon. Dwight Davis, a Republican in the House of Delegates, asked O'Reilly why nothing was done to fix the "inhuman conditions" in the workhouse, but O'Reilly replied that he did not have the authority to remedy the conditions. Davis followed up with a resolution adopted by the House of Delegates, again pressing O'Reilly on the need to relieve overcrowding so that "the Workhouse of St. Louis will no longer be a disgrace to a civilized community."[23]

After the lengthy delay, construction began on a modern addition to the workhouse on May 4, 1909. The new building, well lighted and well ventilated, held fifty-two cells. Superintendent Dawson chose the specs and plans for the new building after seeing similar plans at a meeting of the National Prison Association in Chicago. The plans for the new building included a chapel in the basement with a seating capacity of 650. A *Post-Dispatch* reporter noted that "it is expected to be an improvement over the present cramped and dingy quarters of the workhouse prisoners."[24]

In Dawson's 1909 annual report, he called for the hiring of four new guards, and he recommended the adoption of several major innovations to improve the quality of life in the workhouse. After visiting the Allegheny County Workhouse in Pittsburgh, he urged the creation of a night school, and he recommended the introduction of lectures, musicals, and other forms of entertainment to be held in the new cell house chapel in the basement. In 1908, Mayor Wells vetoed a bill to hire a workhouse physician at an annual salary of $1,200, arguing that it was unnecessary, but Dawson suggested opening an eye and ear clinic with a good dispensary in the workhouse. At the time, the workhouse averaged twelve prisoners in the city hospital daily. Dawson also sought a library, but he recognized that there was no space for one yet. Finally, instead of relying on prisoners to do the cooking, he endorsed hiring a bona fide, competent cook and assistant to improve the quality of food.[25]

While the new cell house was under construction in September 1909, a *Globe-Democrat* writer who interviewed Dawson asked him about criticisms that he was too soft on prisoners. Dawson defended workhouse inmates, including some of his "hardest cases": "These boys here are doing hard work and they are not obstinate about it . . . They make hardly any trouble about it. If they were obstinate, they know they would not be abused, but they would get the dark cell, and they would be made to do the work." Dawson emphasized that the workhouse, with no schools, library, or reading room, was one of the worst in the country in terms of comfort and accommodations. "When the new cell building is completed we will have more room to lock them up in, but we have the only Workhouse now where they have to sleep in chicken houses," he told the writer. "Come around here and I will show you the chicken houses." Dawson led the writer to two crude temporary structures resembling open-air camps, built by prisoners with old lumber salvaged from the torn-down fairgrounds. Upper parts of the walls were left open at the top and were covered in coarse wire netting. Inside the structures were long rows of cots on which Black prisoners slept under the stars.[26]

Besides pointing to the need for reforms, the superintendent called attention to the arbitrariness that governed the police court system and sent so many to the workhouse. He emphasized that "respectable" residents of St. Louis often violated the vast number of city ordinances on the books, but police rarely arrested them. In perhaps 99 out of 100 violations, residents who let weeds get too high in their yards, for example, did not get arrested and fined. "With about ninety-nine in the hundred city ordinances of this kind," Dawson told the *Globe-Democrat* as he referenced the police tool of vagrancy, "there is one left in every hundred which is intended to be enforced all the time against all the 'no-account people' who can be caught violating it. So they are 'vagged' or sent back to the Workhouse in other convenient ways as soon as they become inconvenient to respectable people outside."[27]

The worsening overcrowding in Dawson's workhouse led to a rash of escapes at the time. Among the escapees was Dr. Oscar R. Bullard, whose high-profile case took numerous twists and turns and dramatized the complications of using the workhouse to punish adulterers. The fleet-footed doctor, born around 1881, was a painter in 1902 when he married Rose Stackert in Cairo, Illinois. Rose was about eight years older than him. Her father, Casper Stackert, was a retired merchant who had a little money. The Bullards had four children by the time they moved to St. Louis for Oscar to pursue his ambition to become a physician in the College of Physicians and Surgeons. They received financial help from Rose's father, but they struggled to make ends meet. In July 1908, Rose and the children left St. Louis to live with her parents until Oscar graduated and their financial condition improved.[28]

A year later, when Rose stopped receiving letters from Oscar, she learned on a visit to St. Louis that he was intimately involved with a younger woman. With the children along in August 1909, she confronted her husband and seventeen-year-old Regina Loiseau, deemed a "love pirate" in the press. Regina's father, a French immigrant, operated a restaurant in St. Louis. When Rose found Oscar and Regina together, Regina professed her undying love for Oscar, who begged Rose not to press charges. Oscar told Rose he had stopped writing to her because he failed his medical exams and felt guilty and ashamed to face her. Angry, she notified the police to arrest him for abandoning her and the children. "I worked hard and sacrificed a great deal to help him realize his ambition to become a physician," she complained. "Now when he is about to succeed he has cast me aside as a drag on him and gives his affection and labors to another woman."[29]

At the time of Rose's return to St. Louis, Oscar was employed as an assistant to Dr. Waldo Briggs at the Jefferson Hospital. Oscar, a superb athlete, played right end on the Barnes Medical College football team. He was also known for his boxing skills. According to Regina, she met him at a dinner party in the home of Dr. Briggs in December 1908. Although she came to the party in the company of Briggs's son, there was an immediate attraction between her and Oscar. "It was love at first sight," she exclaimed. "I did not know that he was married until the police arrested him for wife desertion. Then it was too late, for both our heart strings were tangled and we knew we were meant for each other forever."[30]

On September 30, 1909, police arrested Oscar on the charges of abandonment brought by his wife, but he insisted that she left him to go back to Cairo. As his paramour, Regina also was arrested. Judge Wilson A. Taylor of the Court of Criminal Correction released her, but he ordered her to stay away from Oscar, who was sentenced to six months in the workhouse. Regina walked out of the courtroom free, but not before she let Judge Taylor know what she thought of the statutes surrounding matrimony. Her mother, who had left St. Louis in May 1909, whisked her away to Chicago. Rose, who now felt bad about her husband's sentence, asked the judge to parole him, but to no avail. Oscar was admitted to the workhouse and put to work on street crews, driving a cart and hauling rock from the quarry. When he and Regina parted, he promised to divorce Rose and marry Regina upon completion of his workhouse sentence. "He married his first wife because she had lots of money," Regina explained, "but they were incompatible from the start. He had not been near her for a year and a half."[31]

While in the workhouse, Oscar wrote a letter to Judge Taylor to ask for clemency on grounds he intended to finish his medical studies and retake the exams he had failed the year before. When his plea for clemency and release failed, and when he did not receive letters from Regina, who purportedly lacked money for postage, he became desperate. On January 11, 1910, after two months of workhouse confinement, a lovesick impulse led him to make a mad dash for freedom and the loving arms of Regina.

It happened while he was working on a street crew under the supervision of guard George Smith. Using a cart to shield him from Smith, Oscar made a sudden break and sprinted away on Osage Street as rifle shots rang out and bullets whizzed past him. His athletic skills served him well as he dodged the guards' hail of bullets and vanished. Reportedly, he was seen jumping into a milk wagon on Broadway. A full-scale manhunt ensued. Superintendent Dawson jumped into his buggy and joined the search. Bullard hurried to the home of Dr. Briggs and told him he was officially discharged from the workhouse but needed some money. Briggs congratulated him on his release and gave him a small amount of money. Upon hearing afterward of his escape, Briggs noted that under no circumstances would Oscar be allowed to finish his studies and get a diploma at the College of Physicians and Surgeons.[32]

The police department notified Chicago authorities to be on the lookout for Bullard, who was expected to run to Regina. About a week before Bullard's workhouse escape, Regina left her mother's home in Chicago and rented her own apartment in the city. Bullard soon joined her. A mysterious tip led Chicago police to Regina's door, but Bullard was not there at the time. The police took her into custody and continued to search for Bullard.

Through the newspapers, Regina sent Bullard a message, pledging her undying love for him: "I love him and he loves me. He has risked death twice for me and I'll die for him if necessary. The police have no right to keep me here. I'll not tell a thing. I hope he reads what I say now: I love him, love him, love him, and will wait for him forever. I love him as no man ever was loved and he loves me as devotedly."[33]

Later that night, detectives spotted Bullard on the street and tried to arrest him, but he sprinted away once again amid a fusillade of bullets. Three days later, on January 19, police detectives spied him on a street corner with his suitcase and made the arrest. Again he tried to run, but they surrounded him and took him into custody. Reportedly, Bullard was about to leave for South Dakota to file divorce proceedings against Rose. At a police station a few minutes later, he returned Regina's message of love with his own, also using the newspapers: "This is not the end by a long shot, for my fight to gain possession of Regina has only begun. It looks pretty blue just now, but I know everything will come out all right. Have I not Regina's words that I am dearly loved and that no man ever was loved so much before by any woman . . . I would rather go to the bottomless pit than be returned to St. Louis, but there is no alternative, and I shall make the best of it."[34]

When the St. Louis police department and Superintendent Dawson were notified of the arrest, they told Chicago authorities to hold him until they could arrange for extradition papers to return him to St. Louis for further prosecution. After a conference with Dawson, the assistant circuit attorney in St. Louis vowed to prosecute him on a felony charge of breaking jail. Now Bullard was facing not only a return to the workhouse but also a possible two-year stretch in the Missouri State Penitentiary. Regina, distraught, traveled to Springfield in a tearful but unsuccessful plea to Governor Charles Deneen's office not to extradite Bullard to St. Louis. Once the extradition paperwork was fulfilled, Superintendent Dawson traveled to Chicago to bring Bullard back to St. Louis. He arrived in the late afternoon, only to find that Chicago authorities had released him earlier in the day at a habeas corpus proceeding filed on Bullard's behalf.[35]

Dawson and St. Louis chief of police Edmund P. Creecy were furious, blaming Chicago police negligence for the embarrassing snafu. They pointed out that they had sent three telegrams providing the appropriate notifications. Dawson pledged to devote as many resources as possible to recapture and return Bullard to St. Louis. Determined to put an end to the rash of escapes that plagued Dawson's workhouse, the assistant circuit attorney charged Bullard and other escapees with the felony offense of jail breaking. In the meantime, Bullard was now on the lam again in the company of Regina, and Rose obtained a divorce from him.[36]

Oscar and Regina evaded authorities for years, but in 1913 she gave birth to their daughter, Bernice, in Anoka, Minnesota. At some point in the next few years, they lived in Terra Haute, Indiana, but then moved back to St. Louis in hopes that the authorities had forgotten that Oscar was a workhouse fugitive. In 1918, he passed his written medical exams and was granted a license to practice medicine and surgery in St. Louis. Without detection by police, he opened a practice, but his marriage to Regina hit the skids. When they divorced in late 1920, Oscar was required to pay sixty dollars a month in alimony. He paid the first month, but when Regina put Bernice in a distant boarding school, he stopped paying. Oscar complained it was impossible for him to visit his daughter. He suggested a nearby boarding school. When Regina complained to the Court of Criminal Correction in St. Louis that Oscar had failed to provide the monthly alimony, she also turned him in as an escaped workhouse prisoner. Oscar admitted he was an escaped prisoner but pleaded that he had compensated by serving the city as a practicing physician in the past few years.

On December 23, 1920, the judge was sympathetic and paroled Oscar with the stipulation that he resume payment of alimony to Regina. Oscar, pleading that he needed more time to do so, promised to pay later in the month, after a few upcoming scheduled surgeries. On February 2, 1921, Regina returned to court to complain that he still had not paid her the month's alimony. The next day, eleven years after Oscar's dramatic escape from the workhouse, he was sent back to finish his sentence. He was quickly released, after the circuit attorney opted not to prosecute, but five months later, Regina again complained that he was not paying the full alimony. The assistant circuit attorney issued an arrest warrant for Bullard on charges of vagrancy, and back to the workhouse the doctor went to finish serving the sentence that had hung over his head for more than a decade.[37]

In 1910, Bullard's flight from the workhouse was one of countless escapes and attempted escapes that plagued Superintendent Dawson's tenure. Five prisoners crawled through a workhouse sewer in March while the remaining 550 prisoners were eating breakfast. A couple of the escapees stole a skiff from the Western Rowing Club and paddled across the river, while the others disappeared down the Iron Mountain Railway tracks. In a well-organized effort, ten prisoners tried a dramatic escape in August. Only a fusillade of guards' bullets prevented the attempted break, but Dawson armed himself in response and sounded the alarm at the nearby police station. Police surrounded the perimeter of the workhouse, but they were not needed. In both instances, Dawson absolved guards of responsibility and blamed the mass escapes on overcrowding. He had complained repeatedly to the House of Delegates about poor lighting at the workhouse, but it was considered too expensive to install the requested improved lighting.[38]

8

A HALTING PLACE BETWEEN TWO CRIMES

In spring 1910, after the rash of embarrassing escapes by Oscar R. Bullard and other inmates, a subcommittee of the Social Service Committee of the St. Louis Civic League (formerly the Civic Betterment League) investigated the workhouse. The subcommittee, chaired by attorney E. M. Grossman, consisted of some of the city's leading Progressives: Mary E. Bulkley, a suffragist and labor reformer; Hugh M. Fullerton, chief probation officer of the juvenile court; and Roger N. Baldwin, secretary of the executive board of the Civic League. To gather additional ideas and information on practices and procedures in more modern municipal workhouses, the Civic League sent Fullerton to Chicago and Cleveland. The Civic League's executive board, headed by Saunders Norvell, approved the subcommittee's findings and released the report to the public in September 1911. The mayor's secretary, the Board of Public Improvements, and current and past workhouse superintendents all signed off on the report, which laid bare the horrid conditions of the workhouse and recommended solutions to the problems that plagued the institution. The report was ready for release in January, but for tactical and other reasons, the Civic League delayed its release for six months.[1]

The league's report made it clear "that the unfortunate conditions in the care of our offenders committed to the workhouse are not due to negligence or poor administration. They are the faults of a system."[2] In effect, the workhouse functioned as a debtors' prison. While acknowledging recent improvements, the report highlighted a long history of shoddy record keeping, mismanagement, arbitrariness, corruption, and political favoritism in the institution's methods, practices, and prisoner releases. Overcrowded buildings were infested with vermin at the time, and the subcommittee found that the quality of food was inferior and far inadequate for the kind of labor required. Idleness was a continuing problem, especially on rainy days. Women were employed entirely indoors. White women sewed, mended, and made workhouse clothing, but Black women and a few frail men were assigned more menial tasks such as scrubbing, cleaning, making the beds, doing the laundry, and working in the kitchen. The report, noting that institutionalized corruption was hard to root out, called attention to the bribing of guards in exchange for favors, including the smuggling of cocaine and opium into the workhouse.[3]

Included in the report's recommendations was a call to create a board of parole and to hire four probation officers to supervise workhouse admissions and releases. In the course of its duties, the board was to be fully authorized to investigate cases and make recommendations to police courts. In 1910, the mayor's office issued remits for 357 prisoners, most of them at the request of their families. By shifting the power to parole inmates from the mayor's office to the board, the proposal would ease the burden on the mayor's office by replacing the old system of remits that invited corruption, arbitrariness, and political favoritism. If implemented, the proposal would reduce overcrowding by increasing the number of parolees.[4]

The disciplinary methods and practices in the workhouse came under heavy fire in the league's report, which criticized the complete absence of rehabilitation efforts. The chief form of punishment was solitary confinement in the dungeon on a diet of bread and water. The Supreme Court of the United States had condemned the practice more than twenty years earlier, but there were three bull pens in the workhouse, two for men and one for women. The dungeon in the women's quarters was especially dark, with only a tiny hole for ventilation and light. A prisoner's average length of stay in the bull pen ranged from two hours to two weeks. The Civic League's report called for abolition of the dungeon, "a relic of the old method of inquisitorial torture for inspiring goodness." Instead, the report recommended the implementation of a system of rewards for discipline, and it urged the opening of a night school and a system of circulating library books in the workhouse.[5]

Among the Civic League's recommendations was a call for hospital services in the workhouse and the creation of a municipal work farm to be funded by a bond issue. The work farm concept was popular among criminal justice reformers. George B. Mangold, director of the St. Louis School of Social Economy, endorsed the work farm as a place for workhouse prisoners who were repeatedly confined for habitual drunkenness, disturbing the peace, and other misdemeanors. Officers in the workhouse estimated that 75 percent of its prisoners were repeat offenders. While undergoing rehabilitation on the work farm, alcoholics, drug abusers, and others guilty of misdemeanors would be separated from the felons and corrupting influences of the dreary, medieval workhouse. They would benefit from working in a healthier environment under stricter supervision until they were rehabilitated and restored with self-respect. In the words of a *Globe-Democrat* reporter, "Changes along these lines will transform the workhouse from a halting place between two crimes to a place of permanent improvement and restoration."[6]

During the Civic League's investigation, Superintendent Dawson drew attention to the case of Ellen Maher, a "police character" who was repeatedly arrested and confined in the workhouse on the same charge of fighting when drunk. Her sentences, all of which came from police court fines, ranged from twelve days to four weeks. Regarded by police judges as one of the city's worst incorrigibles, she was a model prisoner in the workhouse, where she was confined an average of six times a year, dating back to her first arrest around 1880. Dawson was the arresting police officer at the time of her first arrest. In a workhouse conversation with Maher in 1907, he noted that it must have been at least twenty-five years since he arrested her. "It was more than that, Mr. Dawson," she laughed. "It was most thirty years ago. It was when I first began taking the drink, and I never drank nothin' till after my mother died." He replied, "Well, it was a long time ago anyway. How many times have you been here?" Maher answered, "Lord, Mr. Dawson, I couldn't tell. I lost count 'bout ten years ago . . . I'm a good worker and when I'm out I can always get a place doin' housework. I can cook and scrub and clean up as good as anybody. But I've been here so much it feels jus' like home to me. When I get out this time I'm goin' out to the West End, where there ain't no saloons and find a place, and then maybe I'll repent of my sins and won't come back here no more."[7]

The proposed work farm was largely intended for prisoners like Maher and others confined for disorderly conduct on account of alcohol. Another old-timer in Dawson's workhouse was Molly McGinty, who claimed bragging rights as the prisoner with the next-longest workhouse history of confinement for public drunkenness and disorderly conduct. For "Soapmaking Molly," described by Superintendent Dawson as the "character" of the workhouse, responsibilities as the chief soap maker were sobering. Given full charge of the process, she and her three helpers supplied the institution with two daily barrels of old-fashioned soft soap, which because of its jellylike consistency when cold could be dispensed and easily used via buckets and dippers. Shortly before the expiration of each of her sentences, she made barrels of excess soap to last the workhouse until she returned. Every time she was released, she would say, "Well, I guess that'll last." On a few occasions when the supply of soap ran low while she was on the outside, others made the soap in her absence. Upon her return, she always criticized the quality of the soap manufactured by others.[8]

The Civic League's recommended reforms were consistent with Superintendent Dawson's overall philosophy and recommendations, as the workhouse report duly acknowledged. They also were in line with ideas popular among criminal justice reformers nationwide. When Republican Frederick Kreismann captured control of the mayor's office in 1909, he kept Dawson on as superintendent of the workhouse, but in 1911, he appointed Calvin J. White to replace Dawson, a few months before the release of the Civic League's report. White, a parole officer in the criminal division of the circuit court for the previous eight months, had been in the police department for eleven years as a patrol officer and secretary to the chief of police. The nephew of former chief of police John W. Campbell, he came highly recommended by judges in the circuit court as a man of principle. His wife, soon to become matron at the workhouse, was an accomplished pianist and vocalist who previously took her students to sing to inmates in the workhouse.[9]

Dubbed the Golden Rule Superintendent by the *St. Louis Star,* White set out to create a more harmonious workhouse atmosphere. In his view, a little kindness went a long way, and so did the implementation of an honor system in the treatment of prisoners who showed a willingness to reform. White's wife visited the women's quarters daily, and she often gave women one or more items of clothing when they were released. On Sunday afternoons, she sang for prisoners. For the first time in the history of the workhouse, a large Christmas tree lit up the dining room, where inmates were treated to a traditional Christmas meal after morning religious services in the chapel. White solicited funds from businessmen, politicians, and others for the tree and gifts for prisoners. Guards gave him a diamond pin to express appreciation for his style of management.[10]

Superintendent White, with authorization from the Board of Public Improvements, proposed a back-to-nature experiment to create a miniature version of the work farm model on Chesley ("Hog") Island south of the city, in Jefferson County. On the island, once a site for dumping city garbage where its hogs fed, White proposed to inaugurate a work farm for selected workhouse prisoners. On the fertile island, chosen prisoners whose confinement was due to alcohol abuse planted corn and raised vegetable gardens to supply city institutions. Prisoners under guard supervision built a stockade where they would sleep and work in the open air. Alcohol was banned. Prisoners would benefit from hard work, fresh air, and more sanitary living conditions. Surrounded by the Mississippi, the island's location would make escapes difficult and minimize the need for heavy guard supervision.[11]

In March 1912, the BPI announced plans to tear down the women's quarters and build a new two-story cell house of reinforced concrete for women prisoners. By relying heavily on the use of concrete, the BPI made it possible to employ more workhouse labor than skilled union labor on the construction project. In an L-shaped design, the new building would feature fifteen cells on each floor, with shower baths, exercise corridors, matrons' industrial rooms, enlarged laundry facilities, bathrooms, rooms for matrons, and clothes rooms. The new, better-ventilated building included a solitary confinement room in the attic. The BPI's construction plans, near completion by the end of the year, also included an office building, a section of concrete fence, and a beautified quadrangle for recreational purposes, adorned with shrubbery, flowers, and grass. Thanks to recent mechanization in the quarry, a miniature railroad and machinery were now used to haul rock to the top of the bluff. The mechanization drastically lowered the number of mules used in the quarry. About thirty mules that used to pull wagonloads of rock to the top were no longer needed. The prisoners dubbed the railroad "the BPI."[12]

Despite Superintendent White's good intentions, the release of the June grand jury's report at the beginning of October 1912, and a newspaper exposé two weeks later, revealed a continuing pattern of corruption and abusive treatment of prisoners. The criticisms and recommendations in the report echoed those voiced by the Civic League, grand jurors, and prisoners in the past. In particular, the grand jury criticized the practice of allowing payments to the superintendent for the release of prisoners. The long-standing practice depended entirely on the honesty of superintendents and guards. With no way to keep tabs on the practice, the grand jury recommended the adoption of a regulation to require all such payments to go into the city treasury through the comptroller's office. The jury also urged abolition of the private workhouse store, now run by Superintendent White and two of his guards, each of whom was paid $7.50 each month from city funds to run it. The store sold tobacco, pies, candy, writing materials, socks, and other items to prisoners. The jury, besides praising the work farm initiative on Chesley Island that employed about thirty men from the workhouse, endorsed pending legislation in the municipal assembly for the creation of a parole and probation board in the police courts to help prevent workhouse overcrowding. The city council, too, appointed an investigative committee, headed by John S. Leahy, who made clear the city's obligation to ensure humane treatment of prisoners in the workhouse, which he called a "rat trap" and "pest-hole."[13]

In White's initial dismissal of the grand jury report, he insisted that the grand jury never bothered to visit the workhouse, either collectively or individually. Stung by the criticisms, he charged that the report was based on nothing more than hearsay contained in a letter from the Civic League's Roger N. Baldwin. Soon afterward, White retracted his statement after he learned that the entire grand jury, along with the assistant circuit attorney, had visited the workhouse on a day when he was absent. White emphasized that the food was as good as the city's appropriation allowed without hiring a trained cook or two. The private store, he insisted, did not make a profit. He claimed it was conducted merely for the convenience of the prisoners. According to him, guards said the store netted less than fifteen dollars per month.[14]

On the heels of the grand jury report, a major newspaper investigation unleashed turmoil in the workhouse and led to Superintendent White's stunning, abrupt resignation. Using marked money and taking into its confidence Mayor Kreismann, comptroller B. J. Taussig, and city counselor Lambert E. Walther, the *St. Louis Star* management informed circuit judge William B. Kinsey that several parties expected to profit from the upcoming release of Louis W. Bernard from the workhouse. Bernard was serving a one-year sentence for burglary and grand larceny. The newspaper, using a former railroad detective posing as George Yates, Bernard's uncle, was conducting an undercover investigation into corruption involving the paroling of prisoners at the workhouse. Bernard, a mere instrument in the investigation, knew nothing about what was going on.

Judge Kinsey was made aware in advance that police judge Frank M. Slater, a Republican city committeeman, was the stakeholder in the scheme. Slater was holding $150 in marked money. The money was to be paid to

Charles Kallman, chief clerk in the city's lighting department, who told the undercover detective he could arrange parole for Bernard through Slater. M. Louis Kunifsky, a clothing dealer on South Broadway, along with a former workhouse prisoner and a guard who arranged for Superintendent White to sign Bernard's release, were expecting a cut of the money. By the time White brought Bernard to court on the morning of October 17, the arrangements were in place. All that remained was for Judge Kinsey to give the circuit court's approval for the release. As White sat in the courtroom with Bernard, whose case was first on Kinsey's docket that morning, he was unaware that corrupt shenanigans surrounding the case were about to be exposed.[15]

In the courtroom, Yates laid out the facts of the case, explaining the circuitous route that had led him to the principals involved. A former workhouse prisoner ("Burke") had assured Yates he could introduce him to someone who could secure White's signature to authorize Bernard's release: "He [Kunifsky] has done it many times while I was doing a bit at the Workhouse, and in fact I think he has as much authority over the works as Cal."[16] Kunifsky was cautious at first, but after Burke uttered a secret code, Kunifsky smiled knowingly and took Yates to the workhouse grounds.

A mysterious but familiar face at the institution and an acquaintance of White's for several years, Kunifsky escorted Yates directly to the superintendent's office without interference. Kunifsky, who earlier had arranged parole deals for other prisoners, knew his way around and exercised a certain degree of authority, even taking a few workhouse tools with him as he left. He and White belonged to the same fraternal order. In 1909, when White was on the police force, Kunifsky had been arrested for attempting to bribe witnesses not to show up in court to testify for the state in a larceny case, but prosecutors dropped the charges when he agreed to cooperate.

After a few minutes of conversation in White's office at the workhouse, White signed Bernard's release form without asking further questions. He left blank the space on the form that called for the superintendent to comment on the prisoner's conduct. Next, Burke took Yates to meet Kallman in a prearranged meeting at the American Hotel. Kallman promised to arrange for the court's approval in exchange for $150. After Yates balked at paying the amount outright, it was suggested that he leave it with Judge Slater for safekeeping. When Yates afterward told Slater he intended to secure the release of Bernard, the judge replied, "I remember him, that cripple boy who served in the eleventh precinct."[17]

The *Star* published key documents in the case, including Superintendent White's signed authorization of Bernard's release. Slater claimed he never counted the money that was left with him, but the newspaper published a note from him to Kallman: "Friend Charlie—I hold $150 which is to be delivered to you when you fulfill your part of contract with Geo Yates." According to Yates, Kallman told him the money would have to pass through Slater, who remembered Bernard from three years earlier when he had served as an election judge in Slater's Eleventh Ward. Slater proclaimed his innocence in the matter, insisting that he was a mere stakeholder who knew nothing about the corrupt intent of the money he was holding. According to him, two men came to see him two weeks earlier. One of them was Yates. "The other I don't know," he said, "but I suppose it was this Kallman." Slater emphasized that he was extremely busy at the time Yates and Kallman left the money with him, and he assumed they merely wanted him to hold it until they could arrange for Bernard's release. In no way, he maintained, did he know the money was to be used for bribery.[18]

A political firestorm broke out following the revelations of corruption. Mayor Kreismann summoned Superintendent White to a closed-door meeting with comptroller Taussig and city counselor Walther, who had drawn up a lengthy, formal report with fourteen specific charges against White. The document was signed by Earl J. Howes, a sleuth in the comptroller's office who cooperated with the *Star* investigation. Confronted with possible prosecution, White resigned. After Taussig and Walther left the meeting, Captain Frank J. Primavesi, an employee in the city auditor's office, was summoned to join White and the mayor. After a one-hour meeting, the mayor's office announced White's resignation and the temporary appointment of Primavesi to replace him. At Mayor Kreismann's request, Chief William Young dispatched a heavy police guard to the workhouse to quell possible disturbances by angry prisoners. There were no outbreaks of protest or attempted escapes, only a few catcalls.

White, after his resignation was announced, returned to the workhouse to assist Primavesi in the transition and to clean out his personal items, including a revolver and shotgun. The presence of special investigator Howes, who had come there to look for further evidence while the trail was hot, infuriated White. Detectives warned Howes to leave for the time being. White, angrily complaining of being "double-crossed," made threats against Howes. Purportedly, others at the workhouse did, too.[19]

Mayor Kreismann publicly proclaimed White's innocence of graft charges. He praised his character and record as superintendent of the workhouse, but he emphasized that White was too kindhearted to control his guards. To calm public criticism, city counselor Walther stated that neither White, Judge Slater, nor any court officer was guilty of graft. He complained that White was the victim of a "pure frame-up." The *Star* agreed that White was innocent of graft but called him "grossly negligent in the matter of watching his subordinates, which was one of his most important functions." Circuit judge Kinsey, too, absolved Slater and the courts of any blame in the corruption, which he claimed extended no further than Kallman, Kunifsky, and John Cope, another lighting department employee. Cope testified that he expected $25 of the $150 for his role as a go-between in the scheme.

At the behest of the Board of Public Improvements, Arthur I. Jacobs, supervisor of Cope and Kallman in the lighting department, demanded their resignations. White admitted he had lost control over his workhouse employees. He acknowledged that when he signed Bernard's release, he purposely left blank the portion referring to the prisoner's conduct at the workhouse. Bernard's record at the workhouse was questionable, but as White explained, "I saw the application lying on my desk, and, being in a hurry, just signed my name at the bottom. I had no other interest in doing that than to give a human being another chance in this world, but it seems I made a costly omission."[20]

Mayor Kreismann was especially upset that White had allowed Kunifsky free and easy access to the workhouse, where Kunifsky even gave orders at times and performed services for prisoners as he routinely mingled among them. At the time of the Bernard scandal, White knew that Kunifsky had previously accepted a payment of twenty-five dollars from an uncle of Louis Pappas in Detroit to work for his nephew's parole and release from the workhouse. When Kunifsky failed to deliver, White even went so far as to discourage Pappas from trying to get his money back. After Kunifsky told White he had already given ten dollars to a lawyer and ten dollars to a workhouse guard, White tried to persuade Pappas to settle for a five-dollar repayment from Kunifsky. The superintendent concealed all this information from the mayor at the time. Comptroller Taussig had warned White from the beginning of his superintendency about feeding privately owned hogs with food from the workhouse kitchen, but White did not put an end to the practice, which also came to light again in the *Star*'s investigation. "My big-heartedness got me into this trouble, and I am afraid some of my friends have taken advantage of me," White said when he resigned.[21]

At the time of White's resignation, he bitterly pointed out that he gave up a good career on the police force to take the position offered him at the workhouse. He asked to be reinstated as a patrol officer. About a month later, Mayor Kreismann publicly endorsed his reinstatement: "I stated at the time Mr. White resigned that his only offense, in my opinion, was that he had allowed his organization down there to get away from him. To pursue this matter further would be persecution, I think, and therefore I will advise the [police] board if I attend its session Friday, to appoint Mr. White to the force." At a special meeting of the Board of Police Commissioners at the beginning of December 1912, White was reappointed as a patrol officer.[22]

An editorial in the *St. Louis Republic* called for a deeper probe into the workhouse to determine how far the graft extended. Pointing out that former mayor Rolla Wells had cleaned up city hall considerably in his campaign against the old Ziegenhein machine, the *Republic* complained that vestiges of the machine nonetheless lingered. The scandal revealed that "a set of unclean Republican politicians has been nesting about that institution, fleecing the poor and the unfortunate and corrupting Workhouse and court officials." The newspaper praised Republican Mayor Kreismann's top appointments but condemned the petty Republicans in machine politics who were schooled in "Ziegenheinism." "The small Republican politician in St. Louis is today what he was twelve years ago," ran the editorial. "He looks at city institutions and city business as the pirate looked at the treasure ships from the Spanish Main." In a reference to Calvin White, the newspaper added, "A pitiful part of all this is the corruption of genial, good-natured men, who are not thieves themselves, but who become so accustomed to evidences of graft that they accept it as inevitable and wink at crooked practices to oblige friends."[23]

The *Star's* exposé reached beyond the Bernard case in its revelations of graft and mismanagement, echoing the political analysis provided in the *Republic*'s editorial. The *Star* blasted the workhouse as "a graft farm cultivated by henchmen of the Republican city machine for the production of dollars and burglar votes." Pledging its support for Superintendent Primavesi's mission to clean up the workhouse, the *Star* published numerous stories exposing lax discipline, mismanagement, and corruption on the part of guards in the handling of prisoners and the granting of paroles. David Van Norden, a forger and frequent inmate on a government pension, who kept a tidy sum of money on file at the workhouse, was among those treated like royalty by the guards. On one occasion, he went saloon hopping with guard Bert Rockwell. Another guard, who spotted them, informed Superintendent White, who sent the assistant superintendent to retrieve them. It was well after dark when they returned to the workhouse, where Van Norden was allowed to stay up until midnight talking to guard Leopold Matt. White fired Rockwell but later reinstated him after Rockwell's tearful plea that he had a family to support.

On another outing outside the workhouse, Van Norden, two guards, and Ida Wagner, the workhouse matron, enjoyed a chicken dinner and liquor on the prisoner's dime. Money made special privileges possible, as Van Norden explained: "I went outside with the guards whenever I wanted to and bought whatever I liked to eat and drink. I always set 'em up to the guards that went with me, and they were never sore when they were assigned to this duty, I assure you . . . I made it a rule to treat the guards handsomely and they never assaulted me or abused me in any way."[24]

Fred B. Miller, workhouse clerk, resigned when the *Star* revealed that he took a taxi ride with inmate Moe Solomon (alias Morris Cohen) so that Solomon, a con man flush with cash, could visit his attorney. Solomon, arrested for grand larceny, was allowed by the circuit attorney's office to plead guilty to petit larceny. Instead of a two-year stretch in the penitentiary, he was sentenced to six months in the workhouse. Louis Kunifsky, the mysterious haberdasher in the Bernard release scandal, happened to be at the workhouse on the day of Solomon's arrival. Later, Kunifsky and guard Hurley enjoyed a steak dinner and popped open a bottle of champagne in the guards' dining room to toast the arrival of a prisoner with money. Never mind that wine and liquor were banned in the workhouse. After serving Hurley and Kunifsky, the head waiter left the dining room to allow them privacy. After the dinner meeting, Hurley let the waiter drink what was left in the bottle of champagne. Hurley arranged that Solomon not be sent to the rock pile. Instead, Solomon donned a waiter's uniform to assume the lightest duties and best sinecure in the workhouse.

One morning, Solomon persuaded clerk Miller to take him downtown on a streetcar to see his lawyer and to check on a matter at the Regent Hotel. First, they stopped for a few drinks at the Planters' Hotel bar. Afterward, Solomon arranged for a taxi to take them to the lawyer's office for a consultation. Then they hailed another taxi to the Regent Hotel, where they dined, before taking yet another taxi to Broadway. They returned to the workhouse on a streetcar. Miller confirmed the facts surrounding the outing, emphasizing that Solomon paid for everything. According to Miller, they returned to the workhouse before four p.m., but none of the other prisoners saw Solomon until much later that night. Miller denied they were drunk, but Solomon admitted that he hid somewhere to recover from overindulgence in alcohol. By his estimate, the outing cost him about sixty dollars, but the joyride cost Miller his job when Primavesi took charge at the workhouse.[25]

For prisoners with money on file, the private store operated in the workhouse by White and two of his guards allowed the privileged inmates to eat better than the rest. The infamous concoction of "sweet water" and a soup that contained mostly water and about seven beans remained as longtime mainstays of the workhouse diet. "Cabbage soup" was served two weeks in a row in the summer of 1912. At times, prisoners did "walk arounds" to protest the boiled hominy that was edible only to the privately owned hogs that were fattened from the workhouse kitchen. On evenings of such protests, prisoners took only a hunk of bread and returned to their cells without sitting at the dining room table. Cold mush, considered only slightly less revolting than boiled hominy, was often served too, but very little meat was part of the diet. On Wednesdays or Thursdays, prisoners received no meat at all. Typically, only two meals were served on Saturdays and Sundays, but prisoners did get stew with meat in it on Saturdays, and they enjoyed frankfurters on Sunday afternoons. The workhouse allowed family and friends of prisoners to bring in baskets of food, but the practice was an open invitation to smuggle drugs and weapons into the institution.

Of course, all kinds of delicious pies were for sale in the workhouse store. The workhouse bought them for seven cents each and sold each pie for twenty cents, or by the slice at five cents. The store turned a profit of thirteen cents a pie. At times, the demand for pies was so great that even Superintendent White helped the two guards and the trusties to deliver them to the mess hall tables as fast as they could. Sales shot up from fifty or sixty pies a day from Monday through Friday to about two hundred on Saturdays and Sundays. The less the quantity and the poorer the quality of food served, the greater the profit for the privately run store, a longtime instrument of corruption to fleece prisoners.[26]

The *Star*'s exposé also brought attention to the cruelty of guards while singling out Calvin White's wife and guard John J. McGrath as "Good Samaritans" who opposed such cruel treatment of inmates. During one of many beatings Louis Bernard suffered in the workhouse, guards who did not like his resentful attitude beat him so badly that they broke his artificial leg of papier-mâché.[27] In another case, prisoner Samuel D. Trask, a young clerk whose physical condition was weakened by alcohol and drug abuse, was beaten so badly that he required treatment in the city hospital. Afterward, he ended up in the city sanitarium, where official records noted, "Samuel D. Trask, age 23, threatened with dementia, has hallucinations that he is being persecuted by Workhouse guards."[28]

Leopold Matt, a sixty-five-year-old guard with more than seventeen years of employment at the workhouse, took offense when Trask did not hear a command from him clearly and respectfully replied, "Sir?" According to Superintendent White and the guard's version of what happened next, Matt ordered Trask out of his cell. Matt claimed that when Trask resisted being locked in solitary confinement on bread and water, fellow guards Tony Wotowa and "Big George" came to assist Matt in removing Trask to the bullring. According to this version, Trask continued to resist the three guards, each of whom carried a heavy iron-tipped pick handle attached to his wrist. Matt dealt the first crashing blow to Trask's temple, knocking off his spectacles and damaging a nerve near the ear. Trask suffered a severe injury to his right hip when the guards kicked him down the steps and beat him badly on the shoulders and back. Then the guards dragged him to the bullring and left him on the floor to await the dawn. To keep him from falling asleep, Matt routinely strolled past the dungeon and shouted at him. In the morning, the guards took Trask, beaten, sleep-deprived, and without a bite of breakfast, to the quarry, where he was put to work pushing a stone cart. Trask slipped and fell under the cart, suffering painful injuries when the cart ran over his right foot.[29]

Trask was hurriedly taken to the city hospital, where authorities merely noted without explanation the other injuries on his body. They did not inform his parents or anyone else. His mother, Mary, who regularly took food baskets to him in the workhouse, found out about his hospitalization when she ran into a workhouse guard on the street. The parents were furious at his treatment in the workhouse. The guards' blows left indelible marks and inflicted permanent damage on their son. His father, Samuel A. Trask, was a retired army sergeant employed by the United States Post Office. Walter

Trask, a brother who was a corporal at the Jefferson barracks, confronted workhouse officials, inviting any guard or other workhouse officer to step outside the prison walls to fight him. The family decided to drop the matter at the time, but when they read about their son in the *Star,* they were heartened that public attention was now brought to bear on his case. In the meantime, he was transferred from the city hospital to the city sanitarium. His father, upset by unsavory public remarks about his son attributed to Superintendent White, wrote a letter to the *Star* to thank the newspaper for its efforts: "Our son received a brutal and inhuman beating at the hands of the workhouse guards last July, without cause, from which he is now in the Sanitarium, most likely injured for life. To escape publicity, we took no steps in the matter, thinking it would do no good. However, we have been legally advised we should receive redress."[30]

Between the release of the Civic League's report in September 1911 and the resignation of Superintendent White as a result of the *Star*'s exposé in October 1912, only halting steps were taken to fix what ailed the workhouse. The Civic League emphasized that the problems were systemic, but city officials had few answers. In the *Star,* writer Harry L. Wells called for an entire reorganization of the workhouse along reformatory lines. Lending his voice to those who supported a rehabilitative mission for the institution, he pleaded, "In the name of humanity, in the name of common decency, in the name of their own duty to civilization, St. Louis should do something practical to create decent conditions at the City Workhouse." He reminded readers that the workhouse was not a penitentiary meant to house and punish hardened criminals.

None of Wells's proposed reforms were startlingly new. They followed along the lines of the Civic League's recommendations. But the revelations of the *Star*'s investigation lent a sense of urgency to calls to overhaul the workhouse based on progressive ideas popular among criminal justice experts at the time. Describing the workhouse as a "festering sore," Wells urged residents of St. Louis to pressure the municipal assembly and the mayor's office to do better. "The institution has been bad, awful, and the administration is responsible for its neglect in the matter," he wrote. "This neglect can only be atoned for by better management with what there is available now and an effort to bring about the needed reorganization. Economy at the expense of humanity can never reflect credit on any official or any administration."[31]

9

A THEOSOPHIST AND SOLDIER OF FORTUNE IN CHARGE

Mayor Kreismann's naming of Captain Frank J. Primavesi as acting superintendent to replace White at the workhouse required confirmation by the city council. By forcing White's resignation rather than firing him on October 17, 1912, Kreismann retained the power to appoint his successor. If he had fired White, the sole power to name his replacement would have shifted to the city council. The mayor's appointment of a Bull Moose (Progressive Party) Republican to clean up the workhouse ran into immediate trouble. The council, with several members absent, voted against Primavesi's confirmation by a vote of 7 to 1. The opposition came from old-line fellow Republicans who resented Primavesi's support for Theodore Roosevelt in the national presidential campaign. The candidacy of Roosevelt at the top of the Progressive Party's ticket split the Republican Party, enabling Democratic governor Woodrow Wilson to defeat incumbent Republican president William Howard Taft in the election shortly after Primavesi's appointment. Council member Lorenz E. Lehmberg complained about the acting superintendent's immediate firing of clerk Fred B. Miller and two workhouse guards who were Republican committeemen: "Capt. Primavesi has discharged three good Republicans from his force and has substituted a trio of Democrats."[1]

The *Star,* one of Primavesi's staunchest supporters, attacked the council's opposition to his appointment. On its editorial page, the newspaper suggested that patronage politics was at the root of the Republican opposition. It praised Primavesi's honesty and commitment to cleaning up the workhouse and booting out the grafters and crooks who feasted on its operations. The editorial called on the mayor to reappoint Primavesi in the name of public service and efficiency: "It is a clean, sane and well-made appointment. If the Council is determined to favor some political crook for the job of superintendent of the workhouse, at least we will put the members on record definitely to that effect."[2]

On October 26, Mayor Kreismann, indignant and perplexed by the council's rejection of Primavesi, announced he would reappoint him unless the seven members who voted against the appointment publicly explained their objections satisfactorily. Primavesi promised to vote straight Republican in all cases except the presidential ticket. He denied that politics had anything to do with his firing of workhouse guards. Procedurally, before Kreismann could reappoint Primavesi he first had to make a dummy appointment to fill the position. In behind-the-scenes maneuvering, the mayor named Roger N. Baldwin, secretary of the Civic League as the stand-in. In keeping with the political arrangement, Baldwin, a reformer and former probation officer, agreed to resign if the council approved his nomination. In December, after seven weeks of political deadlock and after the council voted down Baldwin's nomination, Primavesi was confirmed as superintendent of the workhouse by a vote of 9 to 3. Later, he explained that some who opposed him did so because he was a theosophist. "The average citizen didn't know what it meant. Theosophist ends with an 'ist,' like anarchist, and probably some suspected me as an anarchist."[3]

For the next five years, Primavesi, a city deputy auditor since 1909, held the keys to the workhouse. Prior to settling down as a clerk in St. Louis, he had been a soldier of fortune in South Africa's Boer War, and he recruited volunteers in Texas and Oklahoma for the Thirty-Third Infantry as part of U.S. occupation forces in the Spanish–American War. He fought in Cuba and the Philippines as a volunteer and as first sergeant in Company D of the First Texas Cavalry. At war's end, he volunteered for police duty in occupied Havana under General Leonard Wood's command. At that time, his home was Gainesville, Texas. According to the *St. Louis Globe-Democrat,* he also once served as a deputy sheriff in East Texas and worked as a cowboy in West Texas. In St. Louis, he was the captain of a local National Guard machine gun unit.[4]

Born in Prussia on June 24, 1866, Primavesi immigrated to the United States around 1892. At six feet, four inches tall, he brought to the superintendency of the St. Louis Workhouse an imposing stature and a curious amalgam of military authoritarianism and humanitarianism steeped in theosophy and the writings of its Russian founder, Helena Blavatsky. Around 1909, his intellectual quest for answers to the questions of poverty, inequality, and unfairness in the human condition led him to attend a lecture at the St. Louis Theosophical Society. "I was unable to explain the universe to myself. The inequalities, the apparent injustices of existence worried me," he explained. "I could not understand why one man should be happy and another miserable; one person prosperous and another pauperized; one in perfect health and another diseased or deformed, suffering; one an upright and useful citizen and another a criminal, a crook, a ne'er-do-well. I could not reconcile these differences, and consequently human life seemed rather a sorry mess to me."

Primavesi was drawn to the writings of Blavatsky and of Annie Wood Besant, a British social reformer, women's rights advocate, and critic of British colonial rule in India. Besant became Blavatsky's spiritual heir and the international president of the Theosophical Society in 1907. The introduction to theosophy when Primavesi was in his early forties produced major changes in his life. "The bitterness I had felt because of the apparent injustices and cruelties of the world," he recalled, "I felt no longer." He became president of the St. Louis Theosophical Society, gave up meat, tobacco, and alcohol, condemned capital punishment and the killing of animals, and embraced reincarnation. When it came to criminals, he emphasized that they were not immoral but "unmoral." "They are undeveloped souls," he explained. "They are expiating in the present incarnation their errors in previous incarnations." He believed that Jesus Christ as a perfected spirit inhabited the body of Jiddu Krishnamurti, a messianic Indian figure adopted as a child and groomed by Besant to be the "World Teacher." In time, according to Primavesi, inequalities and injustices would be erased as all human souls evolved toward perfection.[5]

At a meeting of the local Theosophical Society, Primavesi met Helen Gardner of Brooklyn, New York. Soon after his appointment to run the workhouse was confirmed, they married. He was forty-five years old and she was twenty-eight. A business manager and clerk in a St. Louis chemical company, she was the first wife of a workhouse superintendent to decline to serve as the institution's matron on the city's payroll. Instead, Helen became the librarian of the local Theosophical Society and organized high-profile opposition to executions. She, too, embraced reincarnation and gave public lectures under the auspices of the Order of the Star in the East, headed by

Krishnamurti. She opposed hangings and all forms of capital punishment on the grounds that ghosts of the executed would return to earth to commit murders and other crimes. As she explained, "The state of emotion in which a person leaves this earth determines his state of mind in the astral plane."[6]

At the time of Captain Primavesi's confirmation as superintendent of the workhouse, the city council sent the city attorney an investigative report on workhouse conditions, conducted weeks earlier. The council called on the attorney to draw up resolutions with several recommended reforms. Among them was a call to abolish the commissary that operated for private profit in the workhouse. The council insisted that the profit be used, instead, to benefit prisoners by providing stationery, stamps, transportation upon release, and other services. To hire a higher quality of workhouse personnel, the council endorsed raising the superintendent's salary to $150 per month, changing guards' salaries from $50 per month with board to $65 per month without board, creating a bookkeeper position at a salary of $75 monthly and an assistant superintendent position at $100 a month, and hiring a cook. Finally, the council recommended that the payment of all fines be shifted entirely away from the workhouse and to the city treasurer's office.[7]

The city council also adopted Judge Karl Kimmel's bill to create a workhouse parole board composed of three police court judges, the mayor's secretary, and the workhouse superintendent. Several women's clubs praised the council's action, but they opposed including the workhouse superintendent on the board. Instead, they called for the inclusion of a citizen unconnected in any way to the institution. The Tuesday Literary Club, composed of three hundred philanthropic women, supported a probation system and parole board but had pushed to amend Judge Kimmel's bill by making the inclusion of a woman probation officer mandatory. Earlier, the Tuesday Club had put forth its own bill in the municipal assembly. "Had such a bill been in operation," insisted Mrs. W. H. Utter, "the trouble at the Workhouse recently brought to public attention could not have occurred . . . Under the old system, these men spend long periods in the Workhouse, come out with no money, no job, and a grudge against society, while during their incarceration their families were subjects of charity. This is the real substance of the effort to establish the parole system."[8]

The Tuesday Club did not get a woman appointed to the parole board, but it received assurances that a woman would be included among the probation officers. After competitive exams in February 1913, the newly created Board of Parole and Probation announced the appointment of chief probation officer John Stradal, a fifty-year-old accountant. His deputy officers were Jessie Lansing Moller, B. Howard Clark, and Adalbert H. Almstedt. Moller, a thirty-two-year-old businesswoman and vice president of the Business Women's Equal Suffrage League, had extensive experience as a social and charity worker. She was chosen from among eleven West End club women who took the exams. Clark, age thirty-two, had three years of experience as a probation officer in the juvenile court, and Almstedt had formerly headed a charity hospital. Those among the thirty-nine applicants who were not selected were put on a waiting list of potential appointees. The duties of the new board, effective March 1, 1913, were confined to supervision of police court cases.[9]

As soon as Primavesi took the reins at the workhouse, he promised a set of new practices and reforms. First, he announced there would be improvements in the quantity and quality of food, with an emphasis on nutrition rather than on what the workhouse hogs liked to eat. The long-standing, surreptitious practice of feeding the privately owned hogs with workhouse leftovers at taxpayers' expense would end, he assured. Working closely with investigator Earl J. Howes of the auditor's office, he examined the caloric content of the workhouse diet, paying attention to how much food was necessary for the kind of labor performed. Although a vegetarian, Primavesi promised to increase the amount of meat in the diet of prisoners and to serve three rather than two meals a day on Saturdays and Sundays.

Effective February 1, 1913, the bill of fare for prisoners included a more varied diet, with three meals a day, seven days a week, and meat offered at two meals each day. The changes, which cost the city $600 a month in added expense, included a ban on bringing food, tobacco, and reading materials into the workhouse. The ban, which came after Primavesi found drugs concealed in bundles of newspapers, food baskets, and tobacco cans and sacks, was part of a crackdown on smuggling. "We have decided to treat all prisoners alike, and to permit no one to receive favors from outsiders," Primavesi announced. "To make up for this we will improve the quality and increase the quantity of the food served at the workhouse tables."[10]

Although the superintendent did not end the private store inside the workhouse, he did announce that the commissary would no longer sell pies, which he regarded as luxuries that benefited inmates with money and bred resentment among others. Furthermore, he refused to take personal profit from the store. The profits would go into a special fund to benefit prisoners in some way. Favoring a more humane overall approach but one with tighter, military-style discipline, he promised an end to the corruption and brutal abuse of prisoners by workhouse guards.[11]

Less than a week after Primavesi took over, a reporter from the *Star* accompanied him on a tour of the workhouse. The *Star,* his strongest advocate, praised the changes he had implemented in such a short time. The sanitary conditions in the kitchen were much improved. So was the coffee, which now was rich in color and tasted like real coffee rather than chicory-flavored water. Cook Robert J. Lark noted that he pulverized the coarse coffee, stopped adding chicory, and included a bit of essence in it. Better-tasting coffee for the same amount of coffee used. At meals, prisoners previously had received a large, thick hunk of bread, about one-seventh of a loaf. Some prisoners wanted but were denied more bread while others who were not hungry left theirs as refuse on the table. After the installation of a bread slicer in the kitchen, Primavesi's workhouse provided three thin slices to each prisoner to start each meal but allowed an unlimited number to prisoners if they later requested more. As happily noted by the *Star* reporter, the innovation meant more food at less cost to taxpayers with less food left on dining hall tables for "the Berkshire and Poland China hogs on Arsenal Island."[12]

Primavesi expressed support for other improvements, including the construction of a concrete wall around the workhouse to replace a board fence after four prisoners escaped at Thanksgiving. His call for higher salaries for all workhouse personnel formed a foundation for the city council investigative committee's report on the workhouse. At the time, guards were paid only fifty dollars a month with room and board at the workhouse. They ate well, but their sleeping quarters were poorly furnished. Only seven beds existed for twenty-seven guards, most of whom lived with their families on the outside. Four foremen, one of whom acted as the assistant superintendent, collected sixty dollars a month. Primavesi recommended the creation of a new position for the assistant superintendent at a good salary. A chief clerk drew a monthly salary of seventy-five dollars. Primavesi told the *Star* reporter that he would use the bullring more judiciously to punish prisoners on bread and water in solitary confinement. When two Black women inmates were seen passing notes to workers constructing a new concrete building, he ordered each of them into the dungeon for an hour and a half.[13]

Contingency funds were available in the mayor's office to help provide selected prisoners with a decent set of clothes when they left the workhouse, but Primavesi was the first to tap into the funds on behalf of a prisoner at the end of his sentence. When prisoner George H. Higgins, age forty-five, walked out of the workhouse on January 11, 1913, he sported a new shirt, work suit, hat, and pair of shoes. During his six-month sentence on a larceny charge, he was assigned as a helper in the blacksmith's shop, where many of the city's teams of mules and horses were shod. A couple of days before the end of his sentence, he had told Superintendent Primavesi that because of his ragged clothes, he feared employers would not hire him. Desperate circumstances, he noted, would likely compel him to steal again. Primavesi, who requested and secured approval to use money from the mayor's contingency fund to buy clothing at wholesale, allowed Higgins to work and reside in the workhouse past his sentence at wages of fifty cents a day. Other selected prisoners soon followed suit. Fifteen days after Higgins finished his sentence, he left the workhouse in new clothes after earning enough to buy them at wholesale cost. The shoes, made in the workhouse, were a gift, a reward for good behavior. Upon release from the workhouse, Higgins went straight to the mayor's office to thank him.[14]

In the quarry, Primavesi continued steps to modernize operations and increase output. Recent efforts included the installation of a number 4 crusher at the eastern end of the quarry floor. The bed of the quarry was about five feet below the river. Although water from the river did not enter the quarry from the east, it did sometimes seep into the quarry from other directions. Formerly, mule-driven carts hauled rock up the incline to the top of the quarry, but the new crusher was located close to a bucket conveyor system that transported crushed rock to the top of the wall. From there, the rock was taken to a screen-and-bin house, where a rotary screen separated it into bins according to the size of the rocks. The bins had chutes for loading crushed rock onto wagons and railroad cars.

Ten steel push cars operated on a portable track at the bottom of the quarry, where a racial division of labor existed. White prisoners loaded rock into these cars and operated three steam drills, whereas Black prisoners did the hand drilling and most of the sledgehammer work. The prisoners were allowed to quit working for the day after they reached a specified quota. Five men pushed the steel cars, which were only about one-third full, up an incline to the crusher. Plans were under way during Primavesi's tenure to install a motorized cable system to pull fully loaded cars up to the crusher.[15]

Soon after Republican mayor Henry W. Kiel was elected in April 1913, he received his first complaint about Primavesi's workhouse. Clarence C. Mason, an inmate whose application for parole was opposed by Primavesi, arranged for a "friendly guard" to smuggle a letter to his attorney, Caroline Thummel, complaining of several instances of cruelty and lack of medical attention in the workhouse. On Mason's behalf, Thummel sent a letter to Mayor Kiel, urging an investigation. Mason, who previously served two years in penitentiaries, was in the workhouse on a one-year sentence for passing bad checks. According to Primavesi, he was also a morphine addict. Kiel appointed an investigative committee of three members: former circuit judge Moses N. Sale, a Democrat; H. W. Blodgett, former Republican member of the Board of Elections Commission; and Sarah Spraggon, president of the National Women's Trade Union League of St. Louis. Spraggon, a leading suffragist, was also a labor organizer for Boot and Shoe Workers' Union Local 338 in St. Louis.[16]

The committee corroborated a few of Mason's allegations but dismissed most of them due to inconclusive evidence. Judge Sale, who dismissed the proceedings as "hokus pokus," concluded that Mason's accusations were entirely groundless. Spraggon, who gave more credence to Mason's claims and favored a more sweeping investigation of the workhouse, publicly dissented from the committee's majority opinion after hearing the testimony of prisoners who complained of cruelty and neglect. In the committee hearing room, she astonished those in attendance by putting Superintendent Primavesi on the stand and grilling him. Mayor Kiel expected a unanimous report, but Spraggon objected to the limited scope of the investigation. "I am very much dissatisfied at the outcome of the whole matter," she complained. "Common sense, not law books, should be used in investigations . . . As to making a unanimous report, I don't see how such can be done. My opinion of the Workhouse charges differ[s] entirely with other members of the committee. I will make my report to the Mayor next week."[17]

The committee's hearings did corroborate Mason's charges that guards beat Fred Klefisch and Harry Parks severely for trying to escape. Mayor Kiel ordered Primavesi to fire chief guard David Hurley and guard Edward Harsch for beating the prisoners before locking them in the dungeon for more than forty-eight hours. Spraggon urged the firing of other guards, too. In deference to her concerns, Kiel ordered the superintendent to draw up a standard code of rules and regulations governing the conduct of workhouse guards. The code was intended to protect prisoners from abusive treatment. At the mayor's request, a bill was introduced in the municipal assembly to create a position for a resident physician at the workhouse. At the time, the law required merely that a physician visit the workhouse for an hour each day, except on Sundays, at a rate of fifty dollars.[18]

At the hearings, Superintendent Primavesi suggested he might have to put Mason in the dungeon for protection from workhouse inmates who were angered by his role as a "snitch." When Spraggon made it clear it was his duty to protect Mason, Primavesi replied, "I'll do the best I can, but I will not be responsible for that man."[19] In response, Judge Sale rose from his seat and instructed the superintendent to assign extra guards if he felt Mason's life was in danger. A couple of weeks later, Primavesi reported that he had learned of at least two plots among prisoners to take Mason's life. According to Primavesi, he then put Mason in the dungeon for his own protection. The superintendent dismissed a recent allegation by Mason that the guards who were fired after the investigative committee hearings were allowed to come back to his cell afterward to try to persuade him to say he lied to investigators. Primavesi announced his intention, with the mayor's approval, to visit the criminal court to ask Judge Ben F. Clark for an alteration in Mason's sentence, allowing Mason's transfer to the city jail or the sanitarium to serve the rest of his time.

It soon became clear that Mason was in solitary confinement not for his protection but for sending a second letter to complain further about his treatment. Primavesi, determined to find out who smuggled the letter out of the workhouse for Mason, put him in the dungeon, promising to keep him there until he revealed the identity of the smuggler. The mayor backed Primavesi in his use of the dungeon to punish Mason for violating the rules. The law forbade keeping a prisoner in confinement for more than twenty-four hours, but the superintendent vowed to put Mason in the bullring for twenty-four consecutive hours every other day. "There is no doubt in my mind but that a guard did it," Primavesi told a reporter. "I am working on a theory that a guard who will smuggle anything out of here will also smuggle things in—drugs for instance. Some of the guards here are soreheads since I have compelled them to do their duty." When the superintendent did release Mason from the dungeon, he claimed he did so after Mason confessed that he had lied when he stated a guard was responsible for smuggling out his letters.[20]

In the immediate aftermath of the investigative committee hearings into Mason's complaints, a bill to abolish solitary confinement was introduced in the municipal assembly. The bill came from a perhaps surprising source: former workhouse superintendent Andrew Scully, now an elected member of the House of Delegates. Scully opposed the bullring on practical, not humanitarian, grounds. In short, he felt it was ineffective. Harry L. Wells, a writer for the *St. Louis Star,* acknowledged Scully's bill and added his own opposition to the dungeon on humanitarian grounds. Wells pointed out that officials and vengeful, callous guards were too wedded to traditions obsessed with inflicting physical punishment on inmates. The *Post-Dispatch* added its editorial support for using the workhouse to reform, not abuse, prisoners, and it reminded Primavesi that the public expected results from him along those lines. The newspaper urged Mayor Kiel and police court judges to keep a close watch on the workhouse lest flagrant abuses continue the way they had after previous investigations. Despite these reformist impulses, the dungeon continued to receive use. In 1914–1915, 251 workhouse prisoners were thrown into solitary confinement.[21]

To improve the quality of life in the workhouse, Superintendent Primavesi, Mayor Kiel, and park commissioner Dwight F. Davis came up with plans to add recreational activities. Prisoners were to build two playgrounds at the workhouse, one for men and the other for women. The playground, under the plan, would include benches, fountains, swings, flowers, and other beautification additions. Primavesi promised to organize baseball teams among the men and to lay out a baseball diamond. "We want to make these people more human," Davis explained. "They should have some form of recreation—something to take their minds from their work and the ever-present realization that they are temporarily denied their freedom. Flowers, trees, green grass and all will tend to soften them and to make upright men and women of these unfortunates."[22]

Primavesi undertook other initiatives to provide educational and cultural programs to prisoners. In late 1914, Professor Holmes Smith of the Art Department at Washington University gave an illustrated lecture in the workhouse chapel. His talk, "Famous Buildings of the World," incorporated the use of lantern slides to show pyramids, Gothic cathedrals, and other buildings. Prisoners enjoyed the talk so much that Primavesi arranged for a monthly lecture by other Washington University professors. He noted that inmates especially enjoyed the lantern slides.

At Primavesi's request, the St. Louis Board of Education loaned 125 textbooks to him for use in night classes at the workhouse, taught by eight volunteer public school teachers, three of whom were Black. Mrs. Atlanta E. Hecker, who formerly taught in the Industrial School, opened the school in the workhouse in the winter of 1915–1916. On a visit to the workhouse one evening in April 1916, Marguerite Martyn, an artist, graduate of Washington University's art school, and a special features writer on the staff of the *Post-Dispatch,* captured some of the poignant images of the voluntary night school classes for readers of the newspaper's Sunday edition. "You could have heard a pin drop when a teacher addressed herself to the whole school," Martyn wrote. She called attention to Charles Rogers, a fifty-five-year-old Black prisoner from a Georgia cotton plantation, who cried because he did not know how to write his name when the classes began. This was his first opportunity at even a rudimentary education. On the evening of Martyn's visit, he wrote his name and read a page from a reader after only five Friday nights of classes in the workhouse.[23]

In an editorial, the *Post-Dispatch* praised Martyn's article and the volunteer teachers but urged the city school system to include such classes and vocational training in the curriculum. Likewise, the Civic League urged the St. Louis Board of Education to operate the vocational school. Providing vocational training not only would reduce the cost of running the workhouse but also would give inmates a chance to make a living. The newspaper pointed out that the workhouse held many young prisoners who had broken parole or who lacked the skills to obtain gainful employment: "To teach these persons profitable trades would be a long step towards their complete reformation. They would learn habits of industry and they would get to feel the pride of ability to be of use to themselves and the community."[24]

Among criminal justice reformers, the concept of a municipal work farm was growing in popularity. In October 1915, Primavesi attended the American Prison Association's convention in Oakland, California, where he noted the rising tide of prison reform that put more emphasis on the reformatory, and less on the punitive, aspects of incarceration. While in California, he gave a speech to the Krotona Lodge of the Theosophical Society in Hollywood on October 19. Comparing prison populations in Japan and the United States, he pointed out that 40 percent of prisoners in the United States reverted to crime after their release but only 7 percent did so in Japan. Primavesi noted that an appointment to head a penal institution in Japan required a background of study in criminology and penology. In contrast, appointments to workhouses and prisons in the United States were determined by who could deliver the most votes and dole out the spoils of office. As a result, he pointed out, graft was at the core of the American system.

Primavesi provided the audience of theosophists with a critical view of police court justice, pointing out the unfairness of the entire system. Judges, at times in a hurry to finish their business for the day, listened only to the arresting police officer before they fined violators of city ordinances. Without money to pay the fine, poor people sentenced to the workhouse embarked on a downhill slide that forever condemned them to a life of poverty, misery, and hopelessness. In the case of a married man, a stint in the workhouse meant added suffering for his wife and children, who were left without resources to sustain them. Primavesi emphasized that in such cases, the city took the breadwinner out of the household and provided him with food and shelter but left the families to root, hog, or die.

In addition, a stigma followed prisoners after they were released. Their trail of shame branded them for life. Even those who did find employment were often hounded by police officers, causing them to be fired after the officers informed the employer that one of his employees was an ex-convict. This stigmatization of prisoners further strained scarce family resources. As Primavesi put it, "When the judge says, 'I send you to prison for one year,' he virtually says, 'I sentence your wife and children to starve, suffer and freeze for one year, while I put you in a comfortable place, into a warm cell where you can sleep comfortably, have plenty of clothes and plenty of good, plain food. Your wife and children must suffer for a year, because that is our system.'"

The absence of a reformatory mission at the St. Louis Workhouse meant that most prisoners left with a sense of bitterness and resentment. Given that the prison population included middle-class professionals and others unsuited for hard labor, Primavesi pointed out the absurdity of assigning them to the rock pile. "In this institution quarry work is the only occupation furnished," he said. "You can imagine how that tends to reform a man! There are, in this place, civil engineers, physicians, professional men of all kinds, even professors and preachers. When they go there they are given a pickaxe, a drill, or some other stone-breaking instrument. Imagine how such a man feels toward Society, and how much this sort of work benefits him after he gets out!"[25]

Primavesi endorsed a municipal farm like the ones recently put in place in Cleveland, in Kansas City at Leeds, and in several other cities. He urged the City of St. Louis to purchase a large two thousand–acre tract of land for the site where a farm would replace the dreary, antiquated rock pile regime of urban incarceration. The farm would include cottage-style living that allowed families of prisoners to live with them in a self-sustaining colony. Prisoners, allowed to choose their work, would receive wages comparable to what they had earned before they were sentenced to the farm. The colony Primavesi envisioned would have its own stores, credit system, amusements, bank, school, and scrip to be used as money redeemable only within the colony. Any surplus scrip earned by prisoners would be redeemed for dollars when they finished their sentences. On the theory that prisoners would not try to escape, given that their families lived with them, Primavesi envisioned a farm without uniformed guards and guard shacks. He favored separating first-time and lesser criminals from the hardened felons. His brand of reform included teaching the wives of prisoners good housekeeping, neatness, and frugality. In his view, the slovenliness of a chaotic household on the part of women often drove husbands to prison. The ultimate objective was the molding of tidy middle-class families, with wives in their domestic role.

All in all, Primavesi's vision of a municipal farm favored the application of a more "human touch" to uplift and rehabilitate prisoners. A campaign to promote public support to replace the workhouse with such a farm extended for several years, well past Primavesi's tenure, but he had all he could handle when it came to prisoner escapes, revolts, and smuggling of drugs into the workhouse. No matter how tight the discipline, Primavesi failed to prevent smuggling. He searched each prisoner about twice a month, typically finding a small quantity of drugs. Friends of prisoners sometimes left drugs for them at prearranged places in the quarry. Primavesi, praised by the *New St. Louis Star* as a strict disciplinarian who also believed in the Golden Rule, repeatedly called for a wall with tangled barbed wire around the quarry to stop the practice and to prevent escapes. "Young boys who come here without bad habits, and have done no great crime," he complained, "are corrupted and become victims of drugs before they serve their sentences out."[26]

On June 3, 1914, the *New St. Louis Star* reported that two mass revolts had been narrowly averted at the workhouse. The first began after a new matron took charge. She removed women from the main dining room to put an end to the practice in which some of the men secretly left pinned notes, tobacco, and cocaine for them under the edges of tables. The women became unmanageable under the influence of drugs they picked up as they passed by the men's tables. As punishment, the matron forced the estimated twenty-five to thirty women to eat in their cells and to wash their own dishes. In protest, they screamed, hollered, refused to work, threatened to fight the guards, and yelled for the men to join them in revolt.

From his office window, Superintendent Primavesi observed a half-dozen trusties afterward burying items in the yard or hiding them in the walls around the yard. He took down the trusties' names and made note of where the items were hidden. About that time in the quarry, guards noticed furtive exchanges of glances between quiet, sullen prisoners who typically engaged in busy conversations as they worked. The guards lined the prisoners against the quarry walls and searched them. Among the buried items found by Primavesi and by guards in a search of prisoners were daggers, crude knives, drugs, chisels, and heavy steel slugs akin to brass knuckles. Afterward, Primavesi showed the cache of thirty-five weapons and drugs to a newspaper reporter. The cache included sharpened steel spikes, razor blades fashioned with leather thongs as handles, a bundle of two dozen hacksaw blades to saw through the window bars at night, six full and six empty bottles of heroin, and a large quantity of cocaine. A couple of days later, male prisoners in the dining room at noon suddenly began to curse loudly and throw bread at each other as a prearranged signal to rush the guards. Typically, only two guards were there to quell dining room disturbances, but in this case a large force of guards on alert rushed in to prevent escalation of a planned riot that otherwise might have led to bloodshed.[27]

About two weeks later, Superintendent Primavesi fired his foreman, John J. McGraw, for negligence in the exercise of his duties. Afterward, an investigation indicated that McGraw had smuggled liquor into the workhouse and failed to keep track of the whereabouts of prisoners. To replace him, Primavesi promoted a guard who was an ex-Army officer.

Circuit attorney Thomas B. Harvey, who interviewed Primavesi about the smuggling of drugs into the workhouse, planned to ask a grand jury to investigate who was supplying prisoners with drugs. To aid the investigation, Primavesi mentioned the name of a nearby drugstore to the *New St. Louis Star.* In the meantime, the Board of Public Improvements notified Primavesi that $500 would be allocated for the construction of a wall around the quarry.[28]

The adoption of a new city charter on June 30, 1914, brought minor changes in the management, administration, and conduct of the workhouse. The new charter, which represented a strand of limited business progressivism, sought to unshackle St. Louis from its fragmented political culture and its history of ward politics, bossism, weak mayors, and unwieldy bicameral legislative structure. The seeds of progressive change were sown in the two administrations of Democratic mayor Rolla Wells, and now the Republicans under Mayor Kiel were pushing to continue modernizing the city's political culture in a new charter.

In 1911, an attempt at charter revision under Mayor Kreismann failed when voters overwhelmingly defeated a proposal to strengthen the power of mayors and to bring professional and business efficiency to city government. Working-class and middle-class voters, influenced by long-standing class and ethnic/neighborhood resentments over neglect of their wards, suspected that the charter revision was a mere ploy by West End elites to deepen their control over the city at their expense. In 1914, however, voters approved the new city charter after the Civic League and other advocates of good government sought greater public input and cooperation from groups who had opposed the 1911 charter revision. The margin of approval was narrow, but the inclusion of the initiative, referendum, and recall helped to sell the charter to voters suspicious of yet another Big Cinch scheme. The new charter, backed by Mayor Kiel, abolished the bicameral municipal assembly and vested legislative power in a board of aldermen and its elected president. The board consisted of twenty-eight members representing the city's wards. Mayor Kiel championed the new charter, which concentrated more power in the office of the mayor.[29]

The charter empowered the Parole Committee to make monthly inspections and to report on conditions and treatment of prisoners in the workhouse. With the aim of rehabilitation, the charter granted the board of aldermen the power to create a municipal farm. Appointees to fill the position of workhouse superintendent would be required to undertake an examination by a newly created efficiency board. The power to appoint heads of the workhouse was vested in the director of public welfare, who oversaw the divisions of health, hospitals, parks and recreation, and correction.

The first to serve as director of public welfare was Emil N. Tolkacz, a German immigrant, distinguished member of the hospital board, and civil engineering graduate of the University of Missouri with a history of service to charitable organizations. He operated an ironworks on the river. In Tolkacz's first annual report to Mayor Kiel, he made clear his support for a bond issue to fund a municipal farm: "It is not going too far to say that our Workhouse as now conducted is merely a kindergarten for our State Penitentiary. We breed criminals there who finally land in Jefferson City. The possibility of reform and redemption is infinitesimal and must remain so until some newer and more modern method is adopted and put into practice."[30]

The charter required the physician assigned to the workhouse to conduct weekly visits at mealtime to make sure the food was sufficient and of proper nutritional value. All prisoners from city courts were checked and treated, if necessary, for venereal diseases upon admission to the workhouse. Dr. Alois E. Turek, in his 1913–1914 report on the medical conditions of workhouse prisoners, noted that approximately 80 percent of the inmates suffered from syphilis. The use of solitary confinement on a diet of bread and water continued to be sanctioned under the new charter, which provided that the solitary confinement cell must allow for adequate light and air. In a long-overdue reform, the daily compensation of prisoners increased from fifty cents to three dollars a day because of the new charter. In a determination by city counselor William E. Baird, the new wage rate applied to those who were sentenced to the workhouse after August 28, 1914, and to those still serving time who had entered the institution before that date.[31]

In Primavesi's 1915 annual report, he recommended salary increases for the forty-two guards employed at the workhouse. To make the raises more economically feasible, he urged an end to providing room and board, since most of the guards were married and lived with their families. The average number of daily prisoners for the 1914–1915 year was 426 (400 men and 26 women). By an overwhelming number, most of the year's 1,094 prisoners who came through the circuit and criminal courts were sentenced on charges of petit larceny. During that year, police and city courts sent 1,506 prisoners to the workhouse for violating city ordinances. On March 31, 1915, there were 311 white men, 143 Black men, 9 white women, and 11 Black women imprisoned in the workhouse.[32]

The number of women in the workhouse dropped steadily during Primavesi's tenure as superintendent. When he first took over the job, the workhouse typically held more than one hundred imprisoned women. By the time he left office, the number had shrunk to twenty-two. At times, there were as few as eight women in the workhouse. Primavesi attributed the declining number to his crackdown on drugs and tobacco and his complete separation of female and male prisoners. When his tenure began, a few men had occupied the women's cell house, and women prisoners, after the installation of a steam laundry, worked with men in the laundry instead of by themselves at the tubs or on washboards. In addition, women prisoners routinely interacted with male prisoners in the dining room, where the men often shared drugs and tobacco with them. Primavesi refitted the women's cell house, created separate dining rooms for men and women, segregated the sexes in their own recreation yards, and banned smoking among the women inmates. Nearly all the alcoholic old-timers stopped coming to the workhouse after a plan was devised to send them to the city sanitarium for treatment for eighteen months instead. Other women who had previously used the workhouse as a kind of "rest cure" stopped coming after Primavesi's crackdown on drugs and the ban on smoking among women prisoners.[33]

In 1917, when Katherine Richardson, a feature writer for the *St. Louis Star,* asked Primavesi about the best way to rehabilitate women prisoners, he proposed as a temporary measure that they be removed from the workhouse and relocated to a vacant building at the Industrial School. He suggested the hiring of a woman as the superintendent and women as guards and social workers, if possible. The prisoners would have no contact with men.

Primavesi, who believed that most of the women inmates were congenital criminals, argued that confinement was the only thing to help them. The youngest woman in the workhouse at the time was a twenty-year-old serving her fourth sentence for shoplifting. Previously, women reformers had tried without success to help her. The last time she left the workhouse, she stole the matron's coat and pawned it. In Primavesi's view, the problem with the St. Louis system was that after sentencing, women had only two options: the workhouse or the Good Shepherd convent. He argued that the workhouse was too rough and the convent was too good for them.

> The women who have come here in my experience have not been immoral—they simply are unmoral, or rather, not moral yet. If they can be taken while yet in the early twenties and kept under strict supervision until they are 30, and taught the benefits to be gained from going straight, the moral fibre will be built . . . After being under the right supervision until they have matured, they can be put under a long parole, say three years. They will have been taught a trade in the meantime, and a social worker or probation officer can keep tab on them and see that they go straight.[34]

The workhouse under Primavesi began to feature weekly movies. In 1914, the Reverend J. L. Lever, the city missioner, continued to bring Christmas carolers to the workhouse, but he had changed the Christmas custom from handing out cigars to men to showing a movie after Christmas. A year later, the workhouse began to show weekly picture shows. Working in tandem with Edward Hidden, president of the Business Men's League, Primavesi arranged to get the necessary equipment, including a secondhand motion picture machine. The league provided films on industrial subjects, purchased from the United States Bureau of Commercial Economies, and Primavesi obtained a comedy to include each week. According to Primavesi, the greatest way to punish a woman prisoner was to take away her movie privileges. "I have found that these women ache for pleasures, of a simple sort," he told Katherine Richardson in 1917. "They want picture shows and they want dances."[35]

Among the women imprisoned in the workhouse during Primavesi's superintendency was Lou West, a notorious pickpocket and shoplifter with countless aliases in other cities of the nation as well as in Canada. The "Queen of Shoplifters" was a "moll buzzer," a criminal who preyed exclusively on other women. With a rap sheet dating back to Milwaukee in 1898, West often dodged lengthy sentences by jumping bail, feigning illness to get out of workhouses, persuading the victims of her crimes or prosecutors to drop charges against her, or intimidating witnesses. The purported head of a nationwide gang of shoplifters, she served three years in the Indiana penitentiary.

Her many friends in the underworld went to great lengths to save her from being locked up. In St. Louis, she was arrested on four counts of larceny on June 18, 1913, after she stole a purse and its baited contents from Kate Phelan, a house detective disguised as a shopper in the Grand-Leader (Stix,

Baer & Fuller) department store. West put up $3,000 bail while her shady friends tried but failed to intimidate witnesses. After a faked illness delayed her trial, she jumped bail and fled to Cleveland, where she was arrested. There, she put up $500 bail and fled yet again. West returned to St. Louis to continue her thieving, but she was arrested for petit larceny and sentenced to Primavesi's workhouse for a year on February 11, 1914.[36]

Primavesi boasted that he did not fall for any of West's tricks while she was a prisoner. Though she had never served an entire sentence in a workhouse, she served a full-year sentence in the St. Louis Workhouse, despite her efforts to shorten it. Her hair was red when she was admitted to the workhouse, but it turned white when the dye wore off. For eight months, she feigned illness. "She was a marvel," remembered Primavesi. "On arising from the dinner table, she could pretend illness, faint, and be revived. No fewer than ten doctors came here to visit her and reported she was in a dying condition." Then Primavesi summoned Dr. Max Starkloff, the city health commissioner, who examined West and concluded there was nothing wrong with her. Once she realized her manipulations would not work, she told Primavesi she would finish the remaining four months of her sentence as a model prisoner. "She boasted that the world owed her a living," Primavesi recalled, "and she said when she got out of the workhouse she would return to her lightfingered friends, and continue to earn her living picking pockets and shop lifting." In 1915, after West completed her sentence and after a hard-fought legal campaign to avoid extradition, she was sent back to Springfield, Massachusetts, where she was sentenced to nine months in the House of Correction for shoplifting in Springfield nearly four years earlier.[37]

10

WOBBLIES IN THE WORKHOUSE

In the winter of 1914–1915, a series of arrests of members of the Industrial Workers of the World (IWW), often called "Wobblies," grabbed headlines in St. Louis newspapers and sent at least two dozen Wobblies to Superintendent Primavesi's workhouse. Members of the IWW, which formed in 1905, were no strangers to city and county workhouses around the country. As political radicals, they were often "vagged" and sent to workhouses or locked up in city or county jails for exercising the rights of free speech. Because of their opposition to World War I, they were often demonized as paid German agents or worse. The federal government used repressive wartime legislation to crush the IWW as a "treasonous" organization. In a roundup of radicals, agents launched a series of raids that led to sensationalized prosecutions and imprisonment of Wobblies and many other war critics.

Authorities in Canton, Ohio, for example, parked Socialists Alfred Wagenknecht, Charles Baker, and Charles E. Ruthenberg in the Stark County Workhouse before sending them to the Ohio penitentiary in 1918 for antiwar speeches. Ruthenberg, as a Socialist candidate, won nearly 30 percent of the vote in Cleveland's mayoral election of 1917. Eugene Debs, presidential candidate of the Socialist Party of America who gave a speech across from the workhouse that housed the three at the time, was soon arrested and sent to the federal penitentiary in Atlanta. The repressive wartime climate also led to the arrests of Alice Paul and militant suffrage activists of the National Woman's Party who were picketing in front of the White House in 1917. The thirty-three women were thrown into the Occoquan Workhouse, where they were beaten and given a bitter dose of workhouse life.[1]

The St. Louis arrests and sentencing of Wobblies to the Point Breeze Workhouse came on the heels of highly publicized free speech campaigns by the IWW on the West Coast and the outbreak of a strike led by the IWW in St. Louis. The revolutionary industrial unionism of the IWW, anarcho-syndicalist in its philosophy, offered a clear radical alternative to the American Federation of Labor (AFL), led by Samuel Gompers. IWW members blasted the limited vision and "business unionism" of Gompers, a bitter enemy, who believed that the way to build a strong, lasting labor movement was to organize workers according to their craft or skill. Wobblies, using fiery, uncompromising rhetoric and a clear message of class unity and unbending opposition to capitalism, sought to organize the working class into "one big union," regardless of skill, race, or gender. Debs and several prominent Socialists joined the IWW but later withdrew.

The IWW dismissed the Socialist Party of America's strategy to capture political power via the ballot box as a swindle and diversionary waste of time, chasing middle-class reforms. From itinerant harvest workers in the wheat fields of Kansas and orchards of the San Joaquin Valley to copper mines in Arizona and logging camps in the Pacific Northwest, the Great Lakes, and Southeast Texas/Southwest Louisiana, class-conscious IWW speakers appealed to the most exploited segments of the working class. The union defied Jim Crow and reached out to the unskilled, uprooted, and dispossessed. In return, Wobblies faced police harassment and death threats, and they were often beaten and run out of town by authorities, citizens' councils, and vigilantes. In some cases, they were lynched or otherwise murdered. Newspapers often distorted and misrepresented their activities, and employers used the IWW as a bogeyman to scare the public into opposing strikes and unionizing campaigns.[2]

In 1911, members of IWW Local No. 84 in St. Louis responded to calls for recruits to join free speech campaigns in Fresno and San Diego, California; Aberdeen, Seattle, and Spokane, Washington; Kansas City, Missouri; and other cities, where they were arrested and thrown into workhouses. The intent was to flood those cities with itinerant Wobblies to protest ordinances that prevented "soapboxing," or public political speaking. The IWW aimed to overwhelm jails and workhouses in large numbers, using passive resistance to get arrested for giving soapbox speeches on the streets. In many cases, local authorities and taxpayers finally became exhausted by prosecuting, feeding, and housing Wobblies. In such cases, compromises were reached and IWW members were released, but not before they gained publicity, new recruits, and support from those who admired their commitment to revolutionary unionism. Often, however, they were confronted by armed vigilante groups who beat, tortured, and ran them out of town.[3]

In Kansas City, the new workhouse at Leeds, highly touted as a model municipal farm by criminologists and penal reformers like Superintendent Primavesi in St. Louis, housed dozens of Wobblies in a free speech fight in 1911, and again in early 1914. Frank Little, an IWW organizer who was in the thick of such fights in western cities, soon painted a much less flattering picture of Leeds. When he arrived from Chicago in 1911, the Kansas City police chief warned city officials not to allow the IWW to speak on street corners. Police arrested Little and threw him into the workhouse for giving a speech on the street. News of his arrest brought a stream of boxcar Wobblies into the city. Soon, two dozen or more joined Little in the workhouse, creating a political problem for city officials and straining the budget. The Leeds officers created a special rock pile for the IWW, segregated from the other workhouse prisoners, lest the others be influenced by the class-conscious songs and rhetoric. In the end, to resolve an embarrassing, counterproductive conflict, city officials stopped arresting Wobblies and worked out a compromise agreement that led to the parole of Little and others with him.[4]

In January 1914, Little was again arrested and put into the Leeds Workhouse in Kansas City's second round of free speech confrontations with the IWW, but upon his release, he went to St. Louis. Also in St. Louis at the time was Adolph Carm, an IWW organizer from Detroit. On February 15, Carm gave a speech on "industrial unionism" under the auspices of the newly formed IWW Local No. 101 at the Socialist Labor Hall at 1717 South Broadway. Several young workers in trunk manufacturing factories, unhappy with low wages, poor working conditions, abusive foremen, and high-handed dictates from management, heard an IWW speaker, and they were impressed with what they heard. They convinced about a dozen other trunk workers to attend an IWW meeting of mixed trades on industrial unionism.

A day or two later, when a foreman for the T. L. Horn Company told a worker to get out if he did not like the decreased wage for a particular job, the fed-up worker walked off the job. Others spontaneously followed him. Twenty-five members of the new IWW local met that night, and by a vote of 19 to 6, they decided to strike. On February 27, 1914, they went to the trunk-making factories and urged a thousand workers at P. C. Murphy, T. L. Horn, and Herkert & Meisel to join them on strike.

According to the *Kansas City Star,* Frank Little headed the strike, but the role of the IWW fit a familiar decentralized pattern that suggested a lack of planning, organization, and leadership. The mass of trunk manufacturing workers expressed a willingness to stand up for their rights and to seek representation by an AFL union, but they rejected the IWW. Workers in one of the factories did not join the strike at that time but indicated that they would go out if led by an AFL union. Edward F. Shilling, general president of the AFL-affiliated Leather Workers' International Union of America, along with organizer Fred A. Lohn, arrived in St. Louis from Chicago on March 4 and met first with an AFL organizer to get the political lay of the land.[5]

The targeted employers refused to grant concessions to the workers. An editorial in the *St. Louis Star* praised their unbending refusal to recognize the new IWW local. The editorial endorsed the use of repressive methods, if necessary, to strangle the new local in its infancy. One of the trunk manufacturers reportedly said, "Before I will recognize the I.W.W., I'll go broke and go back to farming." Within a couple of days after the arrival of Lohn and Shilling, the AFL affiliate won over 158 strikers. The IWW, sensing it was losing control over the strike, held an open meeting to determine whether the trunk makers wanted to continue the strike under the IWW banner or switch over to the AFL. At the meeting, the IWW took a vote and decided to withdraw as leader of the strike, which then continued under AFL leadership.[6]

In the same year as the strike by the St. Louis trunk makers, the IWW created the Bureau of Migratory Workers. In the aftermath of the trunk makers' debacle, local IWW leaders were eager to make St. Louis the storm center of a free speech campaign to draw attention to the plight of unemployed itinerant workers during the winter season. They took to street corners in the factory districts and the slums to exhort all workers to join the revolutionary "one big union," but St. Louis police reminded them who controlled the streets. The free speech campaign followed a similar path as the previous ones in Kansas City and western cities, but in St. Louis it took on an added wrinkle.

On the night of November 11, 1914, St. Louis police broke up a meeting of the IWW at the corner of Seventeenth and Market Streets. Two patrolmen were drawn there by the singing of an IWW parody of "The Ballad of Casey

Jones." A few hundred people were gathered to listen to the singing and a rousing speech by twenty-two-year-old John Miller. According to Captain Martin O'Brien of the Central Police District, the arresting officers considered the music parody objectionable. In "Casey Jones—the Union Scab," the IWW version by Joe Hill in 1911, angels in heaven sent the brave railroad engineer "to Hell a-flyin' . . . for scabbin' on the S. P. Line." The police loaded Miller into the patrol wagon for disturbing the peace. As the wagon drove away, John X. Kelly, age forty, mounted the speaker's stand and began to exhort the crowd. The patrol wagon circled back, the patrolmen slapped the cuffs on Kelly and loaded him into the wagon, and it pulled away yet again. As the street crowd began to disperse, John Cohen, age twenty-five, jumped behind the speaker's stand, and he too was handcuffed and loaded into the patrol wagon. The free speech campaign in St. Louis was under way. All but Kelly were Wobblies at the time. They were arrested for allegedly using obscenity and offensive language in their soapbox speeches and songs.[7]

In city court number 1, Judge Granville Hogan, the son-in-law of Mayor Kiel, fined each of the men twenty-five dollars. When they could not pay the fine, he sentenced them to the workhouse. The arrests marked the opening of a campaign by the IWW to dramatize the plight of hungry, homeless itinerant workers in the cold, cruel grip of wintertime. Forest Edwards, an IWW organizer wired William D. "Big Bill" Haywood, general organizer of the IWW in Chicago, to inform him of the arrests. Edwards told a reporter that the IWW would soon respond to the harassment by the St. Louis police. According to Edwards, Haywood promised that a thousand Chicago workers would arrive soon, and thousands from other cities, too, would hop on freight trains to St. Louis. Reportedly, Haywood was expected to come to the city to take charge of the campaign.[8]

Also taking up the cudgel of migratory workers, free speech, and the unemployed was James Eads How, commonly known as the "Millionaire Hobo." Regarded as an eccentric, he rejected the wealth he had inherited from both sides of his family. His mother, Elisa Eads How, was the daughter of James Eads, architect and engineer of the 1874 St. Louis bridge that bore his name. James F. How, his father, was vice president of the Wabash Railroad. The Millionaire Hobo, founder of the International Brotherhood Welfare Association (IBWA) in 1905, used his money to educate, feed, and clothe the down-and-out. A gentle, messianic-like figure with a humanitarian bent, he went to live among the lowly to understand their needs and struggles.

Well educated, trained in a Universalist seminary in Meadville, Pennsylvania, and a medical doctor who practiced when the need arose, How provided a free children's clinic, a gymnasium for boys, and numerous other services to promote his vision of universal brotherhood. IBWA centers ("hobo colleges") opened in Chicago, New York, and other cities, and How's newspaper, *Hobo News,* connected members and provided an alternative news outlet. Hobo colleges became popular gathering places for migratory workers, particularly during the winter when work dried up. They provided food, shelter, educational materials, and a forum for political discussions of issues important to itinerant laborers. In How's view, the war in Europe was a product of glutted markets due to the lack of purchasing power among workers. The mad scramble for new overseas markets fueled bitter economic rivalries and militarism that exploded into war. He opposed U.S. entry into the war, and like other Social Gospel proponents, he criticized religious institutions for neglecting the poor.[9]

Previously, How had pushed for the creation of a municipal lodging house in St. Louis. The house, which opened in December 1911, was in the basement of the old Four Courts Building at Twelfth Street and Clark Avenue. Lodgers of all races slept on the concrete floor. On January 11, 1913, the workhouse sent fifty-three "double-deck" cots to the lodging house. Once lodgers entered, they were not allowed to leave until the next morning. They were given black coffee and a free doughnut for breakfast, but they were required to work two hours to pay for a lunch. A clerk, superintendent, and guard supervised the admission procedure and operations.

The work requirement, punitive in nature, rankled the IWW and How, who pushed for its elimination. After a conference with How and members of the Legislation Committee of the IBWA, Mayor Kreismann dropped the compulsory work requirement on January 11, 1913, and called for coffee and bread to be given to lodgers on the night they checked in. "The work the men do is of little value to the city," the mayor remarked. "The municipality surely can be generous enough to provide lodging worth about 5 cents and food and drink of equal value to the unfortunate."[10]

Missouri's assistant labor commissioner, James J. Barrett, visited the municipal lodging house many times in the winter of 1913–1914. On one of those occasions, he found eight hundred men sleeping on the cement floor or on iron bunks. After extensive conversations with many of the lodgers, he concluded that 90 percent of them were willing to work and did not want charity. However, St. Louis businessmen whom Barrett interviewed complained that when the city called for five hundred lodgers to shovel snow, only sixteen responded to the call. Barrett believed that their criticism, which echoed a recent newspaper article, was unjust. "The weather was below zero, and out of the 500 men there were not over 20 that had enough clothes on their bodies to keep them warm, or sufficient nourishment in their stomachs to enable them to shovel snow," he pointed out. "The few I found working along the streets were shivering with cold, in many instances without gloves on their hands or socks on their feet, their bare toes protruding through holes in their shoes."[11]

How, too, was arrested on a charge of peace disturbance for giving a soapbox speech near the same street corner where the IWW orators had been arrested. After refusing to pay the fine in a city court, he was held over for the workhouse, but Judge Hogan persuaded him to pay the fine, warning that news of his workhouse confinement might further contribute to his mother's rapidly failing health. How cooperated with the IWW and extended open arms to all representatives of labor, no matter their political orientation, but he made it clear that the IWW and IBWA were separate entities with different philosophies. Although he was often considered a radical, How favored education and reform, not the direct action of the IWW's revolutionary strategy.

There was an IWW faction within the IBWA whose members often ridiculed some of his reformist proposals to improve the living conditions of itinerant workers. Nevertheless, when IWW speakers were arrested in St. Louis, he worked to arrange their release from the workhouse. One of them, John X. Kelly, was an associate of his in the IBWA. When Mayor Kiel was asked to pardon them, he replied that he would not do so unless How secured the signatures of three of the five members on the Board of Parole and Pardons. How secured the signatures of Judge Hogan, Judge John T. Sanders, and workhouse superintendent Primavesi. In addition, How assured the mayor that a compromise had been worked out to allow speakers to use the steps of the old Four Courts Building for public speech.[12]

To undercut radical appeals and to combat the anticipated problems of unemployment and homelessness in the following winter, business philanthropists Albert von Hoffmann and Paul O. Sommer opened a soup kitchen around the beginning of December 1914. Von Hoffmann, an Austrian immigrant, was manager of the National Telephone Company, and Sommer was secretary of the Holman Paper Box Company and president of the St. Louis Turnverein. Club women, Ladies' Aid societies, and church women volunteers ladled soup and did other work at the kitchen.[13]

The notion that club women whose husbands were among the city's business elites were ladling soup to the unemployed, the homeless, and the "unfortunates" rankled the IWW, which launched a campaign that drew widespread newspaper coverage. At noon on December 16, 1914, five IWW members entered Joseph Schertz's restaurant at 350 Grand Avenue, ate about fifty cents' worth of food each, and topped off the meal with ten-cent cigars. When they had no money to pay the bill, Schertz summoned police. One of the men exclaimed as they were being taken away in the patrol wagon, "We will have some place to sleep and eat for a week, anyway." Judge Hogan fined each of them twenty-five dollars and sent them to work off their fines on the workhouse rock pile at a daily wage of three dollars minus food and board costs. The very next day, two men who did not pay after enjoying lunch and cigars in Schertz's restaurant fled after they told an employee to "put it on the Mayor's ticket."[14]

The subsequent Charge It to the Mayor campaign led to a flock of arrests and workhouse sentences before and after Christmas. To contain it, Judge Hogan raised the fines to the maximum of $500, but even that did not deter committed soldiers in the war against capital and its instrument of control, government. The arrests continued, but the campaign generated publicity for the IWW and drew public support for those who were arrested. When anarchist Emma Goldman gave a lecture to an audience of three hundred at the Central Trades and Labor Union Hall on December 5, a police detective was in the audience to spy on her and other radicals who gave short speeches after she finished. In a lecture billed as a speech on prohibition, Goldman digressed to attack bourgeois culture and to blast the "idle, hysterical women" of philanthropic clubs who ladled soup and engaged in other philanthropic activities. John Mowatt, an organizer and spokesman for the St. Louis local of the IWW, was one of the speakers who followed her.

The speeches further stimulated the IWW's momentum in the city. On January 8, 1915, John Hamilton, Meyer Becker, Don Olden, and William A. Connell, known to police as IWW sympathizers, enjoyed a free porterhouse steak, fried potatoes, and full cream for their coffee at a restaurant at 712 Pine Street to continue the Charge It to the Mayor campaign. Sheridan Webster, a Socialist attorney and secretary of the People's League, defended them in Judge Hogan's courtroom. The men refused to enter a plea or to swear on a Bible, emphasizing that they did not believe in it. Judge Hogan fined each of them $500 and sentenced them to the workhouse. In a courtroom filled with about seventy-five supporters, the men dragged their feet to make a rhythmic noise as they were led away to the workhouse.[15]

As the number of arrests mounted, a reporter for the *Post-Dispatch* paid a visit to the sparse IWW headquarters at Seventeenth and Wash Streets. There he found August Dietricht, secretary of St. Louis Industrial Union No. 84 of the IWW, and Mowatt, an organizer and skilled orator from New Jersey who earlier was part of IWW campaigns in New England and the Pacific Northwest. Fresh out of a city jail cell for incendiary remarks on the courthouse steps on January 1, 1915, Mowatt defended himself before Judge Hogan, who freed him. According to Mowatt, St. Louis Local No. 84 had about sixty members, but he predicted that hundreds more would soon arrive to fill the workhouse in response to the Charge It to the Mayor campaign. Hinting that the predicted hundreds might smash storefront windows if officials mistreated Wobblies in the workhouse, he criticized Judge Hogan for imposing the maximum fine on IWW members merely for their failure to pay for a fifty-cent meal. When a reporter asked why they did not become soldiers for pay, food, and shelter, Mowatt retorted that they would rather starve than become soldiers for any country. He blasted militarism and denounced the outbreak of war in Europe six months earlier.[16]

When the reporter left the IWW hall, he went to the workhouse, which housed fifteen Wobblies at the time. Superintendent Primavesi, who offered that he could accommodate a hundred more in the workhouse, took the reporter to the quarry, where the Wobblies were swinging sledgehammers in a quarry work gang of Black prisoners. The reporter learned that their leader, Big Bill Cunningham, had been put into solitary confinement on bread and water for thirty hours. One of the IWW prisoners with a black eye indicated that a guard beat him when he insisted on talking to the superintendent. Cunningham, a sailor thrown out of work due to disruptions in interoceanic commerce caused by the war in Europe, said all of them were unemployed workers. He was adamant that neither he nor any of the Wobblies in the workhouse would accept a mayor's pardon. Primavesi indicated that the group made a lot of noise every night in their cells by singing "Hallelujah, I'm a Bum," "Casey Jones—Union Scab," and other labor solidarity songs, but he added that the other prisoners did not mind. According to the superintendent, he was not having a particular problem with any of them.[17]

According to Judge Hogan, he tried to reach a compromise with the men when it came to giving speeches on street corners. Insisting that some of the language and song lyrics offended women who were passing by, he offered to find designated places in the city where people would not complain about their presence. He even attended some of the IWW meetings to reach a compromise, but he made it clear he had no choice but to fine them if they continued to eat restaurant meals without paying for them. Hogan felt they were good guys misled by a few bad leaders. After discussions, he agreed to speak in the Open Forum to be held at the IWW hall on January 17. The topic was "The Unemployed and the Duties and Purpose of Police Judges and Courts." It was customary at these forums for a speaker to give a talk, answer questions, and listen to five-minute presentations by other speakers. The IWW was eager to present its side of the recent arrests and workhouse sentences, and to make the judge aware of the plight of the unemployed. When Hogan received ongoing threats of damage to storefront windows if prosecution of IWW members continued, however, he backed away from speaking at the Open Forum.[18]

Among those influenced by the activism of IWW members in St. Louis and by the speeches of Emma Goldman on the abolition of poverty and social injustice was Roger Baldwin, a Massachusetts-born Harvard graduate who taught sociology at Washington University and served as chief probation officer in the St. Louis juvenile court. At the time, Baldwin was moving to the left as he became impatient with his work in the Civic League and the slow pace of reform. Still of considerable influence in high circles, he worked behind the scenes to help set up St. Louis's first soup kitchen and municipal lodging house, and at times he acted as a mediator in the standoff between Judge Hogan and the IWW over imprisoned members in the workhouse.

"I attended their meetings and knew their leaders," he later explained. "Some of them became my close personal friends. Sympathizing with their general ideals of a free society, with much of their programme, I yet could see no effective way of practical daily service." The spirit of sacrifice and the idealism of some of the Wobblies impressed Baldwin so much that he considered giving up his position and his respectability for manual labor and membership in their union. "I thought better of it," he later recalled. "My traditions were against it. It was more an emotional reaction than a practical form of service. But ever since I have felt myself heart and soul with the world-wide radical movements for industrial and political freedom—wherever and however expressed—and more and more impatient with reform."[19]

The growing arrests and stream of IWW members to the workhouse created a fast-developing crisis in Judge Hogan's court and a political problem for the city. In frustration, Hogan praised a waiter who had punched Herbert Connell when he, Ed Toombs, William Jones, and Pete Steinkovitch tried to charge their restaurant meal to the mayor. A police officer who arrived on the scene likewise punched Connell. The judge noted that a punch in the nose was the best way to deal with the uncompromising IWW members. Shortly before he fined the four men $500 and ordered them to the workhouse, he asked Connell if he was sorry for trying to steal a meal. Connell replied, "Yes—sorry for the beating I got."[20]

Albert von Hoffmann soon discovered firsthand that the IWW did not think much of his soup kitchen. Frank Bierman and William Gillespie harangued those standing in his long soup line, urging the hungry to reject handouts from the rich. It would be better to steal than to accept a few crumbs from the tables of the wealthy, they argued. "Now, if anyone is allowed to say that," von Hoffmann later noted, "then our soup system falls down like a nutshell." When he intervened to stop harassment of those who stood in the soup line, Bierman allegedly called him names and threatened him, and Gillespie shook his fist at him. Von Hoffmann followed them to Eleventh and Market, where a gathering IWW crowd further threatened him.

On January 2, 1915, Judge Hogan fined Bierman and Gillespie fifty dollars and twenty-five dollars, respectively. As soon as he announced his verdict, a demonstration broke out in the courtroom. Approximately forty IWW sympathizers rushed toward von Hoffmann, the prosecuting witness. They jostled him and shook their fists in his face before a police sergeant and a detail of ten patrol officers hurried over to escort the beleaguered soup kitchen philanthropist safely from the building. The large police presence was the result of an anticipated demonstration in Judge Hogan's courtroom. "That's the gratitude you get," muttered von Hoffmann to the police as he left the courtroom.[21]

On January 5, five hundred marchers protested municipal charity. Led by IWW leaders Mowatt and Dietricht, they marched through the factory and slum districts, picking up recruits among the unemployed as they marched along. Holding signs and placards that read "No Soup—We Want Work," "Soup Means Slow Starvation," and "We Have Fed You for a Thousand Years and Now Ye Hail Us as Unfed," they stopped at various locations and held meetings. Before the march began, the protesters passed a set of resolutions, which included a proposal to tax soup kitchen promoters eighteen and a half cents for each bowl of soup served.[22]

When IWW members John Mosohoe, Archie Abbott, Jacob S. Brown, and John Van Ester were arrested for giving speeches on the steps of the courthouse, Mosohoe denied they were incendiary. He claimed that the arresting police sergeant told him at the time of arrest, "I'd like to take you up an alley and beat your head off." Mosohoe, who indicated he had been arrested many times in different cities, told Judge Hogan he had come to St. Louis to look for work. "And, like 88,000 other men in your city," he complained, "I have been unable to find work." Hogan freed all four of those who were arrested.[23]

By the second week of January, the number of IWW arrests and sentences to the workhouse reached twenty-five. The arrests became such an everyday occurrence, in fact, that they sometimes took on a comedic tone of political theater. On January 12, Carl Fisher and William Geltner were fined $500 for eating thirty cents' worth of food without paying at Robert Belton's restaurant at 11 North Broadway. They said they were tired of eating soup. Fisher claimed he had not eaten a square meal in more than six weeks. A *Post-Dispatch* reporter who covered the courtroom cases noted, "The I.W.W. who said, 'Home, James!' to the driver of the patrol wagon ought to keep the workhouse from being too dull for a while."[24]

By the end of January 1915, the steady parade of IWW members to the workhouse slowed to a trickle. The Charge It to the Mayor campaign petered out and the predicted influx of thousands of IWW itinerants from Chicago and other cities did not materialize. Some who did arrive and found themselves stranded in St. Louis soon sought to leave. On January 27, Sam Afresky, Sam Mendlovitz, Ben Karp, and Isadore Laut led a group of about fifteen men who stormed into the headquarters of the Jewish Charitable Aid Association at 901 Carr Street and threatened its secretary, Oscar Leonard, who in the past had helped them. Admitting afterward to Judge Sanders that they intended to break up the charity by way of "direct action," the four arrested IWW leaders demanded that the association provide tickets for them back to New York, New Orleans, and elsewhere. Judge Sanders fined each of the ringleaders twenty-five dollars and sent them to the workhouse, but he freed the rest of the group who charged into the association's headquarters. The *Globe-Democrat,* nearly a year later, credited von Hoffmann's soup kitchen for putting an end to the IWW's Charge It to the Mayor campaign. Without it, the paper said, the IWW might have attracted more converts among hungry, homeless itinerants in the winter of 1914–1915. The newspaper praised the soup kitchen as "the mayor's shield and protection."[25]

11

PETTY PEANUT POLITICS AND THE DEATH OF REFORM

As the IWW population in the workhouse thinned out in early 1915 after the Charge It to the Mayor and free speech campaigns ended, Superintendent Primavesi was beset with new problems that jeopardized his position and future reform. Backers of his proposal to create a municipal farm continued to push for the project, but his critics and other opponents of reform were determined to push him out of his job. Drugs and whiskey continued to find a way into the workhouse despite the superintendent's efforts to stop smuggling. On May 14, 1915, an incident in the quarry that resulted in the beating death of a prisoner provoked public outrage and put the spotlight on the ongoing use of alcohol and drugs by inmates. The incident, which gave Primavesi's critics political ammunition against him, led to demands for his resignation and a lengthy investigation of his management of the workhouse.

Newspaper reports portrayed the quarry incident as a riot, mutiny, or attempted uprising led by four prisoners under the influence of drugs and alcohol. Michael Crowley, Michael Hart, Bryan Walsh, and Bart O'Donnell reportedly were members of a gang disliked by most of the inmates. At 10:30 in the morning, the ringleaders jumped guard Richard Slawson in the quarry and took his revolver from him. They yelled for other prisoners to join them in the escape attempt. Before they could get away, however, Edward Hoelscher and other guards and prisoners came to Slawson's aid. The quarry foreman, John D. Stratton, was the guard most responsible for overpowering the four prisoners. He rushed from the ledge of the quarry down into its pit and clubbed them into submission. Guards Stratton and Slawson received nonserious wounds, and the four ringleaders, all of whom were serving one-year sentences, were sent to the city hospital with severe scalp wounds. Doctors who treated the wounds and sent the prisoners back to the workhouse the following day reportedly said they were suffering as much from alcoholism as from the scalp wounds inflicted by Stratton. In a search of prisoners, workhouse officials found drugs, alcohol, razors, knives, and assorted crudely fashioned weapons. Superintendent Primavesi blamed the entire episode on the lack of funding for a security fence around the quarry.[1]

On May 21, a week after the quarry incident, workhouse officers found Crowley dead in his bunk. A glassblower whose sentence was to have expired in January 1916, Crowley was serving his third sentence on charges of malicious trespass, burglary, and larceny. In a postmortem examination, Dr. Louis Brandenberger determined that the cause of death was a traumatic brain hemorrhage or blood clot. As the result of a coroner's hearing, the public soon learned contradictory versions of the episode that led to Crowley's death. The hearing included testimony by nine workhouse inmates.

Hart, Walsh, and O'Donnell admitted they were drinking at the time but denied there was trouble before Stratton clubbed them. They testified that there was trouble between Crowley and an unidentified Black prisoner, and between guard Slawson and Walsh earlier on the morning of the beatings. When Slawson's pistol fell to the ground, Crowley picked it up but made no effort to use it. According to Hart, Walsh, and O'Donnell, Stratton did not beat them until he discovered them sitting in a "shade house" in the quarry. The coroner's jurors learned that twenty-nine-year-old Stratton, known in the workhouse as "the slugger," was called upon whenever any slugging of prisoners was to be done. He was hired at the workhouse after finishing a three-year stint as a sergeant in the Sixth U.S. Infantry in December 1913.[2]

Stratton testified that Crowley hit him with an iron bar, but nine workhouse inmates testified that Stratton clubbed Crowley without provocation. According to them, Crowley did not resist or try to hit Stratton. The inmates made it clear that Crowley did not even have an iron bar in his hand. Several testified that he was forced back into the quarry to work after he was beaten. Guard Arthur F. Krausse testified that Crowley cried out repeatedly for a doctor and a priest to attend to him on the night before his death. On May 25, the coroner's jury ruled that Crowley's death was a homicide. Stratton was arrested at the workhouse and taken to the Wyoming Street police station, where he was held for the circuit attorney's office, but there is no indication that homicide charges against him were pursued. He left the workhouse but soon joined the city fire department, where he enjoyed a long career.[3]

The board of aldermen, acting upon resolutions introduced by Gus A. Baur, a Republican alderman from the Fourteenth Ward, ordered an investigation into the management of the workhouse. Baur's only public comment at the time was that certain provisions of the new city charter were not being followed. The *Star*, one of Primavesi's strongest supporters, emphasized that Primavesi was never "one of the boys." The newspaper suggested that his political sin was to devote too much attention to his job and too little time engaging in Republican politics and the ward spoils system. Primavesi, who told the *Star* he was unaware of any conflicts with fellow Republicans, said he welcomed the investigation. At its session on June 4, 1915, the board of aldermen appointed Baur to head a committee of five aldermen to investigate the workhouse, which, as the April grand jury report indicated, was a financial albatross regardless of who managed it. The report recommended a bond issue of $500,000 to relocate the workhouse and convert it into a self-sustaining municipal farm.[4]

The investigation of Primavesi's management of the workhouse dragged on for nearly ten months. Alderman Baur, whose young son worked in Mayor Kiel's office, publicly questioned the legality of the workhouse store operated by Primavesi. Baur complained that the store violated the city charter by allowing a public servant to run a money-making enterprise for private gain in addition to drawing a salary. For a half century or more, the store operated by guards and previous superintendents had come under political fire during endless investigations, but it always survived with a few modifications. On March 15, 1916, the committee summoned Primavesi and Tolkacz, director of public welfare, to answer questions about the store in the presence of city counselor Charles H. Daues. Primavesi indicated that the store netted between five and ten dollars monthly, but he insisted that he used funds from the store to buy supplies for the night school and other educational activities, as well as movies and the purchase of a moving picture machine for prisoners' entertainment and recreation. Tolkacz, who stood behind the beleaguered superintendent, said he did not believe Primavesi used the store for private gain. Although Tolkacz opposed the existence of the store, he emphasized that it had been standard practice at the workhouse for decades. Daues promised to issue a formal opinion of the store's legality, but he suggested offhand that it was probably illegal.[5]

The meeting might have been intended mostly to embarrass and intimidate Primavesi publicly. Baur might well have asked Daues for a legal opinion on the store long before the committee held Primavesi's feet to the fire. On April 14, 1916, the *Post-Dispatch* reported that Baur's committee planned to urge Tolkacz to demand Primavesi's resignation at that evening's session of the board of aldermen. Nothing about the workhouse store, drug smuggling, or the beating death of prisoner Crowley was mentioned in the committee's stated reasons why Tolkacz should get rid of the superintendent. Instead, the committee complained about the declining output of macadam in the quarry, accusing Primavesi of neglect of duty. The committee claimed that during his three and a half years as superintendent, he had visited the quarry only four times. In an additional accusation, Alderman Baur criticized Primavesi for using city materials and carpenters to build furniture for the local chapter of the American Theosophical Society, of which Primavesi was president. Primavesi dismissed the charges as trivial, admitting that he had used materials to build a blackboard and stand for the society, but he emphasized that the lumber was old, discarded lumber of little or no value.[6]

When asked about the committee's recommendations, Mayor Kiel professed to know nothing about the matter. Under the 1914 charter, the power to fire the workhouse superintendent was in the hands of the director of public welfare, but Tolkacz would not fire Primavesi. In fact, when the board of aldermen met in session on April 14, Baur pulled a surprise by announcing that the workhouse investigating committee's report was not ready. Facing ongoing pressure to pay more attention to ward politics and intraparty divisions in his conduct of operations, Primavesi might have bent a little to pressure from meetings behind closed doors. On August 26, 1916, he fired guards George M. Karp and Edward F. Schiera, both of whom had scored high on the city's new efficiency board exam less than a year earlier. Karp and Schiera complained that the firings were purely an act of political retribution. Republican alderman John A. Fett, a member of Baur's workhouse investigating committee, escorted them to the city hall offices, where they complained that Primavesi fired them because they had voted against John E. Swanger for the Republican gubernatorial nomination, and against Mayor Kiel's Eleventh Ward candidate for the Republican city central committee.[7]

The future of Primavesi's superintendency was tied to the political fortunes of Tolkacz. In 1917, Mayor Kiel did not reappoint Tolkacz as director of public welfare, instead picking John M. Schmoll, chairman of the Republican city central committee and a former business partner of Mayor Kiel. Primavesi announced his resignation on May 11, 1917. In the final months of his tenure, he hired Mrs. Harry Denny as the first Black matron at the workhouse. Schmoll chose Colonel Houston N. Morgan, the mayor's longtime right-hand man, as the new superintendent of the workhouse. Morgan, age fifty-nine, was a former deputy sheriff, lawyer, playwright, and vaudeville actor who lost his right arm to a saw in an onstage accident. Upon coming to St. Louis in 1907, he managed a moving picture theater and operated two others. Prior to his workhouse appointment, he had worked as a paving inspector in the street department. His rise in politics began in the election of 1912, when he organized a group of Progressives who later backed Mayor Kiel in his first mayoral campaign. In the city elections of 1917, Morgan produced motion picture films touting St. Louis's civic achievements during Kiel's mayoral tenure.[8]

Schmoll indicated that Morgan's appointment was only temporary and that he would have to compete with others on the efficiency board examination. Schmoll also denied a role in forcing Primavesi's resignation. "I intend to run this department on strictly business efficiency principles," Schmoll said. "All appointees will be men who have passed the Efficiency Board test." In response to criticisms, Schmoll made it clear he expected Morgan to end longtime abusive practices at the workhouse, including the smuggling of drugs.

Before Morgan assumed his duties as superintendent, and within a week of his appointment, he was arrested in a Sunday police raid on the Fraternal Order of the Eagles' club. He was charged with violating the Sunday lid law that prohibited the sale of alcohol on that day. The prosecuting attorney refused to charge him or anyone else arrested in the raid, announcing that there was no proof that any sales of alcohol had occurred. Morgan dismissed his arrest as a "political trick," and Schmoll insisted it would have no impact on his appointment.[9]

Schmoll's rhetorical nod to reform did not fool astute political observers. In an editorial, the *Star* complained that the appointments of Schmoll and Morgan signaled a return to patronage politics. By reverting to patronage appointments, Mayor Kiel was making a mockery of the new city charter he had promoted in 1914. "As the first fruits of this change," the *Star* noted, "we have the squeezing out of Captain Primavesi as superintendent of the workhouse and the appointment of a man who was taken in a lid club raid the very first Sunday after his appointment." The editorial praised Tolkacz and Primavesi as men of vision who brought decency and discipline to an institution that was in a disgraceful condition when they took office. Their replacements, on the other hand, were pure patronage appointments.[10]

Four years later, Tolkacz, a fellow Republican businessman, publicly expressed his own critical assessment of Mayor Kiel. At the time, Kiel was running for a third mayoral term. In a speech opposing the Kiel political machine and endorsing the mayor's Democratic opponent, James W. Byrnes, Tolkacz noted that although Kiel was a "fine fellow," highly likeable and easy to approach, he was in the grip of petty patronage politics. He recalled that when Kiel first offered him the newly created position of director of public welfare under the new city charter, he had agreed to accept it if there were no strings attached. Tolkacz said it took less than six months for the mayor to renege on the agreement. Tolkacz recalled some unpleasant meetings with Kiel, who twice refused to accept his resignation. The only times Kiel ever asked about anything in Tolkacz's department was when he wanted a friend to be appointed to a vacant position. In the end, Tolkacz described Kiel as "the creature of petty, peanut politics, trying to be faithful to those who put him in office."[11]

The exodus of Tolkacz and Primavesi left the workhouse without two of its most passionate advocates for structural reform. The spirit of reform that began with Democratic mayor Wells and continued with Republican mayors Kreismann and Kiel dissipated with the departures of Tolkacz and Primavesi and the entry of the United States into the First World War. As limited as it was, progressivism in St. Louis gave way to the restored system of patronage politics and institutionalized cynicism. The Republican platform on which Mayor Kiel ran for reelection in 1917 did include a plank calling for a municipal farm to replace the workhouse. Schmoll, the new director of public welfare, Morgan, the new workhouse superintendent, and nearly all major civic agencies, organizations, and newspapers, including the new Black-owned *St. Louis Argus,* supported calls for a municipal farm, but the proposal stalled. The Kiel administration prepared a list of many projects with budgetary figures for a municipal bond issue to put before city voters, but bureaucratic delays and ward wrangling over priorities and budget amounts in bond committee meetings held it up until 1920. By then, an earlier figure of $900,000 had been pared to a paltry $400,000. Schmoll protested the cut, but to no avail.[12]

In a $24 million municipal improvement bond election on May 11, 1920, the appropriation of $400,000 for a municipal farm was number seven on a list of eighteen items on the ballot for approval. The bond election came only a year after a concerted effort to recall Mayor Kiel for favorable concessions to the United Railways Company at the expense of the city. Although the St. Louis League of Women Voters and nearly every civic organization in the city endorsed the farm, voters failed to provide the two-thirds majority necessary for approval. Item seven, which called for the municipal farm, fared the worst of all items in the bond issue. One of thirteen items rejected by voters, it lost by a margin of more than three thousand votes. The *Post-Dispatch* suggested that the ballot's misleading wording of the call for a municipal farm "for the care and cure of habitual drunkards and persons adjudged guilty of the violation of city ordinances" doomed it in the context of the recent ratification of the Eighteenth Amendment establishing Prohibition. There was considerable sentiment among voters that Prohibition rendered the municipal farm unnecessary. Whatever the reasons for its failure, the progressive blueprint for reforming the workhouse never got off the ground.[13]

CONCLUSION

When the Workhouse Bell Tolls

In a 1928 report, the Missouri Welfare League described the St. Louis Workhouse as "so old, so overcrowded, so inadequate in every way to meet the difficult task of handling hundreds of men of dissimilar types herded into it."[1] On the league's list of projects was to continue pressing for a new workhouse, but remarkably, the old one at 4200 South Broadway held on until 1966. In 1953, the closing of the quarry, dubbed the "Black Pit" by prisoners, left inmates cooped up with a lot of time on their hands. Three explosive riots in a ten-month period in 1955–1956 brought scores of riot police, tear gas, and firefighters to the workhouse. In May 1955, St. Louis voters approved a $3 million bond issue for a new medium security prison. Alarming newspaper headlines in 1957 about a workhouse narcotics ring, "the Syndicate," further dramatized the urgent need for a new facility.[2]

It took construction of the Ozark Expressway, now Interstate 55, to drive a stake through the heart of the medieval workhouse, condemned by the city circuit court as "St. Louis' No. 1 Public Disgrace." Despite mounting pressure from the planned highway project, which required destruction of the workhouse, the bond issue funds sat idle while city and county authorities quarreled over the site of the future correctional institution. They agreed that they needed one hundred acres, but where would they find an acceptable tract for purchase? St. Louis County had plenty of potential sites, but county officials did not want a prison built in their suburban neighborhoods.

Under pressure after years of persistent bickering and repeated delays for one reason or another, the St. Louis City Plan Commission at last located a tract, but it had to settle for a much smaller site of thirty or so acres. Not surprisingly, the future home of the institution was near the levee once again, but this time on the North Riverfront, east of Broadway at Hall Street and Thatcher Avenue. The newly built St. Louis Medium Security Institution, still commonly but inaccurately referred to as the Workhouse, had a capacity of 514 when it opened on June 9, 1966. Under heavy security, buses transferred 234 prisoners from the old workhouse to the new location.[3]

If a chance ever existed for meaningful reform of the old St. Louis Workhouse, it would have been in the Progressive era before the First World War, but the city's limited progressivism was not equal to the task. As in the past, ward politics and patronage took precedence over reforming a corrupt, disgraceful institution. In the half century after voters rejected the municipal farm on a bond issue in 1920, the workhouse became bogged down even deeper in cynicism, plagued by human rights violations, hunger strikes, riots, civil rights protests, prisoner abuse, and more. The criticisms of the workhouse in the 1850s reverberated like the old mission workhouse bell throughout its entire history. The same fundamental problems went unresolved for more than one hundred years as the workhouse remained a patronage plum of corrupt ward politics.

When Communists were thrown into the workhouse for leading unemployment protests, anti-eviction movements, and poverty relief demonstrations during the Great Depression, their sentences harked back to the First World War era when dozens of Wobblies were imprisoned on Point Breeze. Likewise, when Percy Green and countless civil rights activists were locked up in the new facility right after it opened in 1966, they were part of a history of political prisoners locked up for their principled stand against racial injustice and the inequities of capitalism, dating back to the old Workhouse. Fifty years later, Inez Bordeaux, the ArchCity Defenders, and other community activists who urged closure of the city's Medium Security Institution called attention to the same problems of poverty, racism, and horrid, inhumane conditions that had plagued the workhouse on Point Breeze for more than a century. Their persistence paid off when Mayor Tishaura Jones closed the Medium Security Institution on June 17, 2021. Bordeaux, who was a former prisoner, and many others in the Close the Workhouse campaign represented St. Louis's new voices of dissent against racial, class, and gender injustices in the penal system.[4]

Reportedly made in France, the old 1804 mission bell that once rang when the Black Maria dumped a new batch of prisoners at the old St. Louis Workhouse found a new home at 7600 Hall Street, after considerable wrangling over its fate. Fred Weber Jr., the contractor who tore down the workhouse on Point Breeze, preferred to donate it to the Missouri Historical Society, but after conferring with Mayor Alfonso J. Cervantes, he turned it over to the new workhouse on the promise that Warden Charles A. Head would take care of it. In the mournful tolling of the bell, if one listened just right, it was possible to hear not only the voices of hardened felons who should have been in the penitentiary but also the voices of all who did hard time for criminalized poverty, Blackness, homelessness, and unemployment. The bell tolled, too, for those who defied social norms and political convention. More than a century and a half old, the bell was a reminder of the workhouse's long history and the underside of St. Louis's Gilded Age, Industrial Revolution, and police court justice system.

The workhouse's riverfront location, too, was an indication of where the bulk of its impoverished inmates came from. In each reverberation of the bell, one could hear the moans and groans of yet another steamboat roustabout beaten within an inch of his life by guards. Another Black voter pulled aside by an election judge at the polls, arrested for vagrancy or some other phony violation of a city ordinance, and banished to the "vag pen." Another routine beating of a new Black woman prisoner to welcome her to the political process of the workhouse. The bell rang out the anguish of Mary Duff and countless others in the dark dungeons of solitary confinement. In the bell's reverberations, one could hear outrage, resistance, and the resilient voices of nonconformists, radical women's rights advocates, and other dissenters for whom it tolled. Above all, however, the bell tolled for the victims of St. Louis's full-on scorched-earth warfare against its very own poor people.[5]

NOTES

Introduction

1. Twain, *Following the Equator,* 1:143.

2. *Daily Missouri Republican,* February 6, 1861, 4; *Missouri Republican,* April 7, 1871, 5. On Dickens's use of *Oliver Twist* to criticize England's New Poor Law of 1834, see Richardson, *Dickens and the Workhouse.* For studies of British workhouses, see, for example, Driver, *Power and Pauperism;* Fowler, *The Workhouse.* In Charleston, South Carolina, slave owners sent disobedient slaves to the hidden confines of the city workhouse to be whipped and tortured. The enslavers gave specific instructions as to how many lashes and the degree of torture the enslaved were to receive. See Strickland, *All for Liberty,* 24–54.

3. Dickens, *American Notes for General Circulation,* 238–239. On the booster promotion of St. Louis as "the Babylon of the New World, not standing on the Euphrates, but on the banks of the great Mississippi," see Primm, *Lion of the Valley,* 274.

4. *In re: Medley,* 389.

5. *St. Louis Post-Dispatch,* August 11, 1877, 4, and August 1, 1877, 2.

6. Wetmore and Steffens, "Tweed Days in St. Louis," 586. See also Wetmore, *Battle Against Bribery,* 1904.

7. Primm, *Lion of the Valley,* 304–305; Stein, *St. Louis Politics,* 4–6.

8. Dreiser, *A Book About Myself,* 119. On the Big Cinch, see Primm, *Lion of the Valley,* 347–350, 354–358, 363–364.

9. Dreiser, *A Book About Myself,* 117–118.

10. Dreiser, *A Book About Myself,* 101.

11. *St. Louis Post-Dispatch,* June 23, 1886, 1; Adler, "Streetwalkers," 737–755.

1. Daily Life and Labor in the Workhouse

1. *St. Louis Post-Dispatch,* July 28, 1895, 17. On the workhouse's creation, rules, and regulations, see *Revised Ordinances of the City of Saint Louis* (1843), 477–486. See also *St. Louis Globe-Democrat,* January 8, 1956, 95; Ritter, *Inventing America's First Immigration Crisis,* 118–119.

2. Civic League of St. Louis, *Report on the St. Louis Workhouse,* 2, scanned pages available at https://www.loc.gov/item/ca15001498; *Missouri Republican,* July 30, 1872, 2; *Daily Missouri Republican,* July 8, 1865, 3, and April 21, 1868, 3; Naffziger, "A Brief History of the Workhouse in

the 19th Century"; *Daily Missouri Democrat,* June 21, 1855, 3; Conard, *Encyclopedia of the History of Missouri,* 523. On the length of the workday, see *Revised Ordinances of the City of Saint Louis* (1850), 423. The practice of forcing women inmates to break rock in the quarry drew public criticism. See *Daily Missouri Democrat,* February 26, 1856, 3.

3. *Daily Missouri Democrat,* June 21, 1855, 3; *Daily Missouri Republican,* January 18, 1856, 2.

4. *Daily Missouri Democrat,* January 19, 1856, 3, February 14, 1856, 3, February 15, 1856, 3, February 18, 1856, 3, February 21, 1856, 3, February 22, 1856, 3, February 26, 1856, 3, and February 28, 1856, 3.

5. Stanley, "Beggars Can't Be Choosers," 1265–1293. On vagrancy in St. Louis before the Civil War, see Adler, "Vagging the Demons and Scoundrels," 3–30. On profiling and harassment of roustabouts in the early 1890s, see Handy, *Father of the Blues,* 27–28; Andrews, *Shantyboats and Roustabouts,* 64.

6. *Missouri Democrat,* July 3, 1868, 3, and July 29, 1869, 4; *St. Louis Globe-Democrat,* October 19, 1878, 4; Stanley, "Beggars Can't Be Choosers," 1265–1293. Vagrancy laws were deeply rooted in English and American legal culture. For a study of such laws in Philadelphia in the early Republic, see O'Brassill-Kulfan, *Vagrants and Vagabonds.*

7. Judge Primm's decision reprinted in *Missouri Democrat,* July 28, 1869, 4. On the Hines case, see *Daily Missouri Republican,* December 11, 1868, 3, and December 20, 1868, 3.

8. *Missouri Democrat,* July 29, 1869, 4; Wagner, *Good Order and Safety,* 16–17, 49–65; Primm, *Lion of the Valley,* 265–268. Although he was a Radical Republican, Mayor Thomas sought to restore local control over the board of police commissioners appointed by the Radical Republican state legislature.

9. *Missouri Democrat,* September 16, 1869, 4.

10. *St. Louis Post-Dispatch,* May 4, 1896, 2, May 18, 1896, 5, and October 16, 1897, 4; *New York Times,* February 22, 1897, 1; *Ex parte Smith,* 223–230; *In re: Thompson,* 83–92; Sherwood, *Commentaries on the Criminal Law of Missouri,* 678.

11. *Missouri Republican,* July 30, 1872, 2; "Report of Superintendent of Workhouse," October 10, 1871, 139.

12. *Missouri Republican,* July 30, 1872, 2, and May 26, 1873, 8. For further description of the workhouse and grounds, see *St. Louis Globe-Democrat,* July 19, 1875, 8.

13. *Daily Missouri Republican,* April 21, 1868, 3; Ritter, *Inventing America's First Immigration Crisis,* 119; *Missouri Democrat,* July 3, 1868, 4.

14. *Missouri Republican,* October 12, 1869, 3, and October 26, 1869, 3; *Missouri Democrat,* September 10, 1869, 4.

15. *Daily Missouri Republican,* May 11, 1867, 3, and April 21, 1868, 3; *St. Louis Post-Dispatch,* September 7, 1888, 2.

16. *St. Louis Post-Dispatch,* July 28, 1895, 17; *Missouri Democrat,* July 3, 1868, 4; *Missouri Republican,* May 26, 1873, 8; *St. Louis Post-Dispatch,* June 23, 1886, 1.

17. "Report of Superintendent of Workhouse," October 9, 1872, 4; Civic League of Saint Louis, *Report on the St. Louis Workhouse,* 2–3; *St. Louis Post-Dispatch,* June 23, 1886, 1. In 1866, the city awarded a contract to build a patrol wagon patterned after the Black Marias in London. Before that, a spring wagon was used to deliver inmates to the workhouse. See *Daily Missouri Republican,* May 4, 1866, 2.

18. Civic League of Saint Louis, *Report on the St. Louis Workhouse,* 2–3; *St. Louis Post-Dispatch,* June 23, 1886, 1.

19. *St. Louis Post-Dispatch,* February 4, 1894, 21, June 23, 1886, 1, and April 16, 1905, 62; *Revised Ordinances of the City of St. Louis* (1881), 893.

20. *St. Louis Post-Dispatch,* June 23, 1886, 1.

21. *Missouri Republican,* July 27, 1872, 2; *St. Louis Globe-Democrat,* July 19, 1875, 8; *St. Louis Post-Dispatch,* June 23, 1886, 1.

22. *St. Louis Post-Dispatch,* June 23, 1886, 1.

23. *St. Louis Post-Dispatch,* June 23, 1886, 1, and November 22, 1895, 5; *St. Louis Globe-Democrat,* July 19, 1875, 8; *Missouri Republican,* July 27, 1872, 2.

24. Civic League of Saint Louis, "Report on the St. Louis Workhouse," 5.

25. *St. Louis Post-Dispatch,* November 23, 1880, 4, and November 23, 1880, 4.

26. Civic League of Saint Louis, *Report on the St. Louis Workhouse,* 5; *St. Louis Post-Dispatch,* February 21, 1890, 2, and July 28, 1895, 17; *St. Louis Globe-Democrat,* June 1, 1881, 7. Maher is quoted in *Globe-Democrat,* October 27, 1907, 32.

27. Quoted in *St. Louis Post-Dispatch,* December 1, 1898, 1; Civic League of St. Louis, *Report on the St. Louis Workhouse,* 5; *Revised Ordinances of the City of St. Louis* (1881), 892–893. See also *Post-Dispatch,* February 4, 1894, 21.

28. *St. Louis Post-Dispatch,* June 23, 1886, 1.

29. *St. Louis Post-Dispatch,* October 11, 1897, 1.

30. *St. Louis Post-Dispatch,* December 1, 1898, 1.

31. *Revised Ordinances of the City of St. Louis* (1881), 892–893; Civic League of St. Louis, *Report on the St. Louis Workhouse,* 2; Mangold, "Social Reform in Missouri, 1820–1920," 193; *St. Louis Post-Dispatch,* June 23, 1886, 1.

32. *Revised Ordinances of the City of St. Louis* (1881), 886, 890–892; *St. Louis Post-Dispatch,* July 7, 1879, 2.

33. *St. Louis Post-Dispatch,* June 23, 1886, 1, February 4, 1894, 21, May 6, 1895, 2, and July 28, 1895, 17; "Annual Report of the Superintendent of the Workhouse" (1909), 135–136. For a brief biographical sketch of Reverend Thomas Harvey Hagerty, see *The National Cyclopaedia of American Biography,* 17:54. In 1888, he wrote a booklet, *St. Louis City Institutions: Their Inmates, What Is Due Them, Needed Reform, Incidents, Location, Personal.*

2. Guardians of Brutality

1. *St. Louis Globe-Democrat,* July 19, 1875, 8, and July 9, 1875, 8; *St. Louis Post-Dispatch,* May 8, 1875, 1; City Directory of St. Louis, 1877, for Henry Stussel, 918, U.S., City Directories, 1822–1995.

2. *St. Louis Globe-Democrat,* August 3, 1878, 8; *St. Louis Post-Dispatch,* August 3, 1878, 5; George Stevens, August 3, 1878, City of St. Louis, Missouri, U.S., Death Records, 1850–1931.

3. *St. Louis Globe-Democrat,* August 3, 1878, 8.

4. *St. Louis Post-Dispatch,* February 11, 1879, 3, and March 16, 1879, 4; *St. Louis Globe-Democrat,* February 27, 1878, 3, and February 12, 1879, 8.

5. *St. Louis Post-Dispatch,* July 7, 1879, 2.

6. *St. Louis Post-Dispatch,* June 23, 1886, 1, and August 14, 1898, 19; *St. Louis Globe-Democrat,* September 26, 1898, 10.

7. *St. Louis Post-Dispatch,* May 26, 1907, 30.

8. *St. Louis Globe-Democrat,* September 8, 1912, 32.

9. *St. Louis Globe-Democrat,* January 20, 1880, 3, January 23, 1880, 7, and February 11, 1880, 7; *St. Louis Post-Dispatch,* January 29, 1880, 1, February 6, 1880, 1, April 10, 1880, 4, and April 12, 1880, 8.

10. *St. Louis Post-Dispatch,* April 10, 1880, 4.

11. *St. Louis Globe-Democrat,* January 18, 1880, 8, January 19, 1880, 3, and May 7, 1880, 2.

12. *St. Louis Post-Dispatch,* September 13, 1881, 1.

13. *St. Louis Post-Dispatch,* June 23, 1886, 2, and February 20, 1882, 5.

14. *St. Louis Post-Dispatch,* June 23, 1886, 2.

15. After Ulrich's death, portions of his diary appeared in a Sunday edition of the *St. Louis Post-Dispatch,* October 7, 1894, 18, thanks to his sister in Ohio.

16. *St. Louis Post-Dispatch,* May 8, 1889, 4, and October 7, 1894, 18.

17. *St. Louis Post-Dispatch,* October 7, 1894, 18.

18. *St. Louis Post-Dispatch,* October 7, 1894, 18. On the legal case, see *Ulrich v. City of St. Louis et al.,* November 14, 1892; *Southwestern Reporter* 20 (1893), 466–469.

19. *St. Louis Post-Dispatch,* November 17, 1889, 9. On Carroll's appointment, see *St. Louis Globe-Democrat,* September 7, 1888, 2; *St. Louis Post-Dispatch,* September 8, 1888, 5.

20. *St. Louis Post-Dispatch,* June 23, 1886, 2.

21. *St. Louis Post-Dispatch,* June 23, 1886, 1.

22. *St. Louis Post-Dispatch,* November 19, 1887, 2, and March 5, 1888, 2.

23. *St. Louis Post-Dispatch,* November 17, 1889, 9.

24. *St. Louis Post-Dispatch,* November 17, 1889, 9.

25. *St. Louis Post-Dispatch,* March 12, 1890, 7.

26. *St. Louis Globe-Democrat,* December 3, 1889, 12, and December 10, 1889, 8; *St. Louis Post-Dispatch,* November 11, 1890, 5, and December 9, 1890, 1.

27. Quotes in *St. Louis Globe-Democrat,* July 2, 1890, 4.

28. *St. Louis Globe-Democrat,* July 2, 1890, 4, and July 3, 1890, 11.

29. *St. Louis Globe-Democrat,* July 8, 1890, 12.

30. Kelley is quoted in *St. Louis Globe-Democrat,* July 8, 1890. On the newspaper's quote, see *Globe-Democrat,* July 13, 1890, 13. On Clark's burial in Potter's Field, see Burial Certificate for Nathan Clark, June 25, 1890, St. Louis, Missouri, U.S., Death Records, 1850–1931.

31. *St. Louis Post-Dispatch,* May 2, 1891, 6; Andrews, *Shantyboats and Roustabouts,* 51.

32. *St. Louis Post-Dispatch,* July 6, 1891, 3; *St. Louis Globe-Democrat,* May 23, 1891, 3, May 24, 1891, 9, and October 17, 1891, 8.

33. *St. Louis Globe-Democrat,* May 30, 1891, 8; *St. Louis Post-Dispatch,* July 10, 1891, 5.

34. *St. Louis Post-Dispatch,* July 10, 1891, 5, and December 16, 1891, 5. On wider complaints about tainted meat and stale, wormy foods delivered to the city hospital, see the public letter by its superintendent, Dr. Heine Marks, to Supply Commissioner Gilbert in the *St. Louis Globe-Democrat,* December 29, 1892, 11. See also *St. Louis Post-Dispatch,* June 17, 1891, 3.

35. *St. Louis Post-Dispatch,* July 12, 1891, 19. On Bass, see *The Jewish Voice,* January 30, 1891, 3.

36. *St. Louis Post-Dispatch,* July 14, 1891, 5.

37. *St. Louis Globe-Democrat,* August 7, 1891, 8.

38. *St. Louis Globe-Democrat,* August 27, 1891, 11.

39. *St. Louis Post-Dispatch,* September 11, 1891, 2; *St. Louis Globe-Democrat,* September 12, 1891, 8.

40. *St. Louis Post-Dispatch,* September 11, 1891, 2.

41. *St. Louis Post-Dispatch,* September 12, 1891, 4.

42. *St. Louis Post-Dispatch,* September 17, 1891, 6.

3. The Fiefdom of "Big John" Lohrum

1. *St. Louis Post-Dispatch,* December 15, 1891, 4, and December 19, 1891, 4.

2. *St. Louis Post-Dispatch,* December 19, 1891, 4. The dispute continued. See *Post-Dispatch,* January 11, 1892, 4.

3. Letter to the editor, *St. Louis Post-Dispatch,* December 5, 1892, 2.

4. *St. Louis Post-Dispatch,* September 12, 1891, 2.

5. *St. Louis Post-Dispatch,* November 3, 1891, 5, November 24, 1891, 8, and May 18, 1892, 9.

6. *St. Louis Post-Dispatch,* April 7, 1891, 2, August 7, 1891, 2, April 7, 1892, and October 9, 1892, 5; *St. Louis Globe-Democrat,* August 5, 1891, 4.

7. *St. Louis Post-Dispatch,* May 20, 1894, 24.

8. *St. Louis Post-Dispatch,* July 21, 1893, 1, and February 4, 1894, 21; "City Workhouse, Annual Report" (1893), 40.

9. *St. Louis Post-Dispatch,* October 24, 1894, 6.

10. *St. Louis Post-Dispatch,* October 23, 1894, 1, and October 24, 1894, 6.

11. Homan's report is quoted in *St. Louis Post-Dispatch,* November 7, 1894, 12.

12. *St. Louis Post-Dispatch,* November 7, 1894, 12.

13. *St. Louis Post-Dispatch,* November 10, 1894, 2.

14. *St. Louis Post-Dispatch,* January 3, 1895, 1, 7.

15. Lohrum quoted in *St. Louis Post-Dispatch,* January 9. 1895, 3. See also *St. Louis Globe-Democrat,* January 9, 1895, 5, which claimed that Wilson's real name was C. B. Browning

16. Wilson quoted in *St. Louis Post-Dispatch,* January 10, 1895, 9.

17. *St. Louis Post-Dispatch,* February 16, 1895, 2, and February 18, 1895, 1; *St. Louis Globe-Democrat,* February 22, 1895, 7.

18. *St. Louis Globe-Democrat,* February 19, 1895, 9.

19. *St. Louis Post-Dispatch,* March 26, 1895, 6.

20. *St. Louis Post-Dispatch,* March 26, 1895, 6; *St. Louis Globe-Democrat,* February 19, 1895, 9.

21. *St. Louis Post-Dispatch,* April 6, 1895, 3.

4. Karr's Gang of Guards

1. *St. Louis Post-Dispatch,* April 17, 1895, 6; *St. Louis Globe-Democrat,* April 17, 1895, 7, and May 24, 1895, 12; City Directory, St. Louis, Missouri, 748, U.S., City Directories, 1822–1995; Karr, Nicholas O., U.S., Civil War Pension Index: General Index to Pension Files, 1861–1934.

2. *St. Louis Post-Dispatch,* November 12, 1895, 9. See also *St. Louis Globe-Democrat,* March 13, 1895, 9, and June 5, 1895, 9.

3. *St. Louis Post-Dispatch,* October 17, 1895, 2, October 23, 1895, 1; *St. Louis Globe-Democrat,* October 18, 1895, 9.

4. *St. Louis Post-Dispatch,* October 23, 1895, 1. Marcus indicated he was prepared to give sworn testimony, if requested.

5. *St. Louis Post-Dispatch,* October 23, 1895, 1.

6. *St. Louis Post-Dispatch,* October 24, 1895, 8.

7. *St. Louis Post-Dispatch,* October 26, 1895, 1.

8. *St. Louis Post-Dispatch,* October 24, 1895, 8.

9. *St. Louis Post-Dispatch,* October 25, 1895, 4.

10. *St. Louis Post-Dispatch,* November 12, 1895, 9. On the explosion, see *Post-Dispatch,* November 3, 1895, 1.

11. *St. Louis Post-Dispatch,* July 23, 1896, 6.

12. *St. Louis Post-Dispatch,* July 31, 1896, 3.

13. *St. Louis Post-Dispatch,* July 31, 1896, 3.

14. *St. Louis Post-Dispatch,* July 31, 1896, 3.

15. *St. Louis Post-Dispatch,* April 9, 1896, 3.

16. *St. Louis Post-Dispatch,* April 19, 1896, 27. See also *Post-Dispatch,* April 17, 1896, 3, and April 18, 1896, 3.

17. *St. Louis Post-Dispatch,* August 31, 1896, 7.

18. *St. Louis Post-Dispatch,* September 4, 1896, 7, and September 5, 1896, 8.

19. *St. Louis Post-Dispatch,* March 16, 1897, 9.

20. *St. Louis Post-Dispatch,* February 1, 1897, 2.

21. *St. Louis Post-Dispatch,* August 7, 1896, 5, and August 8, 1896, 8. On Lohrum's use of convict labor for personal gain, see *Post-Dispatch,* December 19, 1891, 4.

22. *St. Louis Post-Dispatch,* December 18, 1898, 7.

23. *St. Louis Post-Dispatch,* May 3, 1898, 6.

24. *St. Louis Post-Dispatch,* December 3, 1898, 1.

25. *St. Louis Globe-Democrat,* December 12, 1898, 7, and December 14, 1898, 5. See also the obituary of Newton Jones in *Cuba Review,* November 25, 1915, 5.

26. Marriage License of William James Wallace and Florence Lee Jones, May 18, 1895, Steelville, Crawford County, Missouri, Marriage, U.S., Marriage Records, 1805–2002; 1900 United States Federal Census for William J. Wallace, ward no. 5, East St. Louis, St. Clair County, Illinois; Death notice of William James Wallace in *St. Louis Star and Times,* November 2, 1927, 17; *Cuba Review,* November 10, 1927, 1; Florence L. Wallace, death date December 10, 1955, burial in Mt. Hope Cemetery, Belleville, St. Clair County, Illinois, U.S., Find a Grave Index, 1600s to Current.

27. *St. Louis Post-Dispatch,* May 7, 1902, 1; *Chicago Chronicle,* March 31, 1896, 7, and May 23, 1896, 4; *Chicago Tribune,* May 24, 1896, 8.

28. *St. Louis Post-Dispatch,* May 7, 1902, 1.

29. *St. Louis Globe-Democrat,* June 8, 1898, 11, and June 16, 1898, 13.

30. *St. Louis Post-Dispatch,* November 29, 1900, 2.

31. *St. Louis Post-Dispatch,* December 4, 1900, 1; *St. Louis Republic,* April 18, 1901, 14.

32. *St. Louis Globe-Democrat,* May 7, 1902, 12.

33. *St. Louis Post-Dispatch,* January 27, 1904, 1. On the escape, see *Jefferson City Republican,* January 14, 1904, 1, and January 15, 1904, 2, 4; Missouri State Penitentiary Database.

34. *St. Louis Post-Dispatch,* July 6, 1898, 9.

35. *St. Louis Post-Dispatch,* October 3, 1897, 6, October 11, 1897, 1, and October 21, 1897, 4; Jerry Reynolds, City of St. Louis, October 20, 1897, Missouri, U.S., Death Records, 1850–1931.

36. "Annual Reports of the Health Commissioner" (1897), 128.

37. *St. Louis Post-Dispatch,* October 13, 1897, 10, and March 7, 1898, 3.

38. Crosby's statement appeared in *St. Louis Post-Dispatch,* December 18, 1898, 7. See also *Post-Dispatch,* November 5, 1897, 7.

39. For further details, see Andrews, *Shantyboats and Roustabouts,* 51–55.

40. *St. Louis Post-Dispatch,* April 29, 1898, 6.

41. *St. Louis Globe-Democrat,* September 26, 1898, 10.

42. "Report of the Christian Willing Workers," Conference on Charitable and Philanthropic Institutions, Saint Louis, February 23–26, 1892, 202–203; *International Good Templar* 10 (March 1897): 85–86; Harris, *Behind the Scenes,* 13; *St. Louis Post-Dispatch,* October 4, 1896, 5, and January 21, 1897, 6; Wagner, *Good Order and Safety,* 316.

43. *St. Louis Post-Dispatch,* December 23, 1896, 1, December 24, 1896, 2, December 29, 1896, 1, December 31, 1896, 9, and January 1, 1897, 7; *St. Louis Globe-Democrat,* December 30, 1896, 4, 9, January 6, 1897, 12, January 15, 1897, 9, and January 22, 1897, 9.

44. *St. Louis Post-Dispatch,* January 22, 1897, 6, January 28, 1897, 7, April 28, 1897, 3, Oct 9, 1897, 2, and November 6, 1897, 6; *St. Louis Globe-Democrat,* January 6, 1897, 7, January 22, 1897, 12, June 9, 1897, 13, July 8, 1897, 12, and November 6, 1897, 12.

45. Wilson quoted in *St. Louis Post-Dispatch,* November 5, 1897, 3. On the Ornes and the case of Jessie Wilson, see Andrews, *Shantyboats and Roustabouts,* 183–188.

46. *St. Louis Globe-Democrat,* May 27, 1899, 11; *St. Louis Post-Dispatch,* July 2, 1899, 10.

47. *St. Louis Post-Dispatch,* January 22, 1898, 7, and August 7, 1904, 3. Karr, who later became a city inspector, made an unsuccessful bid as a Republican candidate to become the Second District representative in the state legislature in the election of 1912.

5. The Little Pine Street Anarchist

1. Duff quoted in *St. Louis Post-Dispatch,* May 17, 1899, 1; Prince, *History of Ewing College,* 6; *Franklin County, 1818–1997,* 43; Aiken, *Franklin County History: Centennial Edition;* Marriage of John Duff and Lucinda Smith, March 28, 1839, Franklin County, Illinois, U.S., Marriage Index, 1860–1920; Lucinda D. Duff, September 27, 1865, and John Duff, 1857, both buried in Drummond Cemetery, Franklin County, Illinois, U.S., Find a Grave Index, 1600s–Current; 1860 United States Federal Census, township 6 south, range 2E, Franklin County, Illinois.

2. Duff quoted in *St. Louis Post-Dispatch,* May 17, 1899, 1; *Post-Dispatch,* February 10, 1879, 2, May 29, 1880, 4, June 11, 1880, 8, and July 15, 1894, 5. See also *St. Louis Globe-Democrat,* February 11, 1879, 7, and February 18, 1879, 8. In 1881, Baldwin married, left St. Louis, and by the mid-1890s opened a law practice in Spokane, Washington. See Marriage Record of Harris Baldwin and Abbie F. Park, December 1, 1881, St. Louis, Missouri, U.S. Marriage Records, 1805–2002; 1880 United States Federal Census, city of St. Louis, district 171, St. Louis, Missouri; Harris Baldwin, Spokane, Washington, 1895 City Directory, 133, U.S., City Directories, 1822–1995.

3. *St. Louis Globe-Democrat,* February 18, 1879, 8.

4. *St. Louis Globe-Democrat,* March 5, 1879, 8; *St. Louis Post-Dispatch,* March 7, 1879, 1.

5. *St. Louis Post-Dispatch,* March 7, 1879, 1.

6. *St. Louis Post-Dispatch,* May 13, 1879, 1, May 15, 1879, 4, and May 16, 1879, 5.

7. *St. Louis Post-Dispatch,* May 15, 1879, 4.

8. The Missouri State Colony for Feeble-Minded and Epileptic opened in Marshall in 1901.

9. *St. Louis Post-Dispatch,* May 17, 1899, 1.

10. *St. Louis Post-Dispatch,* July 15, 1894, 5.

11. On the Haymarket bombing and the anarchist movement in Chicago, see Avrich, *Haymarket Tragedy*; Nelson, *Beyond the Martyrs*; Green, *Death in the Haymarket.*

12. *St. Louis Post-Dispatch,* November 14, 1887, 4.

13. *St. Louis Post-Dispatch,* November 15, 1887, 3; *St. Louis Globe-Democrat,* November 16, 1887, 4; *Inter Ocean,* September 10, 1889, 1.

14. *St. Louis Post-Dispatch,* November 14, 1887, 4.

15. *St. Louis Post-Dispatch,* November 16, 1887, 3.

16. *St. Louis Globe-Democrat,* November 25, 1884, 12; *St. Louis Post-Dispatch,* June 15, 1894, 1. For examples of Mary Duff's newspaper ads, see *Post-Dispatch,* September 16, 1888, Classified Ad section, 12, and August 7, 1889, 6. See also *Globe-Democrat,* May 19, 1889, 18.

17. *St. Louis Post-Dispatch,* December 14, 1889, 2.

18. *St. Louis Post-Dispatch,* December 14, 1889, 2.

19. *St. Louis Post-Dispatch,* December 15, 1889, 3.

20. *St. Louis Post-Dispatch,* February 25, 1892, 8; *St. Louis Globe-Democrat,* July 15, 1893, 4.

21. *St. Louis Post-Dispatch,* July 2, 1892, 3. See also *Post-Dispatch,* June 20, 1892, 5.

22. *St. Louis Post-Dispatch,* July 13, 1894, 1, and July 14, 1894, 2; *St. Louis Globe-Democrat,* July 14, 1894, 7; *Herald and Review,* July 15, 1894, 8.

23. *St. Louis Globe-Democrat,* July 14, 1894, 7.

24. *St. Louis Post-Dispatch,* July 15, 1894, 5; *St. Louis Globe-Democrat,* September 14, 1894, 11.

25. *St. Louis Post-Dispatch,* April 29, 1897, 3. On earlier attempts to evict her from the property, see *Post-Dispatch,* February 20, 1897, 8.

26. *St. Louis Post-Dispatch,* October 5, 1897, 6, and October 13, 1897, 10. On the Humanity Club, see Eliot, "The Change Wrought by the Juvenile Probation System in St. Louis," 162–164; Clapp, *Mothers of All Children,* 92. A brief biographical sketch of Ingalls appeared in the *Post-Dispatch,* April 7, 1895, 34.

27. *St. Louis Post-Dispatch,* October 6, 1897, 1. On Ingalls's appointment, see the *National Bulletin of Charities and Correction* 1 (May 1897): 126.

28. *St. Louis Post-Dispatch,* October 10, 1897, 8. See also *Post-Dispatch,* October 6, 1897, 1.

29. *St. Louis Post-Dispatch,* October 6, 1897, 1. In the same year, city health commissioner Max Starkloff blasted the male quarters of the workhouse as an "outrage on civilization." See "Annual Report of the Health Commissioner for the Year Ending March 31, 1897," 128.

30. *St. Louis Post-Dispatch,* October 7, 1897, 1–2.

31. *St. Louis Post-Dispatch,* October 9, 1897, 2.

32. *St. Louis Post-Dispatch,* October 10, 1897, 8. On Ingalls's career, see the tribute by Nelle G. Burger, president of the Missouri WCTU, in *Union Signal,* February 28, 1918, 11.

33. *St. Louis Post-Dispatch,* October 12, 1897, 5.

34. *St. Louis Post-Dispatch,* October 5, 1897, 1.

35. *St. Louis Globe-Democrat,* August 10, 1905, 14; *St. Louis Post-Dispatch,* August 10, 1905, 11.

36. *St. Louis Post-Dispatch,* November 2, 1896, 8, February 20, 1897, 1, and August 7, 1904, 3; McEwen, "The Unforgettable Daisy Barbee," 106.

37. The exchange between Barbee and Karr is quoted in *St. Louis Post-Dispatch,* April 17, 1899, 8.

38. *St. Louis Post-Dispatch,* April 19, 1899, 3.

39. *St. Louis Post-Dispatch,* April 29, 1899, 3.

40. *St. Louis Globe-Democrat,* July 8, 1899, 16, and July 15, 1899, 16; *St. Louis Post-Dispatch,* July 7, 1899, 9, and August 7, 1904, 3. For the quote, see *Post-Dispatch,* May 17, 1899, 1.

41. *City of St. Louis to use of Mary Duff, Respondents v. Nicholas Karr et al., Appellants,* 85:608–617, at 617. See also *St. Louis Post-Dispatch,* November 20, 1900, 4.

42. *Mary Duff, Appellant, v. Nicholas Karr, Respondent,* 16–22; *Mayor's Message with Accompanying Documents to the Municipal Assembly of the City of St. Louis for the Fiscal Year Ending April 8, 1903,* 186. For a sample of newspaper coverage of the suit, see *St. Louis Globe-Democrat,* October 3, 1899, 14; *St. Louis Republic,* January 11, 1900, 5, March 23, 1901, 8, and April 1, 1901, 4; *St. Louis Post-Dispatch,* October 22, 1899, 31, March 21, 1901, 7, and November 19, 1901, 7.

43. *St. Louis Republic,* September 10, 1904, 1; *Mayor's Message with Accompanying Document to the Municipal Assembly of the City of St. Louis for the Fiscal Year Ending April 8, 1902,* 61. On Barbee's career, see the article by Clifton McEwen in the *St. Louis Globe-Democrat,* October 1, 1950, 106.

44. *St. Louis Globe-Democrat,* August 10, 1905, 14; *St. Louis Post-Dispatch,* August 10, 1905, 11.

45. Quoted in *St. Louis Post-Dispatch,* August 8, 1907, 19. On the fire, pranks, and thievery, see *St. Louis Globe-Democrat,* December 6, 1905, 4, and February 20, 1907; *Post-Dispatch,* August 13, 1905, 14.

46. *St. Louis Globe-Democrat,* October 23, 1908, 14; *St. Louis Post-Dispatch,* October 22, 1908, 24.

47. Mary Duff to the board of supervisors, Madison County, Illinois, December 11, 1908, letter reproduced in *Edwardsville Intelligencer,* January 5, 1909, 1; *St. Louis Post-Dispatch,* July 5, 1908, 35, October 20, 1910, 23, and November 29, 1910, 19.

48. *St. Louis Globe-Democrat,* January 27, 1910, 2; *St. Louis Post-Dispatch,* August 7, 1910, 27, and March 18, 1912, 6; *St. Louis Star,* March 20, 1912, 3. Included in Duff's lectures was a discussion of the recent growth of Emmanuelism, which originated in Boston. For a contemporary sketch of the history of drugless mental healing, including Emmanuelism, see Riley, "Mental Healing in America," 351–363; and Purrington, "The Church's Attitude towards Mental Healing," 719–730.

49. *St. Louis Post-Dispatch,* March 18, 1912, 6, and March 20, 1912, 15; *St. Louis Globe-Democrat,* March 18, 1912, 4; Mary Duff, certificate of death, March 17, 1912, Missouri Death Certificates, 1910–1971, Missouri Digital Heritage.

6. Remit Scandals and a Single Tax Prisoner

1. *St. Louis Globe-Democrat,* April 22, 1900, 42.

2. *St. Louis Globe-Democrat,* April 22, 1900, 42. On the House of Refuge, which opened in 1854, see Stepenoff, *Dead End Kids of St. Louis,* 55–67.

3. *City of St. Louis vs. John J. McCann,* Appellant, Division 2, June 26, 1900, 157: 301–309; *St. Louis Post-Dispatch,* May 14, 1899, 36; McCann quoted in *Post-Dispatch,* July 17, 1900, 3.

4. *St. Louis Post-Dispatch,* July 19, 1900, 6.

5. Dalton's letter, dated July 20, 1900, and Homan's, dated July 18, are among many similar letters reprinted in the *St. Louis Post-Dispatch,* July 29, 1900, 21.

6. *St. Louis Post-Dispatch,* July 29, 1900, 21.

7. *St. Louis Post-Dispatch,* August 25, 1900, 1. McCann's health problems worsened after he was released from the workhouse, and he died a little more than a year later. For brief obituaries, see "John J. McCann," *Single Tax Review,* October 15, 1901, 58; *St. Louis Republic,* September 11, 1901, 12; and *St. Louis Post-Dispatch,* September 13, 1901, 4.

8. *St. Louis Post-Dispatch,* September 18, 1899, 3, and October 31, 1899, 5. Upon learning of the state court's ruling against her, White skipped town and later was apprehended in Louisville, Kentucky. She then served her time in Jefferson City and returned to St. Louis, where she again was arrested. See *St. Louis Republic,* December 8, 1900, 10; *St. Louis Post-Dispatch,* August 31, 1902, 15; Missouri State Penitentiary database. On Raymond, see, for example, *Post-Dispatch,* October 28, 1898, 6, and September 19, 1899, 2.

9. Schawacker and Smith quoted in *St. Louis Post-Dispatch,* October 9, 1899, 10.

10. *St. Louis Globe-Democrat,* September 2, 1898, 8; *St. Louis Post-Dispatch,* September 1, 1898, 9.

11. *St. Louis Republic,* November 27, 1900, 1.

12. *St. Louis Post-Dispatch,* November 27, 1900, 11, and November 29, 1900, 9; *St. Louis Globe-Democrat,* November 28, 1900, 13.

13. *St. Louis Republic,* November 28, 1900, 4.

14. *St. Louis Republic,* November 28, 1900, 4; *St. Louis Post-Dispatch,* November 27, 1900, 4; *St. Louis Globe-Democrat,* November 28, 1900, 13.

15. *St. Louis Post-Dispatch,* November 12, 1900, 3. See also *Post-Dispatch,* December 19, 1900, 2.

16. *St. Louis Post-Dispatch,* December 19, 1900, 2.

17. *St. Louis Post-Dispatch,* December 18, 1900, 1. See also *Post-Dispatch,* December 19, 1900, 2; and *St. Louis Republic,* December 19, 1900, 4.

18. *St. Louis Post-Dispatch,* December 18, 1900, 1. On Fred Ziegenhein's indictment, see *St. Louis Republic,* June 1, 1902, 1, and *Post-Dispatch,* May 27, 1902, 1.

19. *St. Louis Post-Dispatch,* May 27, 1902, 1.

20. Geiger, "Joseph W. Folk vs. Edward Butler: St. Louis, 1902," 438–449; Primm, *Lion of the Valley,* 349–372; *State v. Butler,* 560–582. On Folk's public career, see Piott, *"Holy Joe."*

21. *St. Louis Post-Dispatch,* April 12, 1901, 1; *St. Louis Republic,* May 29, 1902, 2, and February 11, 1905, 5.

7. Faint Heartbeats of Reform

1. *St. Louis Republic,* May 9, 1903, 9; *St. Louis Globe-Democrat,* May 10, 1903, 55; *St. Louis Post-Dispatch,* May 13, 1903, 12.

2. *St. Louis Post-Dispatch,* November 25, 1900, 2.

3. *St. Louis Globe-Democrat,* April 11, 1903, 1; *St. Louis Post-Dispatch,* February 3, 1903, 1, April 11, 1903, 1; *St. Louis Republic,* February 5, 1903, 4. On Robert G. Cochrane, see his obituary in the *St. Louis Post-Dispatch,* August 6, 1905, 16, and his will, dated March 25, 1905, in Kansas, U.S., Wills and Probate Records, 1803–1987, Wyandotte County, frame 777.

4. *Kansas City Times,* February 3, 1903, 1; *Kansas City Star,* January 7, 1906, 15; *Kansas City Gazette,* February 7, 1903, 3. On Barton's long criminal history, see *Monongahela Valley Republican,* March 8, 1906, 1.

5. *St. Louis Globe-Democrat,* April 11, 1903, 1.

6. *State v. Barrington,* 23–133.

7. *State v. Barrington,* 23–133; *St. Louis Post-Dispatch,* June 2, 1907, 55; *St. Louis Globe-Democrat,* April 28, 1907, 37; Missouri State Penitentiary database. At the time Governor Folk spared Barrington from execution, reports of McCann sightings and claims that he was still alive circulated in the public sphere. Others disputed that Barrington was George F. Barton, the English crook with a long rap sheet.

8. *St. Louis Republic,* February 12, 1905, 12; *World's Fair Bulletin,* September 1904, 57; *Fourth Biennial Report of the State Board of Charities and Corrections,* 6.

9. *St. Louis Republic,* February 12, 1905, 12.

10. *St. Louis Post-Dispatch,* April 16, 1905, 62.

11. "Annual Report of the City Workhouse for the Fiscal Year Ending April 10, 1905," 145; *St. Louis Post-Dispatch,* May 24, 1905, 9.

12. *St. Louis Post-Dispatch,* August 19, 1904, 1, 7; Des Moines, Iowa, City Directory, U.S., City Directories, 1822–1995, 157; *Des Moines Register,* August 20, 1904, 3.

13. *St. Louis Post-Dispatch,* August 19, 1904, 7; *St. Louis Globe-Democrat,* August 21, 1904, 1.

14. *St. Louis Post-Dispatch,* August 19, 1904, 7; *St. Louis Republic,* August 20, 1904, 8. Swift sued the Iowa Traveling Men's Association, which refused to pay the $5,000 life insurance policy on grounds that the death of her brother was not an accidental drowning. See *Des Moines Register,* November 11, 1904, 6.

15. *St. Louis Post-Dispatch,* January 15, 1905, 13, and March 1, 1905, 2; *St. Louis Globe-Democrat,* March 2, 1905, 2.

16. *St. Louis Post-Dispatch,* October 10, 1905, 2, and October 12, 1905, 11; *St. Louis Globe-Democrat,* October 13, 1905, 16.

17. *St. Louis Post-Dispatch,* August 25, 1907, 27.

18. *St. Louis Post-Dispatch,* August 25, 1907, 27.

19. *St. Louis Globe-Democrat,* October 27, 1907, 32; Civic League of St. Louis, *Report on the St. Louis Workhouse,* 3, 4. The grand jury's report is quoted in *St. Louis Globe-Democrat,* December 5, 1908, 3, 8.

20. Report quoted in *St. Louis Globe-Democrat,* December 5, 1908, 8.

21. *St. Louis Post-Dispatch,* January 29, 1908, 2, and January 30, 1908, 11.

22. "Annual Report of the Superintendent of the Workhouse" (1909), 135; *St. Louis Post-Dispatch,* October 7, 1908, 16; *St. Louis Globe-Democrat,* October 19, 1908, 10, October 31, 1908, 9, November 15, 1908, 38, and December 15, 1908, 10.

23. *St. Louis Globe-Democrat,* January 16, 1909, 10, and February 10, 1909, 14; *St. Louis Post-Dispatch,* January 20, 1909, 6, and February 10, 1909, 3.

24. *St. Louis Post-Dispatch,* May 4, 1909, 6; "Annual Report of the Superintendent of the Workhouse" (1909), 135.

25. "Annual Report of the Superintendent of the Workhouse" (1909), 136–138; *St. Louis Globe-Democrat,* February 12, 1908, 9.

26. Dawson quoted in *St. Louis Globe-Democrat,* September 12, 1909, 8. See also *Globe-Democrat,* March 28, 1910, 1.

27. *St. Louis Globe-Democrat,* September 12, 1909, 8.

28. Marriage of Oscar R. Bullard and Rose Stackert, 1902, Alexander County, Illinois, U.S., County Marriage Records, 1800–1940; *Cairo Bulletin,* October 3, 1909, 1; *St. Louis Post-Dispatch,* October10, 1909, 30.

29. *St. Louis Post-Dispatch,* October 10, 1909, 30.

30. Quoted in *Chicago Tribune,* January 16, 1910, 1. See also *St. Louis Post-Dispatch,* October 10, 1909, 30.

31. *Chicago Tribune,* January 16, 1910, 1. See also *St. Louis Post-Dispatch,* November 6, 1909, 1; *St. Louis Globe-Democrat,* January 12, 1910, 1; *St. Louis Star,* January 19, 1910, 1.

32. *St. Louis Globe-Democrat,* January 12, 1910, 1, and January 21, 1910, 2.

33. *Chicago Tribune,* January 16, 1910, 1.

34. Quoted in *Chicago Tribune,* January 19, 1910, 3. See also *St. Louis Post-Dispatch,* January 27, 1910, 2.

35. *St. Louis Post-Dispatch,* January 19, 1910, 2, and January 20, 1910, 4; *St. Louis Star,* January 27, 1910, 9.

36. *St. Louis Post-Dispatch,* January 27, 1910, 22, and February 3, 1921, 1; *St. Louis Globe-Democrat,* April 20, 1910, 14.

37. *Journal of the Missouri State Medical Association,* 1918, 64; World War I draft registration card of Oscar R. Bullard, Terra Haute, Vigo County, Indiana, September 2, 1918, U.S., World War I Draft Registration Cards, 1917–1918; *St. Louis Star,* December 23, 1920, 1; *St. Louis Post-Dispatch,* December 23, 1920, 32, and February 3, 1921, 1; *St. Louis Globe-Democrat,* June 4, 1921, 11. Regina and Oscar continued to battle over their troubled daughter, who, at age fifteen, ran from her mother's relatives in Chicago. Chicago police feared she was caught up in a white slavery ring, but she had gone to live with her father, who by now had married E. Ruth Carrington, eighteen years younger than he. Regina objected to ceding custody to her ex-husband. St. Louis police, notified that Bernice was reported missing in Chicago, knocked on Dr. Bullard's door in St. Louis to take her to the house of detention until other arrangements could be made. In September, Bernice's parents agreed to send her to a boarding school. See *Chicago Tribune,* June 27, 1928, 17; *St. Louis Post-Dispatch,* August 30, 1928, 3, and September 6, 1928, 3.

38. *St. Louis Post-Dispatch,* March 28, 1910, 5, and August 29, 1910, 1.

8. A Halting Place Between Two Crimes

1. Civic League of St. Louis, *Civic Bulletin,* September 18, 1911, 1; *St. Louis Globe-Democrat,* September 13, 1911, 6; Civic League of St. Louis, *Report on the St. Louis Workhouse.*

2. Civic League of St. Louis, *Report on the St. Louis Workhouse,* 1.

3. Civic League of St. Louis, *Report on the St. Louis Workhouse,* 1–5.

4. Civic League of St. Louis, *Report on the St. Louis Workhouse,* 7.

5. Civic League of St. Louis, *Civic Bulletin,* September 18, 1911, 1. For the quote, see Civic League of St. Louis, *Report on the St. Louis Workhouse,* 13.

6. Civic League of St. Louis, *Civic Bulletin,* September 18, 1911, 1; *St. Louis Globe-Democrat,* September 13, 1911, 6.

7. Maher and Dawson quoted in *St. Louis Globe-Democrat,* October 27, 1907, 32. See also Civic League of St. Louis, *Report on the St. Louis Workhouse,* 4–5.

8. *St. Louis Globe-Democrat,* October 27, 1907, 32.

9. *St. Louis Globe-Democrat,* April 26, 1911, 3; *St. Louis Star,* April 26, 1911, 2; *St. Louis Post-Dispatch,* April 27, 1911, 14.

10. *St. Louis Star,* December 13, 1911, 3; *St. Louis Post-Dispatch,* June 30, 1911, 20, and December 25, 1911, 11.

11. *St. Louis Post-Dispatch,* July 7, 1912, 44; *St. Louis Globe-Democrat,* June 21, 1912, 18.

12. *St. Louis Globe-Democrat,* March 15, 1912, 14; "Concrete Favored for Workhouse Buildings at St. Louis," 46–47.

13. *St. Louis Globe-Democrat,* October 5, 1912, 9; *St. Louis Star,* October 4, 1912, 1. Leahy quoted in *Star,* November 2, 1912, 1.

14. *St. Louis Globe-Democrat,* October 5, 1912, 9, and October 6, 1912, 2.

15. *St. Louis Star,* October 17, 1912, 1, October 18, 1912, 1, and October 19, 1912, 1. See also *St. Louis Post-Dispatch,* October 17, 1912, 1, October 18, 1912, 13.

16. Quoted in *St. Louis Star,* October 17, 1912, 6.

17. *St. Louis Star,* November 28, 1912, 5. Slater quoted in *Star,* October 17, 1912, 6.

18. On the documents, see *St. Louis Star,* October 17, 1912, 1. Judge Slater is quoted in *St. Louis Post-Dispatch,* October 17, 1912, 1.

19. *St. Louis Star,* October 18, 1912, 1; *St. Louis Globe-Democrat,* October 18, 1912, 1.

20. *St. Louis Star,* October 18, 1912, 17, and October 19, 1912, 3; *St. Louis Post-Dispatch,* October 20, 1912, 27. White quoted in *St. Louis Globe-Democrat,* October 18, 1912, 1.

21. *St. Louis Star,* November 28, 1912, 5.

22. Mayor Kreismann quoted in *St. Louis Star,* November 28, 1912, 5. On White's reappointment, see *St. Louis Star,* December 4, 1912, 4.

23. The editorial is reprinted in the *St. Louis Star,* October 18, 1912, 17.

24. *St. Louis Star,* October 20, 1912, 8.

25. *St. Louis Star,* October 19, 1912, 5; *St. Louis Post-Dispatch,* October 21, 1912, 3.

26. *St. Louis Star,* October 18, 1912, 6.

27. *St. Louis Star,* October 17, 1912, 1, and October 21, 1912, 1.

28. Quoted in *St. Louis Star,* October 21, 1912, 1.

29. *St. Louis Star,* October 21, 1912, 1, 3.

30. Trask's letter is reprinted in full in *St. Louis Star,* October 21, 1912, 3.

31. *St. Louis Star,* October 23, 1912, 14.

9. A Theosophist and Soldier of Fortune in Charge

1. *St. Louis Globe-Democrat,* October 26, 1912, 1; *St. Louis Post-Dispatch,* October 21, 1912, 3.

2. *St. Louis Star,* October 28, 1912, 12.

3. Quoted in *St. Louis Globe-Democrat,* Sunday edition, December 4, 1927, 84. See also *Globe-Democrat,* October 27, 1912, 9, October 29, 1912, 16, November 7, 1912, 1, and December 7, 1912, 7; *St. Louis Post-Dispatch,* December 17, 1912, 1.

4. *St. Louis Globe-Democrat,* May 2, 1934, 22; *St. Louis Post-Dispatch,* May 1, 1934, 10; U.S., Adjutant General Military Records, 1631–1976, Missouri, Roster of Officers National Guard of Missouri, 1910; 1900 United States Federal Census, Military and Naval Forces, Philippine Islands, Bangued, district 0186, 12; *Times-Picayune,* January 19, 1899, 1; *Daily Ardmoreite,* August 2, 1899, 3.

5. Primavesi quoted in *St. Louis Globe-Democrat,* Sunday edition, December 4, 1927, 84.

6. Quoted in *Chanute Daily Tribune,* September 13, 1916, 4. See also *St. Louis Post-Dispatch,* November 24, 1912, 40, and December 17, 1912, 1; 1920 United States Federal Census, St. Louis, Missouri, Ward 12, district 0244; death certificate of Frank J. Primavesi, May 1, 1934, Bexar County, San Antonio, Texas, U.S., Death Certificates, 1903–1982; Marriage License of Frank J.

Primavesi and Helen J. Gardner, December 16, 1912, St. Charles County, Missouri, U.S., Marriage Records, 1805–2002; *St. Louis Globe-Democrat,* October 3, 1916, 18.

7. *St. Louis Globe-Democrat,* December 7, 1912, 7.

8. *St. Louis Star,* October 24, 1912, 5. See also *St. Louis Globe-Democrat,* December 7, 1912, 10; *St. Louis Post-Dispatch,* November 30, 1912, 3. On the background and career of Judge Kimmel, see *New St. Louis Star,* February 11, 1914, 3.

9. *St. Louis Globe-Democrat,* February 25, 1913, 14, and July 13, 1914, 12. After nine months as a probation officer, Moller resigned as the result of an effort to split the parole board into districts, which ignited bitter partisan squabbles in the municipal assembly and among police court judges. The bill to divide the board into districts included abolishing Moller's position. Mayor Kiel vetoed the bill, but Moller resigned. No immediate successor was named. See *St. Louis Globe-Democrat,* October 28, 1913, 5, December 3, 1913, 18, and January 3, 1914, 4. See also *New St. Louis Star,* November 4, 1913, 5, and January 3, 1914, 3.

10. Quoted in *St. Louis Post-Dispatch,* January 25, 1913, 2. See also *St. Louis Star,* October 18, 1912, 1.

11. *St. Louis Star,* October 18, 1912, 1.

12. *St. Louis Star,* October 23, 1912, 1

13. *St. Louis Star,* October 23, 1912, 3; *St. Louis Globe-Democrat,* November 24, 1912, 9.

14. *St. Louis Globe-Democrat,* January 12, 1913, 1.

15. Crutcher, "Quarrying with Prisoners in St. Louis," 809–811; *Engineering and Cement World,* November 15, 1918, 70.

16. *St. Louis Globe-Democrat,* April 19, 1913, 13, and April 24, 1913, 4; *St. Louis Post-Dispatch,* May 11, 1913, 27.

17. Judge Sale and Spraggon quoted in *St. Louis Star,* April 25, 1913, 9.

18. *St. Louis Star,* May 11, 1913, 11; *St. Louis Post-Dispatch,* May 1, 1913, 1.

19. *St. Louis Star,* April 25, 1913, 9.

20. Quoted in *St. Louis Post-Dispatch,* Sunday edition, May 11, 1913, 27. See also *Post-Dispatch,* May 13, 1913, 1; *St. Louis Star,* May 13, 1913, 2.

21. *St. Louis Globe-Democrat,* May 21, 1913, 6; *St. Louis Star,* May 19, 1913, 6; *St. Louis Post-Dispatch,* May 5, 1913, 12; "Annual Report of the City Workhouse for the Fiscal Year 1914–1915" (April 26, 1915), 616.

22. *St. Louis Globe-Democrat,* May 6, 1913, 3.

23. Board of Education of the City of St. Louis, *Official Report,* March 14, 1916, 750; *St. Louis Star,* December 12, 1914, 1, March 9, 1916, 1, and May 29, 1916, 3; *St. Louis Post-Dispatch,* April 23, 1916, 15.

24. *St. Louis Post-Dispatch,* April 25, 1916, 14; *St. Louis Globe-Democrat,* May 28, 1916, 32.

25. Primavesi, "Prison Reform in America," 19–20.

26. Quoted in *New St. Louis Star,* June 3, 1914, 2. See also Primavesi, "Prison Reform in America," 21; *New St. Louis Star,* June 19, 1914, 1.

27. *New St. Louis Star,* June 3, 1914, 1.

28. *New St. Louis Star,* June 19, 1914, 1.

29. Primm, *Lion of the Valley,* 409–410; Stein, *St. Louis Politics,* 10–11. Roger N. Baldwin, secretary of the Civic League, played an important role behind the scenes in building a coalition of diverse civic organization and grassroots leaders to promote public support for the new charter. See Cottrell, *Roger Nash Baldwin and the American Civil Liberties Union,* 38–41.

30. Emil N. Tolkacz, Director of Public Welfare, to Hon. Henry Kiel, Mayor, August 16, 1915, *Mayor's Message with Accompanying Documents to the Board of Aldermen of the City of St. Louis for the Fiscal Year Ending April 12, 1915.* On Tolkacz, see *St. Louis Star,* August 29, 1914, 3; Stevens, *Centennial History of Missouri,* 5:523.

31. "Annual Report of the City Workhouse, 1913–1914" (April 26, 1915), 334; *St. Louis Globe-Democrat,* October 21, 1914, 5. Mayor Kiel and other city officers took the oath of office under the new charter on August 29, 1914.

32. "Annual Report of the City Workhouse for the Fiscal Year 1914–1915" (April 26, 1915), 616–617.

33. *St. Louis Star,* May 15, 1917, 3.

34. *St. Louis Star,* May 15, 1917, 3.

35. *St. Louis Globe-Democrat,* December 24, 1914, 3; *St. Louis Star,* December 2, 1915, 6; Primavesi quoted in *Star,* May 15, 1917, 3.

36. On West's arrest in St. Louis, see *St. Louis Post-Dispatch,* June 19, 1913, 13. On her lengthy criminal history, see *St. Louis Star,* May 15, 1917, 3, October 3, 1923, 6, and June 10, 1926, 3; *Transcript-Telegram,* May 18, 1915, 5.

37. Primavesi quoted in *St. Louis Star,* May 15, 1917, 3. On West's extradition, see the *Berkshire Evening Eagle,* February 18, 1915, 2, May 18, 1915, 14, and February 9, 1916, 6.

10. Wobblies in the Workhouse

1. *Proceedings of the Judiciary Committee,* 2:2171. For a firsthand account of the arrests and treatment of the suffrage activists in the Occoquan Workhouse, see Stevens, *Jailed for Freedom.*

2. For a pioneering study of the IWW, see Dubofsky, *We Shall Be All.* For a recent study, see White, *Under the Iron Heel.* Paul Frederick Brissenden wrote *The IWW: A Study of American Syndicalism* (1919) while the IWW was under prosecution.

3. The *St. Louis Globe-Democrat,* December 26, 1911, 1, reported that 250 members left for Aberdeen the night before. See also *St. Louis Globe-Democrat,* February 20, 1911, 14. The number came from a conversation between the *Globe-Democrat* reporter and Martin Robertson, secretary of the local IWW.

4. Botkin, *Frank Little and the IWW,* 177–182.

5. Botkin, *Frank Little and the IWW,* 177–182; White, *Under the Iron Heel,* 60; *St. Louis Globe-Democrat,* February 14, 1914, 11; *Official Journal of the Travelers' Goods and Leather Novelty Workers' International Union of America,* 11:1–2, 4–5.

6. *Kansas City Star,* February 27, 1914, 5; *St. Louis Globe-Democrat,* February 14, 1914, 11; *Official Journal of the Travelers' Goods and Leather Novelty Workers' International Union of America,* 11:4–5. On the editorial, see *St. Louis Star,* March 6, 1914, 14. The quote is in *Star,* February 28, 1914, 16.

7. *St. Louis Star,* November 13, 1914, 1; *St. Louis Post-Dispatch,* November 12, 1914, 11, and November 20, 1914, 16; *IWW Songs,* 32. On the Bureau of Migratory Workers, see White, *Under the Iron Heel,* 60.

8. *St. Louis Star,* November 13, 1914, 1; *St. Louis Post-Democrat,* November 20, 1914, 16.

9. *St. Louis Globe-Democrat,* March 28, 1915, 63; Adrian, "The World We Shall Win for Labor," 101–128; U.S. House of Representatives, *Volunteer and Conscription System,* 46–51. See also Bruns, *The Damndest Radical.*

10. Quoted in *St. Louis Star,* January 11, 1913, 3. See also *St. Louis Globe-Democrat,* September 17, 1910, 5, and December 18, 1912, 2; *St. Louis Post-Dispatch,* December 31, 1912, 5.

11. Barrett quoted in Missouri Bureau of Labor Statistics, *Thirty-Seventh Annual Report for the Fiscal Year Ending November 5, 1915,* 218.

12. Anderson, *The Hobo,* 172–174; *St. Louis Star,* November 20, 1914, 1; *Chicago Tribune,* October 26, 1914, 15; *St. Louis Globe-Democrat,* November 14, 1914, 3.

13. *St. Louis Star,* October 29, 1914, 1.

14. *St. Louis Star,* December 17, 1914, 1; *St. Louis Post-Dispatch,* November 20, 1914, 16.

15. *St. Louis Post-Dispatch,* December 5, 1914, 2, and January 8, 1915, 1; *St. Louis Globe-Democrat,* December 5, 1914, 4.

16. *St. Louis Post-Dispatch,* January 3, 1915, 1. In an article published in the *St. Louis Star,* January 4, 1915, 7, writer John Regan claimed that the St. Louis IWW local had 250 members.

17. *St. Louis Post-Dispatch,* January 3, 1915, 1.

18. *St. Louis Post-Dispatch,* January 3, 1915, 1, and January 11, 1915, 2; *St. Louis Star,* January 5, 1915, 1.

19. Duffus, "The Legend of Roger Baldwin," 44–45.

20. Quoted in *St. Louis Post-Dispatch,* January 10, 1915, 22. See also *Post-Dispatch,* January 9, 1915, 2.

21. *St. Louis Post-Dispatch,* January 2, 1915, 1.

22. *St. Louis Star,* January 5, 1915, 1.

23. *St. Louis Post-Dispatch,* January 2, 1915, 1.

24. *St. Louis Post-Dispatch,* January 12, 1915, 1.

25. *St. Louis Star,* January 27, 1915, 5; *St. Louis Globe-Democrat,* December 16, 1915, 12.

11. Petty Peanut Politics and the Death of Reform

1. *St. Louis Star,* May 21, 1915, 1; *St. Louis Globe-Democrat,* May 15, 1915, 3; *St. Louis Post-Dispatch,* May 21, 1915, 3.

2. *St. Louis Post-Dispatch,* May 25, 1915, 2; *St. Louis Star,* May 25, 1915, 1. On Stratton's military background, see his file in Missouri, U.S., Pre–World War II Adjutant General Enlistment Contracts, 1900–1941.

3. *St. Louis Star,* May 25, 1915, 1; *St. Louis Post-Dispatch,* May 22, 1915, 4, and May 25, 1915, 2; City of St. Louis, Directory, 1916, U.S. City Directories, 1822–1995, 2126.

4. *St. Louis Star,* June 5, 1915, 2, and June 7, 1915, 7; *St. Louis Globe-Democrat,* June 6, 1915, 8.

5. *St. Louis Globe-Democrat,* March 16, 1916, 20. On Baur's son in Mayor Kiel's office, see *Reedy's Mirror,* October 27, 1916, 690.

6. *St. Louis Post-Dispatch,* April 14, 1916, 10.

7. *St. Louis Globe-Democrat,* April 15, 1916, 4; *St. Louis Post-Dispatch,* August 28, 1916, 6.

8. *St. Louis Star,* May 11, 1917, 3; *St. Louis Globe-Democrat,* April 17, 1917, 11; *St. Louis Post-Dispatch,* May 12, 1917, 6.

9. Schmoll quoted in *St. Louis Star,* May 17, 1917, 9. On Morgan's arrest, see *Star,* May 14, 1917, 3. Morgan's appointment was made permanent on June 23, 1917, after he reportedly had the highest score on the efficiency board examination. *Star,* June 23, 1917, 2.

10. *St. Louis Star,* May 15, 1917, 4.

11. Quoted in *St. Louis Post-Dispatch,* March 31, 1921, 12.

12. On the limited sweep of St. Louis's progressivism and the political legacy of its failure to mount a frontal assault on ward politics as the locus of municipal political power, see Stein, *St. Louis Politics.*

13. On the bond election, see *City Journal,* April 27, 1920, 10; *St. Louis Post-Dispatch,* May 12, 1920, 1. For a brief analysis, see Budenz, "St. Louis Bond Election," 657. Authorized in 1913, Bellefontaine Farms for delinquent boys between the ages of nine and sixteen opened in 1920 on a tract of 359 acres west of the city. Nonpunitive in design, the Farms provided cottage-style living with educational, social, and vocational training as well as a compulsory half day of work. See Stepenoff, *Dead End Kids of St. Louis,* 67.

Conclusion

1. Quoted in *St. Louis Post-Dispatch,* March 13, 1928, 22.

2. *St. Louis Globe-Democrat,* July 10, 1952, 1, June 8, 1955, 1, and April 24, 1957, 1; *St. Louis Post-Dispatch,* November 1, 1955, 1; *St. Louis Argus,* April 20, 1956, 10. Investigative reporting by Robert H. Collins called attention to the Syndicate. See his article in the *Post-Dispatch,* May 9, 1957, 1.

3. *St. Louis Globe-Democrat,* January 25, 1959, 47; *St. Louis Post-Dispatch,* June 9, 1966, 3.

4. Bordeaux, "Radicalized at the Workhouse," provides a compelling personal story about how Bordeaux ended up in the St. Louis Medium Security Institution and turned private anger into community activism. See also Purnell, *Becoming Abolitionists,* 136–139.

5. *St. Louis Post-Dispatch,* July 7, 1966, 35, and July 8, 1966, 6.

BIBLIOGRAPHY

Ancestry.com

U.S., City Directories, 1822–1995
U.S., Civil War Pension Index: General Index to Pension Files, 1861–1934
U.S., Death Certificates, 1903–1982
U.S., Death Records, 1850–1931
U.S., Federal Censuses, 1860–1940
U.S., Find a Grave Index, 1600s–Present
U.S., Marriage Indexes, 1860–1920
U.S., Marriage Records, 1805–2002
U.S., Pre-World War II Adjutant General Enlistment Contracts, 1900–1941
U.S., Wills and Probate Records, 1803–1987
U.S., World War I Draft Registration Cards, 1917–1918

Archives and Libraries

Missouri Historical Society, St. Louis, Missouri
- Penal Institutions Collection
- Photo Collections

Missouri State Archives, Jefferson City, Missouri
- Adjutant General Military Records, 1631–1976, Missouri, Roster of Officers, National Guard of Missouri
- Coroner's Inquest Database
- Missouri Death Certificates, 1910–1972, Missouri Digital Heritage
- Missouri State Penitentiary Database

State Historical Society of Missouri, Columbia, Missouri
- *Missouri Historical Review* archive

Conferences, Proceedings, and Reports

"Annual Reports of the Health Commissioner." *Mayor's Message with Accompanying Documents to the City Council of the City of St. Louis.* 1853–1915.

"Annual Reports of the House of Refuge." *Mayor's Message with Accompanying Documents to the City Council of the City of St. Louis.* 1853–1915.

"Annual Reports of the Superintendent of the Workhouse." *Mayor's Message with Accompanying Documents to the City Council of the City of St. Louis.* 1853–1915.

Biennial Reports. Missouri State Board of Charities and Corrections, 1899, 1905, 1915.

Board of Education of the City of St. Louis. *Official Report,* March 14, 1916.

Charter of the City of St. Louis, Missouri, Adopted by Vote of the People, June 30, 1914.

The City Journal. St. Louis, 1920.

"City Workhouse, Annual Report." *Mayor's Message with Accompanying Documents, to the Municipal Assembly of the City of Saint Louis at Its Session, 1893.*

Civic League of St. Louis. *Report on the St. Louis Workhouse.* St. Louis, 1911.

The Conference on Charitable and Philanthropic Institutions, Saint Louis, February 23d to February 26th, 1892.

Fourth Biennial Report of the State Board of Charities and Corrections. Jefferson City, Mo.: Tribune Printing Company, 1905.

Missouri Bureau of Labor Statistics. *Thirty-Seventh Annual Report for the Fiscal Year Ending November 5, 1915.*

National Bulletin of Charities and Correction, February 1897–February 1902.

The Official Journal of the Travelers' Goods and Leather Novelty Workers' International Union of America 11 (April 1914).

The Ordinances of the City of St. Louis, State of Missouri. St. Louis: George Knapp & Co., 1861.

The Ordinances of the City of St. Louis, State of Missouri. St. Louis: George Knapp & Co., 1871.

Proceedings of the Annual Congress of the American Prison Association. Chicago: Knight & Leonard Co., 1888.

Proceedings of the Annual Congress of the American Prison Association. Indianapolis: Wm. B. Burford, 1914.

Proceedings of the Judiciary Committee, New York Legislative Documents, One Hundred and Forty-Third Session. Vol. 2. Albany: J.B. Lyon Company, 1920.

"Report of Superintendent of Workhouse," October 10, 1871. In *Mayor's Message with Accompanying Documents to the City Council of the City of St. Louis, at Its November Session, 1871.* St. Louis, Mo.: St. Louis Times Company, 1871.

"Report of Superintendent of Workhouse," October 9, 1872. In *Mayor's Message with Accompanying Documents to the City Council of the City of St. Louis.* St. Louis, Mo.: St. Louis Times Company, 1873.

The Revised Ordinances of the City of Saint Louis. St. Louis: Chambers & Knapp, 1843.
The Revised Ordinances of the City of Saint Louis. St. Louis: Chambers & Knapp, 1850.
The Revised Ordinances of the City of St. Louis. St. Louis: The Printing House, 1881.
Scheme for the Separation and Re-Organization of the Governments of St. Louis City and County and Charter for the City of Saint Louis. St. Louis: Woodward, Tiernan & Hale, 1877.
The Union Signal. Woman's Christian Temperance Union.
U.S. House of Representatives. *Volunteer and Conscription System: Hearings Before the Committee on Military Affairs.* Washington, D.C.: Government Printing Office, 1917.

Court Cases

City of St. Louis to use of Mary Duff, Respondents v. Nicholas Karr et al., Appellants. St. Louis Court of Appeals, November 20, 1900. In *Cases Determined by the St. Louis and Kansas City Courts of Appeals of the State of Missouri* 85. Columbia, Mo.: E. W. Stephens, 1901.
City of St. Louis vs. John J. McCann. Appellant, Division 2, June 26, 1900. In *Cases Determined by the Supreme Court of the State of Missouri at the April Term 1900* 157. Columbia, Mo.: E. W. Stephens, 1901.
In re: Medley. In *The Supreme Court Reporter* 10 (October term 1889). St. Paul, Minn.: West Publishing, 1890.
In re: Thompson. In *Reports of Cases Determined in the Supreme Court of the State of Missouri* 117 (en banc, June 19, 1893). Columbia, Mo.: E. W. Stephens, 1894.
Mary Duff, Appellant, v. Nicholas Karr, Respondent. St. Louis Court of Appeals, November 19, 1901. In *Missouri Appeal Reports* 91.
Ex parte Smith. In *Reports of Cases Determined in the Supreme Court of the State of Missouri* 135 (Division 2, June 30, 1896). Columbia, Mo.: E. W. Stephens, 1897.
State v. Barrington. In *Reports of Cases Determined in the Supreme Court of the State of Missouri* 198 (en banc, June 20, 1906). Columbia, Mo.: E. W. Stephens, 1907.
State v. Butler. In *Southwestern Reporter* 77. St. Paul, Minn.: West Publishing, 1904.
Ulrich v. City of St. Louis et al. In *Southwestern Reporter* 20 (November 14, 1892). St. Paul, Minn.: West Publishing, 1893.

Newspapers

Berkshire Evening Eagle (Pittsfield, Massachusetts)
Cairo Bulletin (Illinois)
Carbondale Free Press (Illinois)
Chanute Daily Tribune (Kansas)
Chicago Tribune
Cuba Review
Daily Ardmoreite (Ardmore, Oklahoma)
Daily Missouri Democrat
Daily Missouri Republican

Dyer's Newsletter (Missouri)
Herald and Review (Decatur, Illinois)
The Inter Ocean (Chicago)
Jefferson City Republican (Missouri)
The Jewish Voice
Kansas City Gazette
Kansas City Star
Kansas City Times
Missouri Democrat
Missouri Republican
New St. Louis Star
Reedy's Mirror (Missouri)
Single Tax Review
St. Louis Argus
St. Louis Globe-Democrat
St. Louis Palladium
St. Louis Post-Dispatch
St. Louis Republic
St. Louis Star
Times-Picayune (New Orleans)
Transcript-Telegram (Holyoke, Massachusetts)
World's Fair Bulletin (1904)

Books and Articles

Adler, Jeffrey S. "Streetwalkers, Degraded Outcasts, and Good-for-Nothing Huzzies: Women and the Dangerous Class in Antebellum St. Louis." *Journal of Social History* 25 (Summer 1992): 737–755.

——. "Vagging the Demons and Scoundrels: Vagrancy and the Growth of St. Louis, 1830–1861." *Journal of Urban History* 13 (November 1986): 3–30.

Adrian, Lynne M. "'The World We Shall Win for Labor': Early Twentieth-Century Hobo Self-Publication." In *Print Culture in a Diverse America,* edited by James P. Danky and Wayne A. Wiegand, 101–128. Urbana: University of Illinois Press, 1998.

Aiken, H. M. *Franklin County History: Centennial Edition.* 1918.

Alexander, Michelle. *The New Jim Crow: Mass Incarceration in the Age of Colorblindness.* New York: New Press, 2010.

Anderson, Nels. *The Hobo: The Sociology of the Homeless Man.* Chicago: University of Chicago Press, 1923.

Andrews, Gregg. *Shantyboats and Roustabouts: The River Poor of St. Louis, 1875–1930.* Baton Rouge: Louisiana State University Press, 2023.

Avrich, Paul. *The Haymarket Tragedy.* Princeton, N.J.: Princeton University Press, 1984.

Berger, Henry W. *St. Louis & Empire: 250 Years of Imperial Quest and Urban Crisis.* Carbondale: Southern Illinois University Press, 2015.

Bordeaux, Inez. "Radicalized at the Workhouse." *Inquest,* October 22, 2021, https://inquest.org/radicalized-at-the-workhouse.

Botkin, Jane Little. *Frank Little and the IWW: The Blood That Stained an American Family.* Norman: University of Oklahoma Press, 2017.

Braude, Ann. *Radical Spirits: Spiritualism and Women's Rights in Nineteenth-Century America.* Bloomington: Indiana University Press, 1989.

Brissenden, Paul Frederick. *The IWW: A Study of American Syndicalism.* London: P.S. King & Son, 1919.

Bruns, Roger. *The Damndest Radical: The Life and World of Ben Reitman.* Urbana: University of Illinois Press, 1987.

Budenz, Louis F. "St. Louis Bond Election." *National Municipal Review* 9 (October 1920): 657.

"Concrete Favored for Workhouse Buildings at St. Louis." *Cement Era* 10 (December 1912): 46–47.

Clapp, Elizabeth J. *Mothers of All Children: Women Reformers and the Rise of Juvenile Courts in Progressive Era America.* University Park: Pennsylvania State University Press, 1998.

Conard, Howard L., ed. *Encyclopedia of the History of Missouri.* Vol. 6. New York: Southern History Company, 1901.

Corbett, Katharine T. *A Guide to St. Louis Women's History.* St. Louis: Missouri Historical Society Press, 1999.

Cottrell, Robert C. *Roger Nash Baldwin and the American Civil Liberties Union.* New York: Columbia University Press, 2000.

Crowther, M. A. *The Workhouse System, 1834–1929: The History of An English Social Institution.* Athens: University of Georgia Press, 1982. Originally published in 1981.

Crutcher, Harry M. "Quarrying with Prisoners in St. Louis." *Municipal Journal,* June 4, 1914, 809–811.

Dickens, Charles. *The Adventures of Oliver Twist.* London: Chapman and Hall, 1866. Originally published in 1838.

——. *American Notes for General Circulation.* 3rd ed. Vol. 1. London: Chapman and Hall, 1842.

Dowden-White, Priscilla A. *Groping toward Democracy: African American Social Reform in St. Louis, 1910–1949.* Columbia: University of Missouri Press, 2011.

Dreiser, Theodore. *A Book About Myself.* New York: Boni and Livermark, 1922.

Driver, Felix. *Power and Pauperism: The Workhouse System, 1834–1884.* Cambridge: Cambridge University Press, 1993.

Dubofsky, Melvyn. *We Shall Be All: A History of the Industrial Workers of the World.* New York: Quadrangle Books, 1969.

Duffus, Robert L. "The Legend of Roger Baldwin." *American Mercury* 5 (May 1925): 408–414.

Eliot, Charlotte C. "The Change Wrought by the Juvenile Probation System in St. Louis." In *Children's Courts in the United States: Their Origin, Development, and Results. Reports Prepared for the International Prison Commission,* 162–164. Washington, D.C.: Government Printing Office, 1904).

Flexner, Bernard, and Roger N. Baldwin. *Juvenile Courts and Probation.* New York: The Century Company, 1914.

Ford, Melissa. *A Brick and a Bible: Black Women's Radical Activism in the Midwest During the Great Depression.* Carbondale: Southern Illinois University Press, 2022.

Forret, Jeff, and Bruce E. Baker, eds. *Southern Scoundrels: Grifters and Graft in the Nineteenth Century.* Baton Rouge: Louisiana State University Press, 2021.

Fowler, Simon. *The Workhouse: The People, The Places, The Life Behind Doors.* South Yorkshire: Pen & Sword History, 2014.

Franklin County, 1818–1997. Paducah, Ky.: Turner Publishing, 1996.

Geiger, Louis G. "Joseph W. Folk vs. Edward Butler: St. Louis, 1902." *Journal of Southern History* 28 (November 1962): 438–449.

Green, James R. *Death in the Haymarket: A Story of Chicago, the First Labor Movement and the Bombing That Divided Gilded Age America.* New York: Pantheon, 2006.

Hagerty, Rev. T. H. *St. Louis City Institutions: Their Inmates, What Is Due Them, Needed Reform, Incidents, Location, Personal.* St. Louis: Commercial Print Company, 1888.

"Handling Limestone at the St. Louis Work-house Quarry." *Engineering and Cement World,* November 15, 1918, 70.

Handy, W. C. *Father of the Blues: An Autobiography.* 1941. Reprint, New York: De Capo, 1969.

Harris, Louisa. *Behind the Scenes; or Nine Years at the Four Courts of Saint Louis.* Edited by Major C. A. Bateman. St. Louis: A. R. Fleming, 1893.

IWW Songs. Joe Hill Memorial edition (Cleveland: IWW Publishing Bureau, 1916).

Johnson, Walter. *The Broken Heart of America: St. Louis and the Violent History of the United States.* New York: Basic, 2020.

Kruger, Mark. *The St. Louis Commune of 1877: Communism in the Heartland.* Lincoln: University of Nebraska Press, 2021.

Lause, Mark A. *Free Spirits: Spiritualism, Republicanism, and Radicalism in the Civil War Era.* Urbana: University of Illinois Press, 2016.

Lintelmen, Joy K. "'Unfortunates' and 'City Guests': Swedish American Inmates and the Minneapolis City Workhouse, 1907." In *Swedes in the Twin Cities: Immigrant Life and Minnesota's Urban Frontier,* edited by Philip J. Anderson and Dag Blanck, 57–76. St. Paul: Minnesota Historical Society Press, 2001).

Mangold, George B. *The Challenge of Saint Louis.* New York: Missionary Education Movement of the United States and Canada, 1917.

——. "Public Treatment of Drunkenness in St. Louis." *Washington University Studies* 3 (July 1915–April 1916): 271–309.

——. "Social Reform in Missouri, 1820–1920." *Missouri Historical Review* 15 (October 1920): 191–213.

McCune, Sarah Lirley. "Death of a Prostitute: Suicide and Respectability in St. Louis, 1875 to 1900." *Missouri Historical Review* 109 (January 2015): 108–127.

McEwen, Clifton. "The Unforgettable Daisy Barbee." *St. Louis Globe-Democrat,* October 1, 1950: 106.

McKelvey, Blake. *American Prisons: A Study in American Social History Prior to 1915.* Chicago: University of Chicago Press, 1936.

McQuillin, Eugene. *The Municipal Code of St. Louis (Annotated). Being Ordinance No. 19991, Approved April 3, 1900.* St. Louis: Woodward & Tiernan, 1901.

Muhammad, Khalil G. *The Condemnation of Blackness: Race, Crime, and the Making of Modern Urban America.* Cambridge. Mass.: Harvard University Press, 2011.

Naffziger, Chris. "A Brief History of the Workhouse in the 19th Century." *St. Louis Magazine,* January 28, 2021, https://www.stlmag.com/history/workhouse-history.

Nelson, Bruce C. *Beyond the Martyrs: A Social History of Chicago's Anarchists, 1870–1900.* New Brunswick, N.J.: Rutgers University Press, 1988.

O'Brassill-Kulfan, Kristin. *Vagrants and Vagabonds: Poverty and Mobility in the Early American Republic.* New York: New York University Press, 2019.

Piott, Steven L. *"Holy Joe": Joseph W. Folk and the Missouri Idea.* Columbia: University of Missouri Press, 1997.

Primavesi, Captain Frank J. "Prison Reform in America." *Herald of the Star,* January 11, 1916, 19–20.

Primm, James Neal. *Lion of the Valley: St. Louis, Missouri, 1764–1980.* 3rd ed. St. Louis: Missouri Historical Society Press, 1998.

Prince, Dr. A. E. *History of Ewing College.* Collinsville, Ill.: Herald Printing, 1961.

Purnell, Derecka. *Becoming Abolitionists: Police, Protests, and the Pursuit of Freedom.* New York: Astra House, 2021.

Purrington, W. A. "The Church's Attitude towards Mental Healing." *North American Review* 189 (May 1909): 719–730.

Richardson, Ruth. *Dickens and the Workhouse: Oliver Twist and the London Poor.* New York: Oxford University Press, 2012.

Riley, I. Woodbridge. "Mental Healing in America." *American Journal of Insanity* 66 (January 1910): 351–363.

Ritter, Luke. *Inventing America's First Immigration Crisis: Political Nativism in the Antebellum West.* New York: Fordham University Press, 2021.

Roediger, David. "Not Only the Ruling Classes to Overcome, but Also the So-Called 'Mob': Class, Skill and Community in the St. Louis General Strike of 1877." *Journal of Social History* 19 (Winter 1985): 213–239.

———. *The Wages of Whiteness: Race and the Making of the American Working Class.* London: Verso, 1999.

Sherwood, Thomas A. *Commentaries on the Criminal Law of Missouri: As Defined by the Statutes and Interpreted by the Supreme Court of Missouri.* Kansas City, Mo.: Pipes-Reed Book Company, 1907.

Smith, Thomas Ruys. *Blacklegs, Card Sharps, and Confidence Men: Nineteenth-Century Mississippi River Gambling Stories.* Baton Rouge: Louisiana State University Press, 2010.

Stanley, Amy Dru. "Beggars Can't Be Choosers: Compulsion and Contract in Postbellum America." *Journal of American History* 78 (March 1992): 1265–1293.

Stein, Lana. *St. Louis Politics: The Triumph of Tradition.* St. Louis: Missouri Historical Society Press, 2002.

Stepenoff, Bonnie. *The Dead End Kids of St. Louis: Homeless Boys and the People Who Tried to Save Them.* Columbia: University of Missouri Press, 2010.

Stevens, Doris. *Jailed for Freedom.* New York: Boni and Liveright, 1920.

Stevens, Walter Barlow. *Centennial History of Missouri (The Center State): One Hundred Years in the Union, 1821–1921.* Vol. 5. St. Louis-Chicago: S.J. Clarke, 1921.

Strickland, Jeff. *All for Liberty: The Charleston Workhouse Slave Rebellion of 1849.* New York: Cambridge University Press, 2022.

Thompson, Gail L. "African American Women and the U.S. Criminal Justice System: A Statistical Survey, 1870–2009." *Journal of African American History* 98, no. 2 (Spring 2013), Special Issue: "African Americans, Police Brutality, and the U.S. Criminal Justice System: Historical Perspectives": 291–303.

Twain, Mark. *Following the Equator: A Journey Around the World.* Vol. 1. New York: Harper & Brothers, 1897.

Twain, Mark, and Charles Dudley Warner. *The Gilded Age: A Tale of Today.* Hartford, Conn.: American Publishing Company, 1873.

United States Postal Inspection Service. *Photographs, Descriptions and Records of Persons Charged with Violation of the Postal Laws.* Vol. 2. Washington, D.C.: Government Printing Office, 1916.

Wagner, Allen E. *Good Order and Safety: A History of the St. Louis Metropolitan Police Department, 1861–1906.* St. Louis: Missouri History Museum, 2008.

Wagner, David. *The Poorhouse: America's Forgotten Institution.* Lanham, Md.: Rowman & Littlefield, 2005.

Wetmore, Claude. *The Battle Against Bribery: Being the Only Complete Narrative of Joseph W. Folk's Warfare on Boodlers.* St. Louis: Pan-American Press, 1904.

Wetmore, Claude H., and Lincoln Steffens. "Tweed Days in St. Louis: Joseph W. Folk's Single-handed Exposure of Corruption, High and Low." *McClure's Magazine* 19 (October 1902): 577–586.

White, Ahmed. *Under the Iron Heel: The Wobblies and the Capitalist War on Radical Workers.* Oakland: University of California Press, 2022.

Winn, Kenneth H., ed. *Missouri Law and the American Conscience: Historical Rights and Wrongs.* Columbia: University of Missouri Press, 2016.

INDEX